11/04/93

791.4365 McCarty, John,   c.1
M   1944-

Hollywood gangland.

26.95

DATE			

HOLLYWOOD GANGLAND

HOLLYWOOD
GANGLAND

The Movies' Love Affair with the Mob

JOHN McCARTY

St. Martin's Press

New York

119.5577

Design by MM Design 2000, Inc.

Library of Congress Cataloging-in-Publication Data

McCarty, John.
    Hollywood gangland : the movies' love affair with the mob / John McCarty.
        p.   cm.
    ISBN 0-312-09306-3
    1. Gangster films—History and criticism.   I. Title.
PN1995.9.G3M33   1993
791.43'655—dc20   93-10254
                                                         CIP

First Edition: November 1993
10   9   8   7   6   5   4   3   2   1

C .1

For
"The Goose"
Who Made Me an Offer I Couldn't Refuse

CONTENTS

ACKNOWLEDGMENTS

I would like to thank the following people for their assistance in bringing this history of Hollywood Gangland to the printed page: Lori Perkins; my editor at St. Martin's Press, Cal Morgan; my son, Christopher McCarty, for helping me mine the riches of Albany's labyrinthine State Education Library; Ken Hanke, for sharing some of his research on Hollywood's early talkies with me; Danny Burk, Ray Cabana, John Foster, and Stephen R. Bissette, for helping me find and screen some important rare films; Eric Caidin (Hollywood Book & Poster), Mary Corliss (Museum of Modern Art), and Linda Rauh (Film Favorites), for supplying me with much of the hard-to-find visual material included in this book; and Gordon Van Gelder, also of St. Martin's Press.

INTRODUCTION

Gunslingers to Gangsters: America's Changing Landscape

The gangster, like the gunslinger, is a classic American character—and the gangster movie, like the Western, one of the American cinema's most enduring genres.

In many ways, the two genres are strikingly similar. Gunplay and the violent struggle for power and territory are the thematic linchpins that hold both of them together. In the archetypal Western, however, the focus is typically on the hero—the strong, silent cowpoke, reticent about using his guns, who is ultimately forced to get tough in order to wrest control of the town away from the bad guys victimizing the helpless townsfolk. The archetypical gangster film employs essentially the same ingredients, transposed to a modern, usually urban, setting. But it turns the tables on audience expectations by casting its spotlight not on the good guy cleaning up the town but on the bad guys grappling for power and position over the townsfolk and among one another.

These and other links between the two genres are not just superficial, for the gangster film is not simply an outgrowth of the Western but the legitimate heir to it, cinematically, historically, and culturally. It is the modern continuation of America's story—a story the Western had grown too old to tell.

The Western outlaw, like his opposite number the Western hero, was a product of America's epic nineteenth-century saga—the rugged, often violent settling of the frontier. Likewise, the gangster and his nemesis, the T-man or G-man, emerged with urban America in the twentieth century—a part of our transformation from a wild frontier society to an industrialized one in which the new ethnic groups pouring into America's great, growing cities had to struggle, sometimes violently, to claim their share of the American pie.

Though America's nineteenth-century outlaws such as Jesse James, Butch Cassidy, and Billy the Kid sometimes ran in gangs, they were basically loners. They also were fairly young—in their teens or early twenties. Their lawless exploits symbolized what might be called America's adolescence—that period during which America grew from volatile teenhood to early adulthood. As the country's maturing process continued into the next century, these loner outlaws, reflecting America's changing cultural and physical landscape, transformed into something new and equally mythic: organized gangs whose individual members became popularly known as gangsters.

In an effort not just to survive but to come to grips with one another, America's ethnic enclaves saw the rise of numerous gangs with such colorful names as the Gophers, the Dead Rabbits, the Sydney Ducks, the Whyos, the Bloody Tubs, the Bowery Boys, the Roach Guards, the Potato Peelers, the Plug Uglies, the Vampires, and the Tongs—groups that frequently clashed head-to-head with one another and with the law to achieve economic, political, and social power.

Police forces, buoyed by strong public support, swelled to combat the mounting problem of escalating street violence and the corruption of public officials by these warring gangs, problems that remained fairly localized and controllable until two events occurred that changed things forever: Prohibition and the Great Depression.

At the time Prohibition came into being, the larger and more powerful of these gangs were beginning to lose ground, crumbling under the weight of incessant public and police pressure. But Prohibition enabled them to reorganize and develop even greater muscle by engaging in a now–publicly approved enterprise: bootlegging. The likes of gang leaders such as Al Capone, heretofore looked upon by the public as low-life thugs and menaces to society, now became heroes to that same public because of their flouting of the Eighteenth Amendment, which denied America's thirsty citizens legal access to a simple glass of beer. Thus the myth of the gangster as hero (or antihero) was born.

Reaping huge financial profits from their bootlegging activities, Capone's gang and others flourished and ultimately grew into a powerful national syndicate that moved into a host of illegal and equally profitable activities after Prohibition was abolished. The mob's power began to wane again during the crackdowns of the

Below, left: *Tough guy cop Dan Callahan (Lon Chaney) shows his grit and determination in combating the gangland menace in* While the City Sleeps *(1928).*

Right: *Because of Prohibition and The Great Depression, gangsters assumed the mantels of yesteryear's gunslingers and outlaws. From* Guns Don't Argue *(1957). (Copyright © 1957 Visual Drama, Inc.)*

late 1930s. But the mob got a new lease on life when the government called upon the patriotism of important mob chieftains—such as the deported Lucky Luciano—to assist the Allied war effort by using their muscle to ensure that industries and ports vital to the success of the war effort, at home and abroad, did not fall prey to strikers or saboteurs. As a result, the power of the mob not only revived during the war but got stronger than ever.

The economic downturns of the Great Depression contributed to the country's fascination with another breed of gangster, as well. As heartland Americans lost their jobs or saw their farms foreclosed on by that once-admired symbol of the establishment, the banking system, rural gangs—descended in spirit from America's frontier outlaws such as the James Gang, and led by desperadoes like Pretty Boy Floyd, Baby Face Nelson, and Machine Gun Kelly—rose up to assault that system, often with public endorsement. Like other well-known desperadoes of the period, such as John Dillinger and Bonnie and Clyde, they became mythic figures to a society whose fear had begun to give way to admiration.

Because of Prohibition, the Great Depression, and World War II, gangsters assumed the mantle of yesteryear's gunslingers and outlaws, and the gangster saga replaced the Western as the quintessential American myth. It told the story of *modern* America. And, almost from its inception one hundred years ago, the silver screen has played no small part in telling that story. The medium of film evolved with the phenomenon of American gangsterism itself, and as popular art always does, it took the lead in reflecting images of that phenomenon back to us. And it has done so from the dawn of the silent cinema.

Because of the medium's power to mythologize them and their exploits—and because of the industry's money-making potential—America's gangsters themselves have always had a fascination with the movies and the movie business. John Dillinger was an inveterate moviegoer between bank jobs, one who not surprisingly favored gangster pictures. His undoing came when he was shot to death outside

Below, left: Desperados like Clyde Barrow (Warren Beatty) became mythic figures to a society fearful yet admiring of them at the same time. From Bonnie and Clyde (1967). (Copyright © 1967 Warner Bros. Seven Arts)

Right: Dillinger favorite Clark Gable (left) as the gangster in Manhattan Melodrama *(1934), the last picture the notorious bank robber—and inveterate moviegoer—saw before being shot to death by the feds. (Copyright © 1935 Metro-Goldwyn-Mayer)*

Chicago's Biograph theater shortly after seeing *Manhattan Melodrama*, a gangster picture starring the man he had hoped would one day play *him* on the screen—Clark Gable.

Benjamin "Bugsy" Siegel, the nattily attired mobster who put Las Vegas on the map and inspired the character of Moe Green in *The Godfather*, became something of a star himself while serving as point man for the mob's West Coast operations in the 1930s, during which time he developed close friendships with many Hollywood celebrities. And then there was Mafia kingfish Lucky Luciano, who felt his life story was destined for the movies, and who, perhaps in an effort to make sure he had creative control, spearheaded the mob's first efforts to take over the movie industry in the early thirties. He failed, though rumors persist that the mob's tentacles have finally reached inside the unions and boardrooms of the conglomerate Hollywood of today.

As America comes to grips with what appears to be the next phase of its evolution—its painful transformation from an industrialized nation to a high-tech, skill-oriented, service-based one—gangster films are enjoying a tremendous resurgence. The reason for this, I believe, is that in times of great turmoil or change, Americans tend to look back to the way things were. In terms of entertainment, they opt for the familiar—genre forms that may be as old as time but that still seem both relevant and reassuring. Westerns peaked in popularity during the first half of this century primarily for that reason: They allowed Americans in the midst of great social, political, and economic change to find solace in the familiar images, emotions, and stories of a less troubling time—at a time when those images, emotions, and stories still connected with much of the population. Today, that change has been completed and America is undergoing another. The characters, landscapes, and mythologies of the Western no longer provide the comforting familiarity, the degree of reassurance, they once did, because our western past is now *too* remote; it is no longer relevant to an American population now too young

Below, left: Las Vegas visionary Bugsy Siegel has been the subject of many a gangster movie biography. Here the doomed gangster (Warren Beatty) gets a finger-pointing lecture from mob kingpin Lucky Luciano (Bill Graham). From Bugsy (1991). (Copyright © 1993 Tri-Star Pictures)

Right: Luciano also felt his life story was destined for the movies (which it was). From Lucky Luciano (1974), starring Gian-Maria Volonte. (Copyright © 1974 Avco-Embassy Pictures)

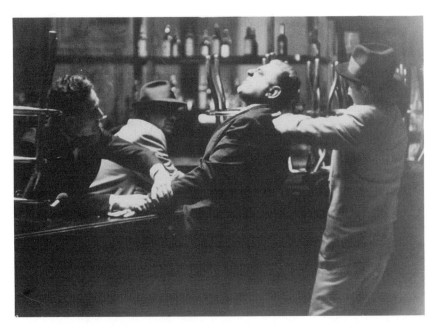

Mafia violence in The Godfather *(1972). (Copyright © 1972 Paramount Pictures Corporation)*

to feel much sense of connection with the past, the *epoch,* the Western conjures up.* Except for anomalies like 1990's *Dances with Wolves,* Kevin Costner's politically correct picture postcard of the Native American frontier experience, and the occasional Clint Eastwood oater—films that are more about past Westerns than our western past—the Western today is as moribund as its epoch. Gone are the best Westerns—the classics of the genre—and the even greater Westerns that transcended the genre to become classics of the cinema. One has to go back almost a quarter of a century to find the last one—and a very late contribution to the genre it was: *The Wild Bunch* (1969), Sam Peckinpah's violent masterpiece about the passing of the West, and, implicitly, of its genre, as well.

Not so the gangster movie. The almost century-old gangster film already boasts a substantial list of genre classics and great films to be sure—*The Regeneration* (1915), *Scarface* (1932), *The Roaring Twenties* (1939), *They Live by Night* (1949), *White Heat* (1949), *Gun Crazy* (1949), *Bonnie and Clyde* (1967), *The Godfather* (1972), and so on.

---

*During the key transitional decades of America's industrialized transformation, the 1930s and 1940s, the Western and gangster film genres even merged occasionally when B-Western heroes such as Tom Mix, George O'Brien, Roy Rogers, Gene Autry, and others found themselves pitted against modern-day gangsters bent on taking over the West rather than against the traditional movie outlaws of old. Even earlier, veteran silent Western movie star William S. Hart saw the handwriting on the wall and himself made a gangster movie, *The Cradle of Courage* (1920), in which he played a reformed San Francisco gangster who becomes a cop. Virtually every other major actor and director who had long been associated with the Western put away the six-guns, took up gats, and made a gangster movie or two, as well—from John Wayne and John Ford to Sam Peckinpah.

But the best is not yet all behind us, for innovative and bold new contributions to the genre keep coming our way. Films such as *The Long Good Friday* (1980), *Once Upon a Time in America* (1984), *GoodFellas* (1990), *Ruby* (1992), and *Let Him Have It* (1991) not only stand tall within their genre but stand out as significant, perhaps even great, works of contemporary cinematic art, as well.

The gangster movie remains very much alive because, from the barrios, ghettos, and boardrooms of America's cities to the drug strongholds of Miami, New York, and Los Angeles, gangsterism itself is still with us. The saga continues. The movies' love affair with the mob, and the audience's love affair with those movies, goes on. The themes, characters, landscapes, and mythologies of the gangster movie have proven resilient enough to be updated, reshaped, and expanded upon to connect with even the youngest among us, the teenagers and young adults for whom most movies these days are made.

And that's what this book is about. The cinematic intersection of Hollywood and one of the darker corners of the American landscape — a place whose signposts are fully recognizable and still with us. A place populated by:

Mobsters and molls

Tommy guns and T-men

Flappers and feds

Bootleggers and bootlickers

Cutthroats and crooked politicians

Mean streets and meaner folks

Heroes and hoods.

A celluloid place called Gangland.

HOLLYWOOD GANGLAND

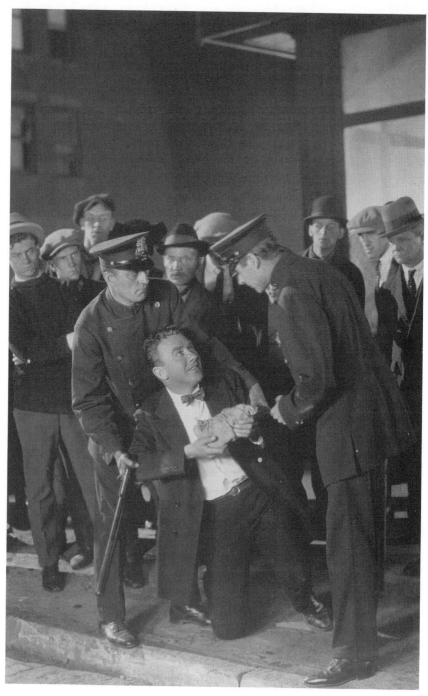

"One of the best "underworlds' ever," wrote Variety, and "a real heartbreaker with fine characterizations," noted director Allan Dwan of his Big Brother *(1924), starring Tom Moore. (Courtesy Museum of Modern Art/Film Stills Archive)*

CHAPTER 1

MUSKETEERS OF
AMERICA'S ALLEYS

By some estimates, as much as 80 percent of the entire output of the silent-film era has been lost to us forever.

The main reason for this monumental loss of our cultural heritage is the decay of the nitrate stock on which silent films were photographed and printed. Though it boasted a sharper image than acetate celluloid, nitrate proved to have nothing of its durability. As a result, most silent films have just decomposed—or ignited and burned—right in their cans in the years since they left general distribution.

But there are other reasons, too—most notably the wanton destruction of these films by the studios themselves. Witness this excerpt from an MGM memo dated December 9, 1931: "This is a partial check-up of the list for destruction of negatives. The following negatives may be destroyed as we own all silent rights: *A Blind Bargain, The Arab, The Wind, After Midnight, Alias Jimmy Valentine, Affairs of Desire, Anna Christie, Baby Cyclone, Becky, The Magician, Fair Co-Ed.*" All the studios— MGM was certainly not alone—regularly destroyed scores of their silents for many reasons: because the talkies had rendered them commercially worthless; because the studios needed more storage space; and because the nitrate stock could be boiled down and the valuable silver it contained extracted.

Thanks to the efforts of film collectors who have diligently sought to acquire prints of many silent films for their own personal enjoyment and edification, many supposedly "lost" films have been saved and miraculously keep turning up all the time—including some of those mentioned above. But the sad truth is that most are genuinely lost, and since many of the earliest gangster films made in America, and elsewhere, are among them, it is now virtually impossible to pinpoint the name or even the year of the very first gangster film.

A reasonable place to start, however, is D. W. Griffith's 1912 Biograph Company one-reeler, *The Musketeers of Pig Alley*, which silent-film historian Kevin Brownlow has called "the first gangster film of any importance to survive," in which "the consciousness of the gangster as social evil, the importance of territory, and the corruption of the police [all characteristics of the gangster film genre as it would soon evolve] are strongly suggested." The Griffith film even offers a harbinger of the type of movie gangster James Cagney would make his own in the 1930s—in the form of Elmer Booth's smilingly vicious character, the Snapper Kid.

Its plot is not what sets *The Musketeers of Pig Alley* apart as a significant early effort in the history of Hollywood Gangland, however. In fact, the plot is pure melodramatic hokum—of a type Griffith had used in many a previous Biograph film. Indeed, it would be surprising if the plot had contained any new ingredients at all, since in 1912 alone the prodigious Griffith turned out sixty-seven one- and two-reelers *in addition to Musketeers*—almost one and a quarter movies a week! No artist can keep up that kind of pace and come up with a wholly original work each time. Griffith would dust off the same plot and use it again in several more Biograph films, refashion it yet again into the modern story of his epic *Intolerance*, and return to the same tenement milieu in his 1931 talkie, *The Struggle*, a tale of poverty, alcoholism, and redemption that would prove to be his directorial swan song.

In *Musketeers*, Lillian Gish plays Griffith's archetypal waif, a child of the slums

Below, left: *Lillian Gish as the child of the slums in D. W. Griffith's* The Musketeers of Pig Alley (1912), *one of the most important early gangster films. (Courtesy Museum of Modern Art/Film Stills Archive)*

Right: *Gish attracts the eye of the Cagney-esque Snapper Kid (Elmer Booth) as another hood (Harry Carey) looks on. From* The Musketeers of Pig Alley (1912). *(Courtesy Museum of Modern Art/Film Stills Archive)*

married to a poor but aspiring musician who wants to give her a better life but can barely put food on the table. She attracts the eye of Booth, the aforementioned Snapper Kid, a fast-talking, nattily dressed ringleader of a small band of thieves and cutthroats whose other menacing members include pugilist Spike Robinson and future cowboy star Harry Carey.

Smitten, Booth determines to give her the better life she deserves out of his ill-gotten gains, and most of the film centers on his persistent efforts (which at one point includes slipping her a mickey) to get the virtuous Gish to bed and make her his own. As passions and plot complications mount, the streets of New York erupt in warfare between Booth's gang and a rival mob. When the gun smoke finally settles, the preyed-upon Gish and her hapless husband no longer have to worry about the Snapper Kid's ardor—her virtue and their marriage are intact—but the "problem of gangsterism" has left its mark upon the environment and their economic situation is not much improved.

Vividly performed and snappily paced, the film crams an amazing amount of action, character development, and plot into its brief ten minutes of running time. But the film is no more skillfully made or exciting, perhaps, than a number of other Griffith "virtuous heroine in jeopardy" melodramas made around the same time—*An Unseen Enemy,* for example, which also featured Lillian Gish and Harry Carey. But it definitely struck a more responsive chord with audiences—particularly in urban areas—due to its topicality and almost documentarylike sense of time and place, the two qualities that make it one of the classic early gangster movies.

At the time the film was made, New York City's various ethnic gangs (*Musketeers'* gangs are predominantly Irish) were beginning to spread their violent wings and encroach not only on one another's turf but on other parts of the city heretofore believed safe from gangland strife. Newspapers and magazines were full of stories about gangland murders, corrupt politicians, gambling operations, and other illegal activities, so the public was by no means in the dark about such things. Griffith simply capitalized on all the notoriety and public attention—as many other filmmakers have since done—by adapting his story right from the headlines. For added realism, he then shot much of the film in the same New York City locales where those headlines were being made. Biograph publicity handouts sensationally maintained that Griffith had even employed real gangsters in small parts to lend the film even more authenticity.

This is by no means an impossible claim; filmmakers such as Griffith, who favored shooting on location, often found themselves forced to pay "protection money" to local toughs and their gangster bosses to film on their turf and to keep potentially troublesome crowds from causing production delays or shutdowns. Very often, these strong-arm types found their way into scenes as background extras, their hardened, nonactorish faces lending the films in question not just authentic local color, but, in retrospect, a certain amount of historical currency, as well.

During the Patents Wars (1908–1913), when certain monied operators attempted to lay claim to the burgeoning film industry by placing a monopolistic stranglehold on the growing number of small independent film companies, the link between Hollywood and gangland grew even stronger. "They began to hire hoodlums to put us out of business—either by destroying the camera, if they could get hold of it, or by burning down our studios if we happened to have one," pioneer director Allan Dwan recalled. "That's one of the reasons most of us went to California, and to distant places, to get away from the packed areas where hoodlums could hide, appear with a gun suddenly and take away the camera."

The reverse also was true, says historian Kevin Brownlow. "The battles between the opposing unions claiming to represent the motion picture operators in Chicago featured gangsters, gunfights and full-scale riots. The Independents simply hired gangsters of their own to combat the Trust's gangsters"—and rewarded their protective on-site efforts by giving the hoodlums small parts as extras in their films.

Though the Patents Wars were finally resolved and most states have long since established film commissions to assist moviemakers in shooting on location without having to hire or pay off hoodlums, gangland pressure and influence continue to exert themselves even in modern-day Hollywood.

Francis Ford Coppola's production of *The Godfather,* for example, drew heavy fire from the Italian-American Anti-Defamation League and Italian-American Civil Liberties League for its use of the word *Mafia* and its portrayal of organized crime as a predominantly Italian-American activity. Both groups marched to protest the making of the film and used their influence to make it difficult for the filmmakers to shoot on New York City locations. Allegedly, there were even threats of union strikes (a subject touched on in the film itself) if the film proceeded or the offending word wasn't eliminated from the script. In a note of supreme hypocrisy, the president of the newly formed Italian-American Civil Rights League was Joe Colombo, the alleged head of one of the Mafia's largest and most powerful crime families. Paramount gave in to the pressure by eliminating all reference to the Mafia from both *The Godfather* and its 1974 sequel, *The Godfather, Part II*—although the offending word finally surfaced in 1990's *The Godfather, Part III.* Ironically, Colombo never got to see his efforts fulfilled. He was gunned down by a hit man belonging to a rival mob family while the first film was still in production. Even later, rumors of mob pressure and/or influence would surround the production of Martin Scorsese's gangster film *GoodFellas* (1990).

And it all started with D. W. Griffith's groundbreaking 1912 one-reeler, *The Musketeers of Pig Alley,* which the Biograph publicity handouts ballyhooed as a "depiction of the gangster evil." A film that even today boasts an atmosphere of undeniable authenticity—captured in black-and-white images that are still sharp and clear—it drives its "poverty breeds crime" message home with conviction and a still-considerable amount of power.

BOWERY BOYS, BIG BROTHERS, AND B GIRLS

Raoul Walsh's *The Regeneration* (1915) is the oldest surviving *feature-length* gangster film; in his autobiography, *Each Man in His Time,* Walsh contends that it was the first full-length gangster film ever made, which may well have been the case. A longer, West Coast variation of Griffith's *The Musketeers of Pig Alley,* called *The Gangster and the Girl,* had been produced a year earlier; still only a two-reeler, however, it was hardly a full-length feature. In any case, *The Regeneration* is definitely the most significant early five-reeler, for it firmly laid the foundation for what the gangster film would become in American culture, melding Griffith's gritty realism and high melodrama into a modern morality play with a much broader and richer canvas than *The Musketeers of Pig Alley.*

Walsh rightly envisioned the gangster film as heir to the Western, and he saw the new genre as a more malleable one in which themes more reflective of America's changing social and moral landscape could be vividly explored. Whereas traditional Western novels and Western movies tended to define their heroes and villains sharply, Walsh felt the gangster story provided the opportunity to do something much more intriguing: combine the hero and villain into a single individual, the antihero, whose struggle to overcome the evil and right the wrongs *in himself* (will he or won't he?) was the core drama. And in *The Regeneration,* Walsh set out to do just that. And virtually every gangster film made since, including those made by Walsh himself (*Me, Gangster; The Roaring Twenties; High Sierra; White Heat*), have followed this pattern.

Critic Andrew Sarris has described the typical Raoul Walsh hero as a man "sustained by nothing more than a feeling for adventure, always plunging into the unknown, and never too sure what he will find there." This is certainly an apt description of the hoodlum protagonist of Walsh's *The Regeneration,* which the director (billing himself as R. A. Walsh) wrote in collaboration with actor Carl Harbaugh, who also plays the part of the district attorney in the film. They based the film on a successful autobiography and play by Owen Frawley Kildare, an illiterate thief and small-time Bowery gang leader who transformed his life with the help of a dedicated social worker and schoolteacher named Marie Deering. Kildare lovingly nicknamed her "My Mamie Rose." Deering taught Kildare how to read and write, and the latter eventually became a successful chronicler of life in the slums from which he sprang; he was known as the Kipling of the Bowery. He and Marie Deering were to have married, but she died of pneumonia before they could, and he dedicated his inspirational 1903 autobiography, *My Mamie Rose: The Story of My Regeneration,* to her memory. Assisted by playwright Walter

Hackett, Kildare turned his book into a popular Broadway drama called *The Regeneration* several years later and producer William Fox acquired the film rights in 1915.

Walsh said of his approach to adapting Kildare's story to the screen: "The plot was basic. Heroine is running a mission in the Bowery for the city's needy. Hero... laughs at her for being a do-gooder. Although he is a gangster, she falls in love with him. From there, play it by ear." His treatment of Kildare's story, though shot on location in New York's Bowery, Chinatown, and in the tenement slums where Kildare grew up, was largely fictionalized. Even the protagnist's name was changed—from Owen Kildare to Owen Conway—though Marie Deering's name was retained.

The plot of this short (barely fifty minutes) but influential film is worth considering in some detail. The film picks up its Bowery hero's story during childhood, when Conway is tossed out on the street by his alcoholic father and forced to fend for himself. He gets a job in an icehouse, but as he grows older, he turns to a life of crime and eventually becomes leader of his own gang. Socialite Marie Deering (Anna Q. Nilsson), who is being courted by the district attorney, suggests a slumming party to the Lower East Side to see some of these much-talked-about gangsters in their native habitat. The DA is quickly spotted by some of the toughs he's been trying to put behind bars, a fracas ensues, and Conway (Rockliffe Fellowes) spirits the pair to safety.

Attracted to the young tough and appalled by the conditions she's witnessed, Marie takes up social work, meets Conway again, and teaches him to read and write so that he'll give up his criminal ways. They fall in love and plan to marry. But the DA intercedes and convinces Conway to give the girl up because he'll never be able to care for her properly, and will likely drag her down to his own level. Conway cuts the relationship off, but Marie, thinking he has gone back to his gang roots, pursues him and falls into the clutches of a rival gang member named Skinny the Rat (William Sheer). Skinny holds her hostage and attempts to rape her. During Conway's attempted rescue, Skinny tries to gun him down, but Marie is accidentally shot and killed instead. Mad with grief and a desire for revenge, Conway grabs Skinny by the neck and starts to throttle the life out of him, but he is stopped by a vision of the dead girl uring him to leave vengeance to God, and he lets Skinny go. Conway's close pal, a hunchback whom Conway once saved from a brutal assault by Skinny, is not quite as forgiving, however. As Skinny attempts to escape across a wash line to an adjoining tenement, the hunchback shoots him and Skinny falls to his death. The film ends with Marie's burial and Conway's commitment to changing his life for good in her memory.

Among the particularly impressive scenes is one where Skinny the Rat sets fire to an excursion barge Marie has hired to give her charges a day's outing on

Marie Deering (Anna Q. Nillson) falls into the clutches of Skinny the Rat (William A. Sheer). From Raoul Walsh's The Regeneration (1915), *the oldest surviving feature-length gangster film. (Courtesy Museum of Modern Art/Film Stills Archive)*

the scenic Hudson River. As the barge is consumed in flames and slowly sinks, Marie and Conway as well as scores of others flee for their lives by jumping over the sides. In his autobiography, Walsh remembered the day the scene was shot: "When the women jumped, their skirts ballooned up and I was almost sure that some of them were not wearing anything underneath. However, they were falling so fast that one body shut out another and I could not be certain. . . . Two days after we finished shooting, the rushes were run in Fox's private projection room. . . . To my horror, what I had suspected was the truth. At least a dozen of the females were naked as jaybirds under their long dresses. . . . If we cut out that part of the sequence, the whole thing would be ruined. If we ran the picture as it was, we'd all go up the river for a long, long time." Walsh ingeniously saved the day by hiring an optical man literally to paint underwear on the women, frame by frame. "Fox was so pleased that he raised me to $800 a week. . . . As a bonus, he threw in a new Simplex car."

The Kipling of the Bowery's sad but uplifting story proved durable enough—and malleable enough—to be retold once more to cinema audiences less than a decade later, when director Irving Cummings refilmed it for Universal as *Fools' Highway* (1924). The remake starred Mary Philbin—who would play Christine to Lon Chaney's definitive *Phantom of the Opera* a year later—as Mamie Rose and Pat O'Malley as the gangster, here named Mike Kildare, who is inspired and reformed by her love. *Fools' Highway* took even more liberties with Kildare's story than *The Regeneration* had: His Mamie Rose is neither a socialite nor a social worker but a

Mamie Rose (Mary Philbin) finds herself trapped in a similar situation in Fools' Highway *(1924), a loose remake of Walsh's* The Regeneration. *(Courtesy Museum of Modern Art/Film Stills Archive)*

mender in a Bowery clothing shop. She befriends the hoodlum Kildare and the two fall in love; over the protests of Kildare's fellow gang members, she manages to persuade Kildare not just to give up his gangster ways but even to join the police force. Despite its almost complete bowdlerization of Kildare's story (capped off by a phony happy ending), however, the film — which regrettably seems to be among the lost — apparently did share at least some of its predecessor's realistic ambience.

Raoul Walsh's next and last underworld drama of the silent era, *Me, Gangster* (1928), was yet another reworking of the old *The Regeneration* material, though not strictly a remake. The film was based on the life of another hoodlum turned reformer and writer, Charles Francis Coe, who first told his story in a series of *Saturday Evening Post* articles, later published in a 1927 best-seller called *Me — Gangster*. Anticipating another potent hit on the order of *The Regeneration*, William Fox quickly scooped up the rights and assigned Walsh to direct. Coe collaborated with Walsh on the screenplay.

Though *Me, Gangster* lacks the on-location atmosphere that had contributed so much to *The Regeneration*'s authenticity (it was filmed entirely on the West Coast in Fox studios), it nevertheless bears striking similarities to the earlier film. Like *The Regeneration*, *Me, Gangster* follows its gangster hero, Jimmy Williams (Don Terry), from youth through early adulthood. A slum victim with no formal education, Terry turns to petty thievery to survive and gradually makes a name for himself with the local gangs, who turn him on to bigger and badder things, including

Raoul Walsh's last underworld drama of the silent era, Me, Gangster (1928), fictionalized the life of another hoodlum turned writer and reformer, Charles Francis Coe, played by Don Terry (center).

armed robbery. Terry decides to go it alone, and he scores a whopping fifty-thousand-dollar haul, which he stashes in a safe hiding place. The police catch him, though, and when he refuses to tell where the money is, he's sent up the river for two years.

While he's in prison, Terry's mother dies in poverty. Embittered at first, and determined *never* to reveal the location of the money, he undergoes a moral transformation through the influence of a kindly young woman named Mary Regan (June Collyer), with whom he falls in love. When he's paroled for good behavior, he decides to give the money back, but his former gangland associates, who have long drooled over his solo score and tried to discover its whereabouts, have different ideas. When Terry and his girl retrieve the loot to give it back, the gang kidnaps them and holds them captive in a rundown tenement. Like *The Regeneration*'s angelic Marie Deering, Collyer is assaulted by one of the gangsters, prompting her lover to fly into action. In the fast and furious finale, he overcomes the hoods and goes off into the sunset with his girl.

Though *Me, Gangster* did well at the box office, it didn't repeat *The Regeneration*'s success with the critics, and Walsh himself neglects to mention it in his auto-biography. Wrote *Variety*'s critic:

> Raoul Walsh had full opportunities for a crook epic, but whether it is the fault of the director or Coe's own transmutation, the yarn read better

than it screens. Walsh has striven hard to inject little niceties. One such is the prison visiting room with a fellow inmate deterred from passing a chocolate bar to his baby, brought in by the convict's wife, because of a placarded warning against the exchange of articles between visitors and prisoners. The guard comes over when signalled and passes the harmless confection to the baby, creating one of the all too few heart-throb moments which a frank morality theme such as that in *Me, Gangster* should possess.

The film, which is lost, was among the first silents to be released with the novelty of a synchronized music track. "With or without sound [however]," noted *Variety*, "it makes no difference, none of its [the film's] values being enhanced or detracted either way."

Allan Dwan's 1923 production *Big Brother* earned a much different reception. Based on a fictionalized account of the Big Brother (later Big Brother–Big Sister) movement by the prolific Rex Beach, *Big Brother* was the emotional tale of a tough gang leader, Gentleman Jim Donovan (Tom Moore), who is redeemed by his commitment to caring for the orphaned boy (Mickey Bennett) of a dead underling. Shot on Lower East Side locales as was *The Regeneration*, and employing real gangsters as extras just as Griffith was said to have done in *The Musketeers of Pig Alley*, the picture was so realistic in its depiction of urban gangsterism and slum life (even including a constantly doped-up "cokie" played by Raymond Hatton) that even the reviewers took notice of its documentary value. Commented *The New York Times*: "Mr. Dwan impresses his atmosphere on all those who see this film. He shows trains on the elevated railroad, above and below, the Queensborough Bridge, street after street of hopelessly squalid dwellings and line after line of freshly laundered flannel and linen hanging on roofs and in open spaces. It is a splendid picture told with unusual sincerity."

Many decades later, Allan Dwan described the making of the film to critic/ director Peter Bogdanovich. Dwan had insisted on shooting on location, even though such shooting was fast becoming the exception rather than the norm:

The basic thing was that we worked in real environments. We didn't build sets. There were two gangs who were bitter enemies—the Hudson Dusters and the Gas House Gang—and, through diplomacy and some money, we got them both to bring their girls and come up to a big famous dance hall at the edge of Harlem. And we laid it on the line with the two gang leaders, and asked them, since they were being paid, to do exactly what we asked and nothing else. And they agreed—shook hands on it. But the police department—just in case—sent up their famous hard-arm squad—the toughest gang of policemen you'll ever know. They

Tom Moore and Edith Roberts in director Allan Dwan's lost classic Big Brother *(1923).*

were standing by. Just as we were ready to start a big dance number, my cameraman [Hal Rosson] decided he needed more light, so to his electricians and grips he called out loudly, "Take the silks [scrims] off the broads [klieg lights]." Well, in gangland, "silks" are dresses and "broads" are girls, so they heard this command, thought it was an order — "Take the silks off the broads" — and started to [undress the girls]. Well, the girls revolted and ran for their lives, the guys got tangled up with each other and the fight was on. Somebody blew the whistle and the hard-arm squad came in and started to lay their clubs down, and we photographed it all. Nearly took all the police ambulances in New York to take these guys away to get patched up. It was the most vivid gangfight I've ever seen. And I had to go back and write it into the picture. But we got a very seedy, very authentic background for the picture and it was a real heartbreaker with fine characterizations.

Reviewers agreed. "One of the best 'underworlds' ever screened," one critic wrote. "One little detail will suffice to illustrate the knowledge of gangdom by the author [Paul Sloane] and director. The leader of the rival gang arrives [at the dance hall] with his 'moll.' He wanders inside and is promptly 'fanned' for his 'rod' by two bouncers. He is 'clean,' for he had previously slipped the gat to the dame. She had it planted conveniently in her handbag. Even in gangdom it is

unethical to search a lady." The critic concluded, "It is a realistic, melodramatic triumph and a really great picture." Unfortunately, modern audiences will never know, since Paramount failed to preserve the film's negatives and prints and *Big Brother* is lost to us forever.

William Wellman's *Ladies of the Mob* (1928) and Irving Cummings's *A Romance of the Underworld* (1928) were among the few important films of the era to turn the spotlight on the distaff side of the gangland problem.

The Wellman film, which is lost, starred "It" girl Clara Bow, one of the most popular romantic comedy stars of her day, in an atypically dramatic role—that of a young woman whose gangster father is sent to the chair for robbery and murder. To avenge herself against society, Bow's mother raises the girl to become a master crook. Bow partners with youthful offender Richard Arlen and other, more hardened criminals to pull off a daring bank raid. But when she and Arlen fall in love, Bow undergoes a moral transformation. To prevent her beau from going down the same road as her father, she steers Arlen away from the robbery—which leads to much bloodshed at the last minute—and the two of them decide to go straight thereafter. *Ladies of the Mob* was a huge financial success for Paramount; nevertheless, the studio returned Bow to making comedies, and she never appeared in a film quite like it again.

Based on a popular 1911 play by Paul Armstrong, *A Romance of the Underworld* picked up on a similar theme to the Wellman film. Mary Astor stars as a country girl who goes to work as a prostitute (or "hostess," as she is more politely called) in a seedy dance hall and speakeasy frequented by gangsters and other lowlifes. When the place is raided and she's almost jailed, she decides to better her life, working as a laundress and waitress while taking courses in stenography.

She lucks out and lands a job as personal secretary to John Boles, an up-and-coming businessman from a well-to-do family who knows nothing of her past. They fall in love and plan to marry, but her past rears its ugly head in the shape of dapper Derby Dan Manning (Ben Bard), one of the gangsters she'd known during her "hostess" days. When Bard threatens to expose her, Astor finds herself at a moral crossroads: Should she give in and likely be bled dry and dragged down again in the process, or continue on her redemptive road by turning the problem over to the kindly police detective she'd met the night the speakeasy was raided? She chooses the latter course, the detective makes short work of Bard, and the reformed Astor and Boles get married and live happily ever after.

Though it wasn't considered to be in the same league as the harder-hitting gangster morality plays *The Regeneration* and *Big Brother* (or even *Me, Gangster*, for that matter), *A Romance of the Underworld* at least gave audiences the chance to view the underworld from a slightly different perspective. Critics called the character study "a quiet, even if absorbing picture," and commented on its subtly evoked atmosphere: "Even the night club isn't overdone. It's meant to be a cheap joint and that's what it looks like." Befitting the technical and artistic sophistication of silent films by this point, *Romance of the Underworld* is slickly made. It is beautifully photographed, boasting many subtle camera moves, deftly edited, and credibly acted, particularly by Astor, who is luminous as the wayward girl regenerated.

Despite such successes as *Ladies of the Mob* and *Romance of the Underworld*, however, the gangster film would remain a male-dominated genre throughout the silent era and beyond, much like the very underworld society that studios and directors were spending more and more time and money trying to capture.

THE MOBSTER OF A THOUSAND FACES

Determining the cinema's first gangster movie is a lot more difficult than pinpointing the first full-fledged gangster movie star. That distinction belongs to the silent cinema's immortal "Man of a Thousand Faces," Lon Chaney.

Though Chaney is more famous now for his classic portrayals of Quasimodo in *The Hunchback of Notre Dame*, the title character in *The Phantom of the Opera*, and many other grotesques, he played quite a few crooks, "underworlders," and gangsters during his seventeen-year career as one of the silent film's most versatile, esteemed, and highest-paid performers. At the time of his death of throat cancer in 1930, Chaney ranked alongside Garbo as MGM's most popular star. Had he lived, it is

The cinema's first gangster movie star, Lon Chaney, strikes a Cagney-esque pose as Black Mike Sylva in Tod Browning's Outside the Law *(1921). He even snarls, "You dirty rat!" at one point.*

likely his star power would have endured, for unlike many actors of the silent screen, the stage-trained Chaney had no fear of the microphone. As *The New York Times* reported, Chaney even welcomed the chance to expand upon his persona as the cinema's Man of Mystery in the new medium of the talkies. "[Chaney] realized the microphone would prevent him from indulging in the make-ups which had won him the sobriquet of the 'man of a thousand faces,'" the *Times* wrote on the eve of Chaney's talkie debut in the underworld drama *The Unholy Three*, a remake of one of his biggest silent successes. "He had secured most of his facial distortions by holding foreign substances of divers shapes and sizes in his mouth. However, Chaney had made up his mind that if he couldn't indulge the genius for make-up which had earned him his unusual position in the cinema world, he would develop a new talent, that of voice disguises for the talking pictures."

Commented Chaney:

Even as a prop boy, I used to watch Richard Mansfield and Robert Mantell and others. Those old actors never showed the audience themselves, but really donned the personality of the character they were playing. From the beginning of my acting career, I always strove to bury my own personality in my part. That is my idea of acting. And there is no question that talking pictures are bringing back the old style of acting. I want to talk in at least two voices, or dialects, in each picture.

In *The Unholy Three,* he kept his word, using not just two more voices but four — those of an old woman, a ventriloquist's dummy, a talking parrot, and a young woman in the courtroom gallery where the film's climax takes place — in addition to his own (one assumes) as the gang leader of the unsavory trio of jewel robbers that calls itself "the unholy three."

Judging by Chaney's compelling looks, demeanor, and particularly his voice as the film's gangster antihero, it is easy to believe that if he'd lived, he might have gone on to become the first great gangster movie star of the talkies, as well. One can envision him playing Edward G. Robinson's Rico Bandello in *Little Caesar* (1930), the part of Tony Camonte (Paul Muni), the underworld antihero of *Scarface* (1932), or even some of Humphrey Bogart's gangster roles, especially that of the doomed Roy Earle in *High Sierra* (1941). Only the gangsters played by the more youthful and pugnacious James Cagney (who, like Chaney, began his career as stage hoofer) would probably have eluded him — though Chaney strikes a very Cagney-like pose in *Ouside the Law* (1921), one of his earliest gangster film successes. Cagney, of course, later played Chaney himself in Universal's powerful and affecting but by no means "warts and all" biography of the star, the 1957 *The Man of a Thousand Faces.*

The Penalty (1920) offered Chaney one of the genre's meatiest early mobster roles, and Chaney used the opportunity to create an indelible portrait of one of the gangster movie's archetypes: the victimized youth who turns to crime for revenge, becoming his city's top gang boss. A violent, psychotic "lord and master of the underworld," *The Penalty*'s protagonist, called Blizzard, is a Little Caesar and Phantom of the Opera rolled into one. Indeed, Blizzard is both little — as a boy, his legs had been unnecessarily amputated by an inexperienced doctor following a traffic accident, filling him with a desire for revenge against the doctor and society — and a megalomaniac who in a moment of frenzy grandiosely calls himself "a modern Caesar." He is also an accomplished musician who takes to soothing his savage breast now and then on the piano, soaring into flights of romantic rapture as one of his molls, perversely stationed beneath him, works the pedals for him with her hands. It's no wonder Universal considered no one but Chaney for the part of the Phantom when it came time to cast the picture a few years later; in these scenes, Chaney's performance seems almost like a warm-up for his most famous role.

Not all of Chaney's contemporaries were enamored of the man's abilities, of course. The acerbic director Josef von Sternberg, who would contribute as much to the genre as Chaney with his groundbreaking 1927 gangster film, *Underworld,* called him "a man who poisons wells," who confused makeup with acting and indulged in "extravagant histrionics." It's true that many of Chaney's vehicles were full of contrivances and improbabilities and are not great films. Many of his roles were rooted in some kind of gimmick that enabled him to appear in a different guise each time, thereby cementing his reputation and box-office appeal. But von Sternberg's accusation that Chaney was a man who confused makeup with acting is unfair; for however mediocre many of his films may have been, his performances—particularly in gangster roles—are as subtle and believable as they are "extravagantly histrionic."

The Penalty is a good example. The plot, as most reviewers noted even at the time, is wildly implausible, its final twist stretching credulity to the limit. But Chaney delivers a powerful, multishaded performance that's much more than bravura stunt work. Commented *The New York Times:* "When Chaney appears with both his legs sawed off above the knees, some will exclaim, 'How in the world can he do that?' but after they have followed his acting for awhile, and felt the force of his presence on the screen, they will take it as just a part of his role that his legs are missing. But in all he does, the man he is supposed to be is present."

It's true that the viewer can't help but gape in wonder at Chaney's physical prowess and endurance, as the actor, his limbs trussed tightly behind him and concealed beneath a long coat, hops about on crutches, jumps to the floor from platforms, landing on his knees, walks up stairs, slides down poles, and hoists himself up a pegged wall hand by hand to spy into an adjoining room. But that's not all there is to his performance. He's equally impressive in the less flamboyant scenes, when the camera focuses just on his expressive face—features grim but eyes twinkling—as he wrestles with the rising tide of evil in himself, aware that his urges are desperately sick yet eager to surrender to them at the same time. We see his pain when he spurns with barely concealed horror and distaste the advances of the woman who loves him—because her actions remind him that the woman *he* loves looks upon him as a freak. And when he fantasizes about his grand scheme to bring the city to *its* knees, he reveals the full measure of his wounded pride, a revelation that shocks even his closest underling. The scheme involves rousing thousands of the city's disgruntled foreign laborers (Reds) to armed insurrection so that the police and the army must combine forces to stop them—during which Blizzard and his men will move in and loot the city's treasury.

Even the laughable ending—the doctor who crippled him operates on Blizzard's brain, removing the "contusion at the base of the skull" that has driven the inherently good man to evil—manages to pack a punch due to Chaney's skill and firm grasp of the character. A reformed man, he sits at his beloved piano with his wife by his side, fantasizing about how he will dismantle the criminal empire he has created. But a quivering drug addict named Frisco Pete, whom Blizzard had reduced to subservience by threatening to withhold the man's dope supply, shoots Blizzard in the back because he's afraid the reformed criminal will snitch on the gang. As Frisco Pete escapes, Blizzard calmly realizes he's paying the penalty for his past misdeeds. "Don't grieve, dear," he tells his tearful wife. "Death interests me." And he falls dead at the piano.

It's a remarkable performance that lifts what is otherwise an uneven, albeit slick, early gangster film to near-classic status.

Chaney followed the Samuel Goldwyn production of *The Penalty* with another strong, but very different, gangster role for Universal in Tod Browning's *Outside the Law.* Chaney had worked with Browning before, in the 1919 crime picture *The Wicked Darling,* in which Chaney played a small-time crook named Stoop. *Outside the Law* reunited him with both Browning and Priscilla Dean, who was fast becoming a popular fixture in Universal gangster films; she not only played the titular lady in the Browning film but starred in two other underworld dramas for the studio — *The Wildcat of Paris* (1918) and *Pretty Smooth* (1919) — during the same period.

Chaney's association with Browning — a director as "obsessional" (in the words of a contemporary magazine writer) in his choice of subject matter as the actor was in his selection of and commitment to his roles — formed a perfect match between star and filmmaker. It would extend to eight more collaborations in the coming decade, four of them gangster films: *The Unholy Three* (1925), *The Blackbird* (1926), *The Road to Mandalay* (1926), and *The Big City* (1928).

In *Outside the Law,* Chaney plays two parts, the first a smilingly vicious Cagneyesque gangster in bow tie and fedora named Black Mike Sylva. At one point, he even snarls, "You dirty rat!" — the phrase that would later become most associated with Cagney. Chaney also plays Ah Wing, the watchdog servant of the Confucius-spouting reformer of the crooks of Frisco who helps the film's main leads, Molly Madden (Dean) and Dapper Bill Ballard (Wheeler Oakman), go straight. Chaney's dual characters — particularly Ah Wing — get little screen time, since the film's primary focus is the evolving relationship between Dean and Oakman and the events that spur their rehabilitation. Black Mike and Ah Wing are really just supporting roles. They only take center stage during the gun-blazing finale, when Black Mike and his gang try to get even with the lovers for a double cross. As Chaney's Black Mike attempts to throttle the life out of Oakman, his Ah Wing fires a bullet into Black Mike's black heart and the villain crashes through a railing, falls from a balcony (a stunt Chaney appears to have performed himself), and expires from his wounds shortly thereafter. With the aid of clever cutting, Browning gave audiences the chance to watch one Lon Chaney kill another.

Critics termed the lightweight but fast-paced and efficient little potboiler "real underworld stuff [that] begins with action and ends with action, and carries

Lon Chaney played Little Caesar and Phantom of the Opera rolled into one as the crippled gang leader Blizzard in The Penalty *(1920).*

a strong moral: that virtue or honesty has its reward"—a message typical of the crime films of the period.

Browning later made a talkie version of *Outside the Law* (1930) that neither begins with action nor ends with it. If anything, it's even more languorous than the director's *Dracula*, made the following year. Despite a fair amount of camera movement, which itself was unusual for Browning, the film is extremely stagy, and, though only eighty-two minutes long, seems to go on for a couple of hours. The youthful cast moves the same way, shuffling along like geriatrics—one can almost hear the sound man ordering Browning to slow the actors' movements to a crawl because the tyrannical microphone wasn't picking up their footsteps—and speaks its lines in the halting manner people usually reserve for foreigners or those who are hard-of-hearing.

Set in San Francisco, like the original, the remake features Edward G. Robinson in Chaney's fashion-plate gangster role, although his character is renamed Cobra Collins. Ah Wing was dropped, as were many other important characters, but an attempt was made to retain the Asian angle by turning Cobra into a Chinese-American. As Robinson wears not the slightest daub of makeup even to indicate he's part Chinese, this revelation, which comes when he introduces an Asian woman as his mother, is so jaw-droppingly improbable that we can't help but wonder whether the filmmaker is pulling our leg. He isn't, but our incredulity persists to such a degree that at the conclusion of the film, when Cobra is killed and the hero (Owen Moore) calls out to the cops, "There's a half million bucks and a dead Chinaman waitin' for you up here," the audience skips a beat, wondering whom the hell Moore is referring to.

Moore and Mary Nolan are much more convincing as the young crooks who are reformed by the love of a child and decide to seek a new life on the straight and narrow as soon as they put in a one-to-five-year stretch in the pen for bank robbery. The casting of Nolan was ingenious, for the actress, much like her character, had escaped a scandalous past to seek a new life, although for very different reasons. As a rising star of the *Ziegfeld Follies* in the mid-1920s named Imogen Wilson (the press called her "the most dazzling flower in the Ziegfeld hot-house"), the attractive blonde had become involved in a love affair with the *Follies'* top funnyman, the married Frank Tinney, who apparently had a fondness for beating the young woman up during their frequent liaisons. Following a particularly brutal beating, Wilson finally decided she'd had enough and called the police. News of the scandalous affair erupted into the headlines. Tinney's career was destroyed; Wilson was fired from the *Follies*. She made her way to Hollywood to pick up her life, acting in the movies under the pseudonym Mary Nolan.

Chaney followed his back-to-back gangster-film successes with other crook roles in 1922's *Flesh and Blood*, directed by Irving Cummings, and Lambert Hillyer's

Edward G. Robinson played the Chaney role in Browning's talkie remake of Outside the Law *(1930) although his character is renamed Cobra Collins and is supposed to be part Chinese.*

The Shock (1923), in which Chaney plays a cripple in the employ of Christine Mayo's Queen of the San Francisco Underworld. Mayo uses Chaney to exact revenge against a banker (William Welsh) who caused her to be sent up the river for a time. But her villainous underling refuses to carry out his mission when he falls in unrequited love with the banker's daughter (Virginia Valli) and undergoes a spiritual transformation. Not to be outfoxed, the vengeful Mayo lures Valli to San Francisco in the hope of sullying her reputation. But the Great San Francisco Earthquake intervenes to thwart Mayo's plans, and Valli, if not the city, is saved from "ruination." In one of the most improbable of all happy endings, the "shock" also cures Chaney of his deformity, so that he can at last satisfy his love for Valli.

Chaney reunited with Tod Browning for the first version of *The Unholy Three* (1925), the most successful collaboration, critically and commercially, of their careers. Though not as deliriously perverse as some of his later films with and without Chaney, *The Unholy Three* is nevertheless quintessential Tod Browning. Based on a novel by the British writer Clarence "Tod" Robbins, who also provided the source for Browning's classic chiller *Freaks* (1932), the film begins in typical Browning territory—a carnival sideshow replete with tattooed ladies, Siamese twins, sword swallowers, and other assorted human oddities. As the crowds surge to gawk, Chaney, a sideshow ventriloquist, has his accomplice (Mae Busch) move among them, pickpocketing their valuables. The show's midget attraction (Harry Earles) angers the crowd by kicking a child making fun of him. When his protector,

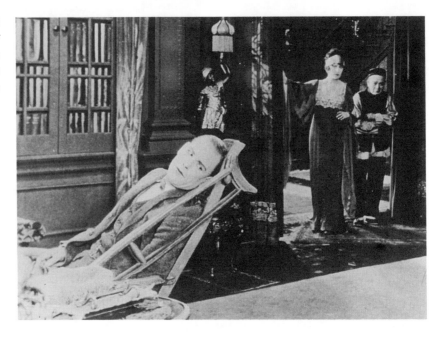

Chaney as a crippled gangster in the employ of Christine Mayo's "Queen of the San Francisco Underworld" in The Shock *(1923).*

Hercules the Strongman (Victor McLaglen), rushes to the midget's aid, a free-for-all breaks out, and the police are called in, bringing a quick finish to Chaney's scam.

Tired of petty hauls—a watch here, a wallet there—Chaney forms an unholy alliance with the midget and the strongman and opens an exotic bird shop to be used as a front for luring wealthy patrons. Disguising himself as a kindly gray-haired grandmother, Chaney uses his skills as a ventriloquist to convince customers the birds can speak. (Browning cleverly shows the birds "speaking" by using comic-strip word balloons superimposed over the birds' heads.) When delivery is made to the customers' homes, Chaney and his cohorts use the opportunity to case the surroundings for expensive jewels and other valuables, returning later to rob the houses.

To make the shop appear as innocent and aboveboard as possible, the strong-man poses as Granny's son-in-law and chief delivery boy, while the midget convincingly disguises himself as her infant grandson, dressed in swaddling clothes. Pretending to be Granny's daughter, Busch works as a clerk in the shop, assisted by the dim but honest Hector (Matt Moore), who is completely ignorant of the group's illegal activities and falls for the girl. When she falls for Moore in return, Chaney grows jealous—for he's in love with Busch, as well—and the successful operation shows its first signs of cracking.

When a customer rings up to complain that the parrot he'd bought no longer talks, Chaney and the midget pay a friendly house call, where Chaney uses his ventriloquist skills again to give the parrot a voice. He also witnesses the delivery of a valuable ruby necklace. The unholy three make plans to steal the necklace on Christmas Eve, but Chaney's unease at the prospect of leaving Busch and Moore alone for the evening decorating the shop Christmas tree prompts him to postpone the burglary for several hours. Impatient to get his hands on the necklace, the greedy midget manipulates the strongman into pulling the job without Chaney; during the course of the robbery, the owner of the necklace is murdered.

Chaney berates the pair for the killing but is pleased with their haul and stashes the necklace in a toy elephant for safekeeping until the heat's off. In the film's most suspenseful scene, a detective almost stumbles upon the necklace, but the strongman grabs the toy elephant away from him and, upbraiding the detective for "teasing the baby," returns it to the wailing midget's outstretched hands. The close shave with the cops prompts Chaney to shut down operations and disappear to the gang's mountain hideout. Before skipping, however, he orders the midget to plant the necklace in Moore's apartment, and the young man is later arrested. When Busch threatens to blow the whistle to save her lover, the unholy three tie her up and take her along.

At the mountain hideout, Busch offers to marry Chaney if he'll get Moore off the hook. Posing once more as Granny, Chaney attends the trial and slips Moore a note urging him to take the stand in his own defense but to say nothing, just silently mumble the Lord's Prayer. Meanwhile, Chaney throws his voice into Moore's mouth, revealing the details of the bird-shop scam, the theft of the necklace, and the murder. The ploy backfires, however, and when it looks as if Moore will be convicted anyway, Chaney keeps his promise to Busch by standing up and making a full confession, naming the midget and the strongman as the genuine culprits.

At the cabin, the midget and the strongman have a falling-out and are killed (the latter by Chaney's pet gorilla), and Busch escapes. She rejoins Chaney, intending to keep her part of the bargain, but the reformed gang leader has a change of heart and allows her to go to the exonerated Moore instead. Chaney then returns to his former job as a sideshow ventriloquist—apparently with the blessing of the authorities, who've chosen to forgive him for all the other crimes in which he *did* take part.

Perhaps because it was one of the more bizarre gangster dramas turned out by Hollywood during what one contemporary reviewer prematurely labeled "the golden age of underworld stories," the film inspired more acclaim than it seems to merit today. It boasts some unusual images: the vision of Chaney whipping off his Granny wig and transforming into his gangster self—forgetting that Granny's earrings are still dangling from his lobes—and that of the midget relaxing in his crib with a cigar stuck in his mouth. But structurally, the film isn't very well worked out, and at times it seems almost disdainful of the audience.

Harry Earles, Victor McLaglen, and Lon Chaney as the crooked title characters in the silent version of The Unholy Three *(1925).*

The ape that kills the strongman isn't introduced to the viewer until the moment it's unleashed. Coming out of nowhere, it seems hardly more than a contrivance thrown in by Browning to give the audience a last-minute frisson while getting the strongman out of the way. Similarly, little is made of the fascinating relationship Browning sets up between "the greedy bit of flesh" midget and the strongman, his beefy but cowardly protector. The film intriguingly hints at a homosexual undercurrent to the midget's behavior — particularly in the scenes where he and Busch reveal a mutual loathing for one another — but gives only hints; Browning gives no definite evidence. And the conclusion, where Chaney confesses all and is let off scot-free, is not only implausible but seems only to serve the design of leaving audiences with a happy ending. Though cleverly rendered through title cards and pantomime, Chaney's ventriloquism scenes don't really work in a silent-film format. They cry out for sound, which is why the story became such an ideal vehicle for Chaney's talkie debut.

The talkie remake, directed by Jack Conway, is superior to the silent version in every respect, although one would not think so judging from the very different critical reaction the two versions received. *Variety* called the silent version "a wow of a story [in which] Lon Chaney stands out like a million dollars." And yet five years later, it said of the remake: "[The] weakness is that the story doesn't adapt well to the talkie technique. Skill in make-up permitted Chaney to get away with the impersonation of the old woman before, but his handling of dialog destroys all plausibility."

Conway's talkie follows Browning's silent fairly closely, even recreating whole scenes from the earlier film shot for shot. But the talkie fleshes out the story and characters more, and the medium of sound allows the characters to engage in some hilarious repartee. At one point, Elliott Nugent's Hector (who is still sappy but nowhere near as stupid as Matt Moore's) marvels to his girl (Lila Lee), "It's wonderful the way your grandma can make those birds talk!" To which Lee caustically responds, "Hector, she could make Coolidge talk!" Contemporary reviewers felt that Lee wasn't "nearly as convincing as Mae Busch in the silent picture," but Lila Lee breathes more sparkle and personality into the role, giving the character of Rosie a hard-edged yet vulnerable quality similar to the later bad/good–girl roles of Glenda Farrell, Joan Blondell, Claire Trevor, and, of course, Bette Davis. The writers also make more of the implied undercurrents in the midget and strongman's relationship; in a priceless exchange, the midget disdainfully says, "You're the one that shoulda been the old woman"; the strongman replies, "I'm not that kind of guy."

Variety to the contrary, Chaney's handling of his dialogue and vocal impersonations is not only convincing but quite impressive; no one voice sounds like another, and yet they all belong to Chaney. Believing audiences might be skeptical of this, the actor even made out a legal document testifying that the voices were his, a deposition widely circulated prior to the film's release. Witnessed by a prominent Los Angeles notary public, the statement contended: "I, Lon Chaney, being first duly sworn, depose and say: In the photoplay entitled *The Unholy Three*, produced by Metro-Goldwyn-Mayer Corporation, all voice reproductions which purport to be reproductions of my voice, to wit the ventriloquist's, the old woman's, the dummy's, the parrot's, and the girl's [a member of the sideshow audience], are actual reproductions of my own voice, and in no place in said photoplay, or in any other of the various characters played by me in said photoplay, was a 'double' or substitute used for my voice."

The remake also lays the groundwork for the strongman's murder by Chaney's pet gorilla by introducing the creature to us in the opening carnival sideshow scenes. Fearful of the strongman's strength and the possibility that he might someday turn against him, Chaney cages the beast (which the strongman took joy in mistreating) and keeps it in the back of the bird shop throughout the film — and later takes it to the mountain hideout — "just in case."

Lon Chaney and Lila Lee in Jack Conway's superior remake of The Unholy Three *(1930), Chaney's last film and only talkie.*

Also much improved is the courtroom denouement. The remake throws out the contrived ventriloquism scene and has Chaney, in his Granny disguise, take the stand in Nugent's defense. As the DA bears down on the old woman's assertion that the midget and the strongman committed the robbery and murder, Chaney gets flustered, lapses into his real voice, and is unmasked. Chaney nobly lets Lee out of her bargain just as he did Busch in the silent version, but rather than going back to his old life as a sideshow ventriloquist, he's more realistically sent to prison, and promises to send Lee a card now and then.

The Browning-Chaney team followed the silent *Unholy Three* with *The Blackbird* (1926), in which Chaney plays an even more intriguing dual role. The film stands up better today than the more acclaimed silent version of *The Unholy Three,* and it may be Browning's very best picture. It, too, would have made an excellent vehicle for Chaney's talkie debut, for its plot also centers on the gangster protagonist's ability to disguise both his appearance and his voice.

The film is set in London's seedy Limehouse District. Chaney takes two challenging roles: the villainous, morally crippled gang leader and thief, the Blackbird, and his kindly, physically crippled brother, the Bishop, beloved by all in Limehouse for his work on behalf of the poor. In reality, they're the same person: Whenever the cops put on the heat, the Blackbird pulls a fast fade, dons the Bishop's clothes and crutches, throws his hip and arm out of joint, and assumes the identity of the Bishop. The Blackbird further cements the masquerade by assuming two voices, conducting frequent loud altercations with the Bishop behind the locked doors of the Bishop's room in the district's mission house.

The Blackbird and his gang ply their trade by robbing wealthy Londoners who visit Limehouse for an occasional low-life night on the town. The wealthy are encouraged to join these slumming parties ("I say we all go down to Plum Alley to see the Chinkies smoking") by the Blackbird's high-society partner in crime, dapper West End Bertie (Owen Moore), who acts as tour guide for his wealthy friends. After they've been relieved of their valuables, he and the Blackbird split the take.

The smooth operation begins to fall apart, however, when the Blackbird and Bertie fall in love with the same girl, an attractive French lass named Fifi (Renée Adorée), who does a puppet show in one of the slum's dingy cabarets. When it becomes clear that Fifi has eyes only for Bertie, the jealous Blackbird dons his kindly Bishop guise and counsels the vulnerable young woman to forget the scoundrel. Fifi confronts her lover, and when Bertie agrees to go straight, she consents to marry him. Furious, the Blackbird frames Bertie for the murder of a policeman. Believing Bertie innocent, Fifi asks the Bishop for help, and the Bishop hides Bertie out. When he and Bertie are alone together, however, the Bishop manipulates Bertie into believing that Fifi and the Blackbird are carrying on an affair.

Jealous to get her man back (even if he gets a stretch in prison), the Blackbird's ex-wife (Doris Lloyd) tells Scotland Yard that the Blackbird is guilty of the policeman's murder. Fifi and Bertie are reunited when she convinces him of her genuine devotion, and the police let him go. Informed that the Blackbird is hiding out in the Bishop's digs, the cops attempt to break down the door. The Blackbird fakes a shouting match and a fight between himself and the Bishop, tossing furniture about the room and making it sound as if he's giving the Bishop a terrible beating. Simultaneously, he struggles into the Bishop's clothes, then tosses open a window to convince the police the Blackbird has flown. Throwing his hip and leg out of joint to complete his disguise, he hobbles to the door to let the police in, but just as he gets there, they burst inside and he's accidentally knocked to the floor, landing at an awkward angle and breaking his back.

Lloyd arrives as the police go for a doctor. Not knowing how bad his wounds are, the Blackbird/Bishop clues his startled ex-wife in on his dual identity, and, to avoid being unmasked during the doctors' physical examination, persuades her to stall the doctor long enough for him to regain his strength and get back on his feet. She suggests that he pretend to be asleep and resting comfortably so that the doctor will put off disturbing him. While doing so, he slips into unconsciousness and expires from his injuries, with the tearful woman by his side, whispering, "You fooled 'em to the end."

Although it was only a moderate box-office success, *The Blackbird* reveals the Chaney/Browning team at peak form. Chaney is not only physically and temperamentally convincing as the brother opposites, he is astonishing at times in his ability, with only minimal use of makeup, to make even the facial features of the Blackbird and the Bishop appear dissimilar.

Atmospherically photographed by Percy Hilburn, beautifully designed by Cedric Gibbons and A. Arnold Gillespie, and sharply edited by Errol Taggart, *The Blackbird* is one of Browning's most striking productions. The pictorial qualities of the film alone make it worth seeing; the surviving prints have been well preserved and are still gorgeous to behold. And for a Browning film, the plot is not only well worked out and plausible but credibly sustained throughout. And it ends, unlike

Limehouse gangster Dan Tate (Lon Chaney), a.k.a. The Blackbird (1926), *splits the take with his high-society partner in crime, dapper West End Bertie (Owen Moore).*

Lon Chaney as the scarfaced gang leader and smuggler Singapore Joe in The Road to Mandalay *(1926). With Rose Langdon.*

the two versions of *The Unholy Three,* with a twist that is genuinely surprising, grimly satisfying, and emotionally powerful.

Like most early gangster films, *The Blackbird* offers the familiar moral that crime doesn't pay. But it also looks forward to the later, more anarchic underworld films of the thirties, particularly those made by Warner Brothers, by offering viewers a gangster hero who is not only unrepentant of his violent and crooked ways but who keeps to those ways right to the bitter end.

Nineteen twenty-six also saw the release of another Browning/Chaney gangster film, *The Road to Mandalay.* Set in the Orient, the film is part underworld story and part domestic drama, with the emphasis on the latter. Chaney plays a scar-faced gang leader and smuggler named Singapore Joe, whose shop clerk daughter (Lois Moran) is not only unaware that he's her father but is repelled by the man's grotesque appearance and unsavory reputation. When the innocent young woman falls for one of Chaney's criminal associates (Owen Moore) and the two plan to marry, Chaney's paternal instincts kick in and he sets out to disrupt the wedding. Diverted from his criminal activities, he finds his criminal empire threatened by a brutal rival (Sojin) and must fight to hold on to his kingpin status. Sojin puts the moves on Chaney's daughter, tries to rape her, and Chaney is killed in a knife fight, saving her virtue and her life. Only then does she learn who Chaney really is and how much he obviously loved her.

Coming right after the superlative *The Blackbird, The Road to Mandalay* is something of a letdown. Events unfold rapidly but often without motivation; the entire construction of the film seems haphazard. But this assessment may be unfair, since the only surviving print of the film is an abridgment of the original seven-reel release.

Browning and Chaney's last gangster film together, *The Big City* (1928), returned the duo to the landscape of their earlier underworld successes—the streets of modern-day America. Its merits—and position in the Browning/Chaney gangster-film pantheon—cannot be adequately judged, however, since the film is on MGM's "lost list." Over the years, MGM managed to preserve most of the films Chaney made for them; their track record is certainly superior to that of any other studio. Of the eighteen silent films Chaney made for MGM, only four are presumed lost: *The Tower of Lies* (1925), *London After Midnight* (1927), *The Big City* (1928), and

Thunder (1929). Otherwise, the picture is rather bleak. "Of Chaney's over 150 billed appearances, a mere 29 of his films exist in a more or less complete form," says Chaney historian Jon Mirsalis. "Another six exist minus a few reels. That leaves over 110 of his films [almost three-quarters of his film career] completely missing."

All we have to go on today in assessing *The Big City* are a few surviving stills and the opinions of some reviewers, which don't always stand the test of time. Sporting no makeup, Chaney again played a flashily dressed big-city crime boss (a figure fast becoming a staple in Hollywood gangster films) who finds that his successful jewel-robbery operation is being undermined by gang rivals. With the help of his girlfriend (Betty Compson) and a loyal lieutenant (James Murray), Chaney turns the tables on his rivals, then he and his two cohorts decide to go straight.

One reviewer wrote, "*The Big City* begins at a swift gallop and ends at a lazy lope. The first half is filled with ingenious ideas, with surprise following surprise, but when Mr. Browning attacks the reformation of the leading gangster he permits the pace of his story to slacken until it becomes slightly tedious." *Variety* concluded: "The heavy publicity should be placed on Chaney as himself, without disguise, just to see the difference. For the picture itself, the best that may be said of it is that it ends with a laugh. When the chief crook reforms and tells his girl he's going to marry her, she's overwhelmed. Rushing toward him for a pleasurable hug, he repulses her, saying: 'Listen! I ain't going to buy you nothing. I'm just going to marry you.'"

Though its only known prints are missing an entire reel and are marred by print decomposition, Chaney's last silent gangster film, Jack Conway's *While the City Sleeps* (1928), remains one of his best. Again wearing no makeup (except, perhaps, for a hairpiece designed to make him appear a little thin on top), he delivers one of his most sensitive and moving performances as a veteran Irish cop in New York City's plainclothes division who suffers from chronically sore feet and, despite his gruff exterior, a sentimental and lonely heart. Known throughout the city for his dedication to duty and his ability to turn youthful offenders onto the straight and narrow, he falls for a girl twenty years his junior when he assigns himself to protect her from a mob hit. While she is hiding out in his cluttered bachelor apartment, Chaney gradually reveals his feelings toward her. Out of gratitude for all he's doing, she agrees to marry him, despite being in love with another, younger man (Carroll Nye), a small-time hood Chaney had given a break in exchange for his promise to move to another city and get into an honest line of work.

Nye mends his ways and returns to New York to marry the girl. When he finds her living in Chaney's apartment, he flies into a jealous rage, hurls her to

Above, left: Cop Lon Chaney takes on the mob with a Gatling gun in the exciting finale to While the City Sleeps *(1928), a crackerjack gangster picture of the silent era.*

Right: Lon Chaney and Lydia Yeamans Titus in the moving final shot of While the City Sleeps *(1928).*

the floor, and accuses her of two-timing him with the older man. Once she explains things, he apologizes for his ugly behavior and agrees to stand aside, since he, too, is in Chaney's debt. He encounters Chaney on the stairs, admits that he'd asked the girl to marry him, then lies that she turned him down becasue "she really loves you." Overjoyed, Chaney goes up to the room and realizes the truth when he hears the girl weeping unconsolably.

After tracking the gang leader targeting the girl (she witnessed his killing of a policeman) to his lair and running him to ground in an exciting rooftop shoot-out, Chaney reunites the two young lovers, convincing them that his marriage proposal was a sham designed to keep the girl out of harm's way until the gang leader was captured or killed. The joyful couple go off together arm in arm; the film's moving final shot shows the tough detective standing beside his adoring landlady (Lydia Yeamans Titus) and waving good-bye. As Chaney's arm circles the woman's shoulder, the young lovers look back and happily conclude that their aging friend and benefactor has at last found love of his own; but the barely concealed longing on Chaney's expressive face as he gazes at the younger woman tells all.

Though it drew only a mixed reception at the time, *While the City Sleeps* holds up today, even in its truncated form, as a really crackerjack gangster picture of the silent era. It is full of wild fights, furious gunplay (the film was released with a synchronized effects track so that audiences could hear all the popping of bullets), exciting chases, and underworld ambience. But it's the humanness of Chaney's performance that gives the film its texture and its punch.

As styles in filmmaking and in America's social climate changed over the years, the motives and behavior of the movie gangster would also change — but not a great deal, for these early silent gangster pictures — Chaney's particularly — had defined his essential character. He is an undisciplined child, fascinated with the forbidden, who never grew up and still bitterly resents the "parental" authority of the police because of the control it represents over him; a violent Peter Pan who justifies his every antisocial act, even murder, as debts owed to him; an innate loner, no matter how much company he keeps, and grandiose schemer determined to acquire wealth and power by the shortest route possible — who invariably sees that route through the barrel of a gun.

Frank McHugh, James Cagney, and Humphrey Bogart in Raoul Walsh's ambitious chronicle of the lawless decade from Prohibition through to The Crash, The Roaring Twenties *(1939). (Copyright © 1939 Warner Bros.)*

CHAPTER 2

THE

ROARING TWENTIES

The Roaring Twenties—which, it can be argued, extended into the early 1930s—began with Prohibition and came to an ironic close with the national hangover that was the Great Depression.

Along the way, the "noble experiment" (in the words of Herbert Hoover) of the nation's Dry Warriors to get Americans off the booze contributed more to the growth of crime—and especially organized crime—in America than poverty and many other social ills put together.

As historian Herbert Asbury said in his chronicle of the Dry Decade, *The Great Illusion:*

> The American people had expected to be greeted, when the great day came, by a covey of angels bearing gifts of peace, happiness, prosperity and salvation, which they had been assured would be theirs when the rum demon had been scotched. Instead, they were met by a horde of bootleggers, moonshiners, rumrunners, hijackers, gangsters, racketeers, trigger men, venal judges, corrupt police, crooked politicians, and speakeasy operators, all bearing the twin symbols of the Eighteenth Amendment—the Tommy gun and the poisoned cup.

INVISIBLE GOVERNMENT

Determined to flout the law, America's thirsty millions turned to the professional law flouters—the gangsters, for whom Prohibition was the "big chance." Bootlegging activities mushroomed and thrived. Nightclubs and speakeasies proliferated and flourished. In *The Lawless Decade*, Roaring Twenties historian Paul Sann wrote:

> In New York in 1929 Police Commissioner Grover Whalen's men counted the speakeasies and came up with a nice round number: 32,000. But that was admittedly a low figure for the number of illicit oases serving the teeming metropolis of 6,000,000. You couldn't count the speaks because there were too many of them—in the basements of fashionable Manhattan mansions, in penthouses off Park Avenue, in Greenwich Village cellars, in Wall Street office buildings, in brownstone rooming houses, in two-family dwellings in the Bronx, in Bay Ridge hardware stores . . . the speak was everywhere; all you needed to know to get the hard stuff was the right word(s), or maybe the right wink.

Police forces swelled to enforce the Prohibition statutes set forth in the 1919 Volstead Act. Judgeships increased to handle the ballooning caseload. And America's gangsters, rolling in cash like never before, were able as never before to pay off crooked officials and buy the influence they'd always needed to boost their power and position—and cement that power and position for many years to come. Thus America's "invisible government" was born.

The prevalence of political corruption and the evolving specter of an invisible government run by gangland had been touched on in gangster films from the beginning; as early as 1920, audiences needed no further explanation when gangster Lon Chaney winked at the cops and they winked back in *The Penalty*. But this image of collusion didn't become a fixture of the gangster-film story until the middle of the Roaring Twenties.

Exclusive Rights (1926) was one of the earliest gangster films to push this theme to the fore. It was also atypical in that it was made and released outside the major studio entente. By the mid-twenties, all the studios (or seeds of the studios) that would dominate American filmmaking for the next sixty-odd years were solidly in place. This may be why independently made *Exclusive Rights* tackled such a daring subject so explicitly: To attract audiences and win theater space away from the bigger Hollywood releases, the filmmakers had to offer audiences and exhibitors something a bit more sensational. And political corruption and gangland influence in government, both subjects much in the news, seemed like ideal material.

Producer J. C. Bachmann purchased Jerome N. Wilson's controversial book *Invisible Government* to use as the basis for his screen treatment of the subject, but he backed away from Wilson's more sensational title, replacing it with the obscure (and much less exploitable) *Exclusive Rights.*

The film chronicles the efforts of a crusading governor played by Gayne Williams to bring down a powerful mob boss (Charles Mailes) by exposing Mailes's gangland activities and politicial manipulations. He gets his opportunity when Sheldon Lewis, a member of Mailes's gang, is convicted of murder and sentenced to death. In exchange for Lewis's turning state's evidence against the mob kingpin, Williams offers to overturn his death sentence, but for the moment Lewis's lips stay sealed. Knowing that Lewis will probably break down and confess everything as his date with death nears, the wily Mailes uses his political influence to advance a bill for the abolition of capital punishment in the state. The bill gains popularity and support from many quarters, including the governor's own fiancée (Lillian Rich). But the governor refuses to sign it.

At his nightclub headquarters, Mailes frames Raymond McKee, a loyal aide (and wartime buddy) of the governor, for the murder of a rival gangster. When the innocent McKee is tried and condemned to death, the besieged governor finds himself torn between concern for the fate of his friend and his dedication to duty. Over the protests of his fiancée, he still refuses to sign the bill that would let Lewis and his boss off the hook, and his seeming heartlessness prompts her to break off their engagement.

But the wily governor has an ace up his sleeve. In the end, he tricks the gang leader and Lewis into believing that McKee's execution was carried out, and when Lewis realizes the honest governor is not to be swayed, he breaks at last and signs a statement revealing the full range of his mob boss's activities, including the corruption of government officials.

Critics took special note of the film's "high powered melodramatic [death-row] climax," but wondered "whether the brutality of the death chair passage will revolt or attract." Apparently it attracted, for *Exclusive Rights* was a success that paved the way for numerous major studio productions about invisible government, notably *The City Gone Wild* (1927) and *The Racket* (1928), both released by Paramount and starring Thomas Meighan.

In *The City Gone Wild*, Meighan plays what is commonly called a "mouthpiece," a defense lawyer to the mob who is continually getting his gangster-clients off on a technicality. His closest friend, and professional enemy, is the district attorney. Both men are in love with the same girl (Marietta Millner), who, like the DA, is unaware that her wealthy father (Charles Mailes again) is the brains behind the city's erupting gang warfare. On the verge of marrying Meighan but disapproving of his criminal practice, she urges him to give it up or lose her. When he hesitates and gets another of the city's hoods off on a technicality, she finally turns her back on him and agrees to marry the DA instead.

The DA discovers that Millner's father has masterminded the city's crime wave, and he is murdered when he refuses to be bought off. Out of loyalty to his dead friend and honest adversary—and determined to get revenge—Meighan gives up his practice, has himself appointed district attorney, and rounds up all the gangsters he'd once worked to set free, including the actual killer (Fred Kohler). Kohler's moll (Louise Brooks) threatens to expose Millner's father publicly unless Meighan agrees to let her lover go. Still in love with Millner, Meighan agrees to Brooks's demands, but his conscience prompts him to consider resigning from his job. In the end, Brooks has a change of heart, tips Millner to the truth, and all ends happily for everyone but Millner's corrupt father and the rest of his gang.

Reviewers dismissed the James Cruze–directed *The City Gone Wild* as "a slow moving, unoriginal, machine-made picture of gangsters and corruption in a city that remains nameless," and the film was not a hit. Its lackluster perrformance aside, *The City Gone Wild* nevertheless remains an important early underworld film for the new spotlight it cast on a Roaring Twenties character heretofore left lurking in the background of most gangster films—the quick-witted, fast-talking legal mouthpiece, whose services were as vital to the success of the mobster's operation as those of his gunman. Just as he would in real gangsterdom, the mouthpiece became an important fixture in Hollywood underworld stories from 1927 on, frequently taking center stage from the gangster himself—especially in the thirties, when the tale of the corrupt-turned-honest mouthpiece became virtually a subgenre all its own thanks to the talkies' new ability to exploit verbal courtroom theatrics. (The cynical, wise-cracking newspaperman seeking to expose the mob, and some-times compromised by it, would become a staple character of the gangster film in

Below, left: Good girl Helen Twelvetrees wakes mob mouthpiece John Barrymore to a sense of public duty in State's Attorney *(1932).*

Right: Warren William played a histrionic lawyer who will do anything to get his mob clients off in The Mouthpiece *(1932).*

such early talkies as *The Front Page* and *The Finger Points*—both 1931—for similiar reasons.)

In David O. Selznick's 1932 production *State's Attorney*, for example, John Barrymore chews up the courtroom scenery in the title role of a corrupt mouthpiece for mob boss William "Stage" Boyd. Barrymore maneuvers himself into the district attorney's chair to help his employer out, then sets his sights on the governorship. But good girl Helen Twelvetrees finally wakes Barrymore up to his sense of public duty, and he ruins his chances of becoming governor by exposing Boyd and his own devious past in court. The film was effectively remade in 1937 as *Criminal Lawyer* with Lee Tracy in the Barrymore role of the cynical, alcoholic, power-hungry mouthpiece who ultimately ruins his political chances by deciding to come clean.

More definitive yet of this type of Roaring Twenties underworld saga was Warner Brothers' *The Mouthpiece* (1932), in which Warren William played an even more histrionic underworld defender, who at one point gulps down a vial of poison—the state's only incriminating evidence against his client—to ensure an acquittal. When the aghast jury sees that the liquid has no ill effect on the lawyer, it drops the charges against his guilty client on the spot. Moments after the courtroom has been cleared, however, Williams hurries to a waiting private ambulance and has the deadly stuff pumped from his stomach. Based on actual New York City attorney William J. Fallon, William's character is a man who would do *anything* to get his underworld clients off. Like Barrymore and Tracy, however, William is felled by love and a resulting crisis of conscience, and he finally uses his courtroom tactics to send an important mob leader to jail. In the end, he pays for it not with his professional ruin but with his life, when the mob leader's loyal lieutenants rub him out for turning his back on them. A tough, exciting, and rather downbeat gangster melodrama, *The Mouthpiece* was remade as *The Man Who Talked Too Much* (1940), starring George Brent, and again as *Illegal* (1955), with Edward G. Robinson in William's role.

Much better than *The City Gone Wild* seems to have been was Thomas Meighan's follow-up film about municipal corruption and gangsterism, *The Racket* (1928), produced by Howard Hughes.

The Racket was based on a sensational 1927 play by former Chicago society and crime reporter Bartlett Cormack, who would later team with director Fritz Lang on *Fury*, the classic 1936 film about a different kind of mob rule. Future movie gangster Edward G. Robinson played the role of Cormack's tough gang leader, Nick Scarsi, on the stage but was passed over in favor of the more brutish Louis Wolheim when the film version was cast. The play's realistic portrait of gangsterism and political corruption in the Windy City proved so controversial that performances of it were banned there when *The Racket* went on the road.

The film version of *The Racket* pitted Meighan's tough, incorruptible cop,

Above, left: *Thomas Meighan's incorruptible cop Captain McQuigg and Louis Wolheim's Capone-like gangster Nick Scarsi square off in* The Racket *(1928).*

Right: *Dapper bootlegger Nick Scarsi (Louis Wolheim) and his pals in* The Racket *(1928), one of the most acclaimed gangster pictures of the silent era.*

Captain McQuigg, against Wolheim's Scarsi, a big-city bootlegger and gang leader "who rides in high-powered cars and dresses in gaudy suits and overcoats." Scarsi was one of the earliest screen gangsters to be based on the legendary Chicago crime kingpin Al Capone, whose nickname, Scarface, the fictional Scarsi not coincidentally calls to mind.

When McQuigg decides to get Nick, Scarsi uses his close ties with the city's most powerful politician, nicknamed the "Old Man" (Burr McIntosh), to get McQuigg transferred to traffic duty in another precinct. A pair of scoop-hungry crime reporters goad McQuigg about allowing himself to be transferred voluntarily due to fear of reprisal from the gangster. But McQuigg angrily counters that the switch was engineered by Scarsi's politician cronies, for it is the gangster who is really afraid of *him.* When the reporters publish this tidbit, the war between Scarsi and McQuigg begins.

Scarsi's younger brother (George Stone) falls for a torch singer (Marie Prevost) whose "B girl" kind Scarsi loathes. Not wanting the kid mixed up with the singer, Scarsi does his best to break off the relationship, incurring the singer's enmity and desire for revenge. When Stone is picked up by one of McQuigg's patrolmen on a hit-and-run charge, McQuigg sees an opportunity to lure the volatile Scarsi out into the open and finally bring him down. Since she was with Stone the night the hit-and-run occurred, the singer is held by McQuigg as a material witness. When she leaks the story to the press, Scarsi pays a visit to the precinct where she's being held, runs up against the patrolman who arrested his brother, and kills him in a fight. McQuigg arrests Scarsi for murder, prompting a quick visit from the city's corrupt district attorney. When Scarsi threatens to blow the whistle on the Old Man and every other crooked politician in the city unless he's set free, the DA, who is under orders from the Old Man to silence the violent, loose-cannon gang leader, manipulates Scarsi into making a break for it, and Scarsi is shot down trying to escape with an unloaded gun.

To achieve a sense of authenticity, director Lewis Milestone followed the lead of Griffith, Raoul Walsh, and Allan Dwan and hired real bootleggers and gangsters to serve as "technical consultants." They apparently revealed so much about the workings of gangland that after the film was released, Milestone's "consultants" did everything they could to prevent it from being shown—including issuing death threats against stars Meighan and Wolheim, Howard Hughes, and Milestone. Notes film historian Kevin Brownlow: "Nothing happened. After all, once the picture was out, there was little point in shooting the men who made it—that would merely arouse the newspapers to give it massive publicity. The only sensible course was to get it banned via the politicians. [In] this [they] proved more successful." Like the stage play, the film version of *The Racket* was banned in Chicago; through the influence of gang leaders and crooked politicians around the country, it was heavily censored in many other American cities, as well.

In newspapers and industry trade journals, *The Racket* received virtually unanimous critical applause. *The New York Times* called it "one of the most entertaining pictures in quite a time [and] a high mark for other melodramatic aspirants to shoot at." Wrote *Variety:* "*The Racket*, like all great pictures, started with a great yarn and a director alive to its possibilities. It grips your interest from the first shot to the last and never drags for a second." Whether a print of the film exists today is not known.

Hollywood rewarded *The Racket* with a Best Picture nomination at the first (1927–1928) Academy Awards ceremony, but the film lost to *Wings*.

Howard Hughes remade *The Racket* for his own studio, RKO, in 1951, updating the story to the fifties, with Robert Mitchum cast as Captain McQuigg and Robert Ryan as McQuigg's gangster nemesis, whose surname was changed from the Caponian Scarsi to the more ambiguous Scanlon. Also ambiguous was the film's setting, a nameless city somewhere in America. Hughes probably updated and remade the film to capitalize on the Kefauver (later McClellan) committee investigations into organized crime, which were capturing the attention of millions of Americans at the time through the new medium of television. Compared to the shocking revelations of the televised hearings, which exposed the existence of the Mafia and the tentacled reach of organized crime into businesses and legislatures from coast to coast, the remake of *The Racket* was tame stuff indeed.

The film follows the plot of the silent version fairly closely. With the help of the Old Man (who is referred to but never seen in the remake) and other corrupt officials, Nick Scanlon gets the incorruptible McQuigg bounced from one precinct to another to keep him out of the way. As before, McQuigg finally gets to Scanlon through the gangster's kid brother when a cop belonging to McQuigg's

elite squad of honest crime fighters nails the kid on a grand larceny charge, to which the kid's singer girlfriend (Lizabeth Scott) was a witness. Scanlon pays a visit to the jailhouse to get at the girl, encounters the cop who arrested his bother, and shoots him. The incident is witnessed by a cub reporter, and McQuigg arrests Scanlon on a murder charge. A mob henchman in line for an important judgeship and a corrupt member of the police force's special investigation team arrive on the scene, and when the belligerent Scanlon says he'll sing if they don't get him out of this mess, they manipulate him into trying to escape and then shoot him down. At the end of this 1950s version, however, a special crime commission puts the screws to the men who murdered Scanlon, the implication being that the Old Man and all the other racketeers in the city will soon be brought to justice.

Unlike Lewis Milestone's acclaimed direction of the silent version, John Cromwell's helming of the remake is rather listless and stagy. It has been suggested that with his contract running out, Cromwell undertook the film just to complete his obligations to Howard Hughes. And Robert Mitchum's performance as the firebrand McQuigg is so laid-back that the character generates little excitement or empathy. The film really belongs to Robert Ryan, who gives a charismatic if overwrought performance as Scanlon, an old-time mob boss (despite his youthful looks) who refuses to give in to the syndicate's "new techniques" of nonviolence and political double-dealing and has to be eliminated. Where the original apparently captured the audience's attention through the freshness of its subject matter and flavor of authenticity, though, the remake seemed leadenly familiar — a dish served up one too many times.

UNDERWORLDERS

A popular silent gangster film that employed real underworld types not only as "consultants" but as actors was the 1928 *Dressed to Kill*, directed by Irving Cummings. The clever title refers to the fondness of Roaring Twenties gangsters for dressing to the nines even when carrying out the most nefarious activities. The picture stars Edmund Lowe as a gallant, polite, and ultimately endearing gentleman thief in the Raffles vein called Mile-Away Barry for his ability to be miles away from the scene of his crimes before the cops get there. (The mob chieftain pursued by Lon Chaney in *While the City Sleeps*, released the same year, bore the same nickname. Later, James Cagney's character in *Doorway to Hell*, 1930, his first important gangster film, would assume the name, as well.)

Variety's typically in-depth review of March 14, 1928, its slangy prose probably inspired by the picture itself, gives a good account of what the film offers:

> [*Dressed to Kill*] has several angles to vary the stereotyped crook story. [The] heroine [Mary Astor], instead of turning out to be a detective, is a girl seeking to recover bonds for the theft of which her lover is in prison. Another difference is that the polished crook [Lowe] works with a gang of tough gorillas, and in the end has to sacrifice his life to their hate to save the girl.
>
> Much of the action takes place in a night club used as a rendezvous by the "mob" . . . and is the basis for some excellent underworld melodrama, such as [the] discovery of a stool piegon and "taking him for a ride"; [and] cool verbal fencing with police officials who crash in with threats of arrests. The grim atmosphere of desperate criminals is nicely established, even to a certain ominous humor that runs through the sequences. Such is the passage where the gunmen bump off the stool pigeon, and then appear in elaborate mourning garb at his impressive funeral, with the baffled detectives watching them.
>
> [The] whole story is told against a background of elegance. [The] master crook lives in a mansion. The crook's crimes are always graceful and unhurried, symphonies of social grace which lend them a disarming attractiveness. Even at the end when the hero gives himself up to the machine gun fire of the gangsters to save the girl (with whom he has fallen in love, of course) he does it in the same debonair fashion, and

drops dead before a propaganda billboard reading "You Can't Win," an impeccable figure in faultless evening dress.

The New York Times wrote:

[*Dressed to Kill* is] a splendid crook story . . . that lives up to the letter of its title. The fun is chiefly afforded by the sartorial equipment of the modernized safe-crackers and killers. These Beau Brummell burglars are marvels at shrouding suspicion. [They] go to their bank robberies in evening attire, but to accomplish the deed they take off their silk hats and don caps and turn up their coat collars. Once they are in possession of the swag they return to their expensive automobiles and turn down their coat collars. This aristocracy of the underworld, so to speak, seeks relief from [its] exciting early morning adventures by playing golf. One of the many good ideas in this film is that of having a distinguished looking man who travels under the sobriquet of "the Professor" [R. O. Pennell]. He looks the part and would never be taken for a crook [except that] in one of the subtitles it is set forth that this gangster is a "Doctor of Larceny and a graduate of the third degree."

Most gangster films of the period were not quite as lavish as *Dressed to Kill*. Poverty-row studios such as Columbia, which had yet to ascend to the ranks of the majors, exploited the growing popularity of the genre by grinding out potboilers like *The Beautiful Sinner* (1924), *Birds of Prey* (1927), and *Stool Pigeon* (1928) as quickly and inexpensively as possible in order to turn a fast buck. *Birds of Prey* may have been given a somewhat larger budget than the typical Columbia gangster film, however, since it climaxes with the bad guys getting their comeuppance from a spectacular earthquake rather than from the long arm of the law.

Much less fanciful and far more characteristic of the gritty, straight from the headlines–style gangster film that would soon become the style in Hollywood was Josef von Sternberg's *Underworld* (1927), which many historians have erroneously pointed to as the first gangster movie. Von Sternberg himself contributed to the perpetuation of this myth when he claimed in his autobiography that *Underworld* "was untried material, as no films had as yet been made of this deplorable phase of our culture." Similarly, many historians point to the film's lead, George Bancroft, as the first gangster movie star—an indefensible slight to the career of Lon Chaney.

Underworld's renown and importance stem largely from its huge popularity—which proved to the Hollywood moguls that the infant genre was far from played out—and from the fact that it was the first gangster film to marshal the many disparate elements of the burgeoning genre into a collective model for other

Evelyn Brent, George Bancroft, and Clive Brook in Josef von Sternberg's influential Underworld *(1927), from a story by Ben Hecht.*

filmmakers to emulate. Corrupt politicians and the specter of invisible government are absent from *Underworld,* but virtually every other element is present: the antihero mobster with a personal code of honor; the gaudy atmosphere of nightclubs and speakeasies; secret hideouts; gang rivalries; speeding roadsters and pursuing policemen on motorcycles; and the requisite flapper heroine, who forsakes her mobster sugar daddy for the love of the upright and decent hero. As important as the film's marshaling of the genre's many surface ingredients was its artistic purpose; von Sternberg intended the film as "an experiment in photographic violence and montage." Befitting the film's title—and anticipating the film noir gangster and crime films of the forties—the director's gangland is different from that of most other gangster films of the era. It's a forbidding landscape shrouded always in darkness. From first frame to last, daylight never intrudes.

The film was derived from a story by Ben Hecht, who based his tale (as his friend Bartlett Cormack had done with the stage play and subsequent film version of *The Racket*) on events he'd witnessed as a newspaper reporter in the crime-ridden city of Chicago. Von Sternberg said he scrapped most of Hecht's scenario "because of my ignorance of the behavior pattern of criminals" and concocted a new story set in a (typically Sternbergian) world of light, shade, smoke and mist referred to only as "A great city...." When he saw the completed film, Hecht reportedly requested that his name be removed from the credits. Fortunately for him, Parmount denied the request; *Underworld* went on to win Hecht the 1927–1928 Academy

Award for Best Original Story, launching him on his career as one of Hollywood's most prolific and talented screenwriters.

Since Hecht's original scenario is lost, there's no way of telling how different the film version is. Visually, *Underworld* is von Sternberg all the way. Most reviewers credited Hecht with the film's in-the-streets realism; wrote *Variety:* "*Underworld,* without mentioning Chicago as the scene of the ensuing machine gun warfare between the crooks and the cops, evidently is a page out of Ben Hecht's underworld acquaintance with the Cicero and South Side gun mob. The 'hanging by the neck' death sentence is another tip-off that New York, at least, is whitewashed, and it makes one wonder how the Illinois and other midwestern censors will feel about some of the niceties of highway robbery, foot-padding, double-crossing, martial warfare with the authorities, and other fine points in underworld misbehavior."

The film's ending, where gangster Bull Weed (George Bancroft) is trapped in his tenement hideout with his mistrusted lover as the police cordon off the streets and riddle the place with tommy-gun bullets, is also likely one of Hecht's surviving contributions, since he used the same scene with only slight variation for the conclusion of his classic 1932 *Scarface.*

As *Underworld* begins, a has-been lawyer turned drunken derelict (Clive Brook) witnesses Bancroft's robbery of a bank late one night. Instead of rubbing him out, Bancroft takes a liking to the affable young man, whom he nicknames "Rolls-Royce" on account of his courtly manners and gift of gab, and gets him a job sweeping the floor of a local nightclub, the Dreamland Cafe. At the club, Brook meets and is immediately attracted to Bancroft's flapper girlfriend, Feathers (Evelyn Brent). He also encounters Bancroft's gangland rival, Buck Mulligan (Fred Kohler), who offers him money for a drink, then maliciously tosses the cash into a spittoon (a scene director Howard Hawks lifted for his 1967 western *El Dorado*). An aptly named bull of a man who can bend silver dollars with his bare hands, Bancroft easily intimidates Kohler into backing off, and the vengeful Kohler vows to get even with both men. Bancroft gets his licks in first, however, by framing Kohler for a jewel robbery, although the man is later released for lack of hard evidence.

Bancroft buys Brook a sharp new set of clothes and sets him up as his mouthpiece. Brook's office does double duty as a front for Bancroft's steel-lined hideout. Brent pays several visits there with and without Bancroft, and as she and Brook spend more time together, they find themselves falling in love. Out of loyalty to Bancroft, however, they keep their amorous feelings in check.

During the gangsters' annual armistice, a confetti-strewn gala of "booze and broads" at which the gangsters vote for their favorite flapper as Queen of the Ball, Brook and Brent dance together and Bancroft jealously ostracizes his former pal. Rival gangster Kohler later makes a drunken pass at Brent himself, prompting Bancroft to follow him to his lair and shoot him in cold blood.

Arrested for Kohler's murder, Bancroft is tried and sentenced to death by hanging. While he is languishing in prison awaiting his date with the hangman, Brook and Brent finally give in to their feelings for one another, and when Bancroft hears rumors of their open affair, he repudiates the pair for their disloyalty and vows to get even. The lovers decide to pack up and start out fresh in another city. At the last minute, however, they come to the realization that they can't turn their backs on Bancroft in his hour of need ("We can't just double-cross him; we owe him everything") and enlist several members of Bancroft's gang in a daring plan to break him out of prison. The plan misfires, but Bancroft manages to break out on his own and holes up in his steel hideout. Brent shows up and the police subsequently surround the place. Bancroft accuses her of leading them to him and roughs her up, then attempts to flee through the steel door at the rear of the hideout. Finding it locked and realizing his ex-pal Brook has the keys, he's convinced more than ever that the pair has set him up.

The police clear out the adjoining buildings, rain gunfire and tear gas on Bancroft's hideout, and a real battle royal ensues. Brook arrives and is shot as he hurries to the rear of the hideout to unlock the door. As the badly wounded man enters, Bancroft immediately attacks him for being a no-good double-crosser and, in between bursts of machine-gun fire at the police, announces that now the three of them will all die together. The girl insists to the gangster that she and her lover had only been trying to help him—Brook had even taken a bullet to come to the gangster's aid—and Bancroft is finally convinced of their friendship and loyalty to him. Realizing the error of his ways, he helps them escape, then locks the door behind them and goes out the front to give himself up to the police.

As the cops lead Bancroft away to his delayed appointment with the prison hangman, one of them remarks that all the gangster got from his escapade was one more hour of freedom. The changed man's reply: "There was something I had to find out—and that hour was worth more to me than my whole life."

Though not in a class with von Sternberg's silent masterpieces *The Last Command* and *The Docks of New York* (both 1928; the latter starred George Bancroft), *Underworld* shares many of their qualities: resplendent cinematography and lighting, vivid use of montage in action and dialogue sequences alike, and strong, believable performances by all concerned. George Bancroft is excellent as the coarse, brutal, jovial, ignorant, conceited, generous, loving, pathetic, and, in the end, self-redeeming tough guy* whom Clive Brook admiringly, if sadly, likens to "Attila the Hun at the gates of Rome." ("Who's Atilla?" Bancroft snaps back at him. "The head of some wop gang?") Evelyn Brent makes a tough, attractive, yet vulnerable and

*An archetypical gangster movie character brought to vivid life in *Underworld* by Bancroft and one that he would continue playing throughout his career in such films as *The Mighty* (1929) and *Blood Money* (1933), and the model for Wallace Beery's very similar portrayals in *The Big House* (1930) and *The Secret Six* (1931).

endearing Feathers. And as the regenerated Rolls-Royce, Clive Brook matches them every step. "It is, if anything, a more difficult part to portray," noted critic Mordaunt Hall. "Mr. Brooks' make-up is effective, for even after the drunkard dodges the cause of his downfall, Mr. Brooks shows by greasepaint the effect of Rolls' intemperance."

Reviews were almost unanimously favorable. A WHALE OF A FILM YARN! headlined *Variety.* "*Underworld* is a film of integrity on the part of director, scenario writer, actors and cameraman, done with back-bone, which is to say, strength and grit," echoed the *National Board of Review Magazine.* "Best of all, at least for those looking for cinema growth on our native screen, it is a film made in America, with an actor and a director who need take off their hats to none."

This unexpected—to modern eyes, anyway—burst of America-first pride was a response to the widely held view, even in America, that European films, especially those made by the great German directors F. W. Murnau, Ernst Lubitsch, Fritz Lang, and E. A. Dupont, far outshone those of their American colleagues in technical virtuosity and artistic merit. Believing America's dominance of the young industry to be slipping from their grasp, the heads of the major studios began luring many foreign talents to Hollywood—just as conditions in Europe began to stir artists there by the thousands to seek greener pastures. Von Sternberg had come earlier: Born Jonas Sternberg in Austria in 1894, he came to the United States in 1911, making his first film in 1924. But at the suggestion of a producer, he changed his name to Josef and added the von to capitalize on the prevailing attitude toward European filmmakers, helping him get work at the major studios.

Underworld was such a surprise and substantial hit that Paramount executives gratefully dished out a ten-thousand-dollar bonus to the fledgling director, and, not unexpectedly, requested a follow-up. A year later, von Sternberg offered up *The Drag Net*, also starring George Bancroft and Evelyn Brent. This time around, Bancroft played not a gangster but a cop—Two-Gun Nolan—a big-city captain of detectives who turns to the bottle after accidentally killing his erudite partner, a sleuth nicknamed "Shakespeare" (Leslie Fenton). The actual party responsible for the murder is gang boss Dapper Frank Trent (William Powell). When Powell's moll, an alluring flapper known as the Magpie (Brent), becomes attracted to Bancroft and reveals Powell's involvement, the despairing detective finally swears off the booze and sets about bringing Powell and his gang to heel.

Though it made money, *The Drag Net* failed to live up to the box-office expectations created by its successful predecessor, and it drew mostly modest or mixed reviews. How well it stacks up against *Underworld* artistically is now impossible to say, for this film, too, is lost. Von Sternberg himself failed to mention it in his autobiography. And von Sternberg scholar Herman G. Weinberg has said little of it either, except to note that "For the second time, Sternberg inserted a ballroom scene frenetic with flying confetti and paper streamers (previously seen in *Underworld*), which was to become a favorite pictorial element with him." As with so many lost films, all we have to go on are some contemporary reviews, which are not always discerning as to a film's genuine merits but which can often be instructive as to the tone and content of a film. *The New York Times* review is worth noting:

> Notwithstanding George Bancroft's derisive laugh, Evelyn Brent's striking plumed headgear and Josef von Sternberg's generous display of slaughter, *The Drag Net* is an emphatically mediocre effort, one that is most disappointing after anticipating something like *Underworld*, Mr. von Sternberg's prize production.
>
> Mr. von Sternberg has a number of weird ideas in this film. He depicts the stunning girl, known to her entourage of murderers and burglars as the Magpie, on more than one occasion trying to outdo Two-Gun Nolan in volleys of epithets. With evident relish, a crook's banquet is pictured. The guests are all arrayed in faultless black and white, and when one or two of them are called upon to address the gathering it is quite obvious that they would sooner face a policeman's pistol. Dapper Dan Trent, the big boss of the underworld, decides before the dessert that indiscreet chatter is a capital offense and he forthwith puts a bullet through one of his own pals, who looks as if he rather enjoyed his summary dismissal from this mundane sphere.
>
> In the [end], Trent goes to his death with a smile and Nolan and the Magpie are both wounded.

Von Sternberg returned to the gangster genre in 1929 with *Thunderbolt*, the final installment in the director's unofficial gangster trilogy and his first talkie. George Bancroft plays mobster Jim Lang, the title character, whose nickname refers to his powerful right fist, capable of killing a man with a single blow. Lang's moll, Ritzy (Fay Wray), decides to go straight and dumps him for a decent younger man, Bob Moran (Richard Arlen), who works in a bank. The possessive Bancroft refuses to let her go ("You an' me'll never be through, Ritzy, get that straight") and threatens to pay a visit to Arlen's apartment and kill him. As Bancroft stealthily enters the apartment building, he's followed by a friendly dog that rouses Arlen with its bark. As Bancroft gently quiets the mutt so he can proceed with his plans, the cops (whom Wray had alerted) show up and arrest the mobster, who's wanted on robbery and murder charges in eleven states.

Bancroft is tried and sent to prison to await death in the electric chair. Wray and Arlen make plans to marry, but the nuptials are stalled when Arlen is framed for bank robbery and murder. Tried and sentenced to death, as well, the innocent man winds up in the cell opposite Bancroft's. With the help of the DA, Wray and Arlen's mother try to persuade Bancroft into confessing that he had engineered Arlen's frame-up out of jealousy. Bancroft emphatically denies this,* insisting that it's not his style to let the state do his dirty work for him, and Arlen's sentence is allowed to stand.

As their respective dates with the electric chair near, Bancroft unexpectedly befriends Arlen and the young man lowers his guard—Bancroft's secret plan is to kill Arlen with a blow from his thunderbolt fist when saying good-bye to him through the bars on the way to the chair. At the last second, however, Arlen springs the news that it was Bancroft who had actually stolen Wray away from him—the two were sweethearts before Wray picked up with the gangster—and the basically decent Bancroft changes his mind and confesses the frame-up, letting Arlen off the hook.

"I always did have a peculiar habit of taking things that didn't belong to me—that's why I'm here," Bancroft reflects with a smile. "You're kinda crazy about her, aren't you?"

"I love her, Jim," Arlen answers.

"Well, I guess I do, too. I still do," Bancroft admits. "Good luck, kid. Good luck to you both. Give her my love—and take care of her, whatever you do."

On his way to the death house, the bemused gangster bids good-bye to his dog (which prison officials had allowed him to keep in his cell after Bancroft had helped them restrain a crazed inmate) and makes a final stab at guessing the name of his Irish guard. It turns out to be Aloysius, prompting Bancroft to go to his death with a loud guffaw.

Herman G. Weinberg has described *Thunderbolt* as "a work of realism, un-prettified in the slighest degree." But this is scarcely the case. Von Sternberg's stylish black-and-white photography is starkly pretty indeed. And despite some dollops of suspense and outbreaks of violence, mostly during the prison sequences— which take up roughly half the film—the film is more surreal than real, and laced with enough gallows humor and loopy dialogue to make it an outright comedy. When Bancroft's Thunderbolt arrives on death row, for example, the first thing he's asked by one of the other doomed inmates is whether he can sing tenor (the convicts have a death-house quartet whose tenor recently walked the last mile, leaving a vacancy); the amused gangster sneers back, "I kill tenors!"

---

*In an amusing reference to the legendary feud between Al Capone and rival mobster George "Bugs" Moran, whom Capone denied trying to rub out in the St. Valentine's Day Massacre and on several other occasions, as well, Bancroft elaborates with a grin: "I make it a point never to kill any Morans."

With just seventeen minutes to go before Bancroft's execution, the frazzled warden (Tully Marshall) suddenly remembers that the doomed man hasn't been granted a favorite last meal, and Marshall offers him anything he wishes. Bancroft spurns the offer, however, since gulping down a meal in the time remaining will only give him indigestion "later on." He requests a shot of liquor instead. "I can't, unless you're sick," the warden replies tremulously. "You are sick, aren't you?" Bancroft kicks back his heels and grins: "Warden, I feel like I'm going to die." But when the warden extends the shot glass through the bars with a nervous hand, Bancroft pushes it back to him, saying, "Here, I think you need this more than I do." The humor continues even as Bancroft is being led to the execution chamber after letting Arlen off the hook. The perplexed prison chaplain, whose spiritual services Bancroft has continually spurned throughout his incarceration, stands idly by, not knowing what to do with himself—until Bancroft cracks, "Come on, Chaplain, I'll give you a break, too."

Reviewers took note of the film's offbeat humor and situations, but some didn't know what to make of them. A *New York Times* critic wrote:

> In *Thunderbolt*, there is a queer idea of humor, that of what the producers esteem to be the lighter side of the death cell. The greater part of this production is of scenes in an aisle of barred cells, with a privileged negro slayer entertaining his colleagues in crime by playing the piano and singing hymns. Another convict warbler is wont to render a song heralded as *Broken-Hearted*, when one of the condemned men is about to shuffle off this mortal coil.
>
> There also is in this talking film yarn a unique specimen—a comic warden—who talks about the electric chair as if it were a suite of rooms in a specially cool corner of a hotel. It is this official who calls upon Thunderbolt to quiet an obstreperous criminal [Fred Kohler] who has acquired a pistol. Thunderbolt snatches the weapon from the man and bangs him over the head with the butt. The dangerous man topples off into a corner as somebody in another cell sings *Rockabye Baby*.

Unprettified realism? Hardly. (Von Sternberg even stages a death-house wedding at one point.) With *Thunderbolt*, the director apparently decided he'd taken the gangster film—his type, anyway—as far as it could go, and he decided to play around with the genre's grim ingredients instead. The year-old Academy of Motion Picture Arts and Sciences, however, took the film seriously enough to nominate Bancroft as the year's Best Actor (he lost to Warner Baxter in the first all-talking Western, *In Old Arizona*). Audiences took to it seriously, as well, and the deft and amusing *Thunderbolt* became a sizable hit for Parmount and for von Sternberg, who nevertheless from then on avoided the genre to which he'd contributed so much.

Thunderbolt is not without its flaws—quite a few of them, in fact. Fay Wray is awfully delicate and waifish for a moll, even a reformed one. And Richard Arlen is rather a lunkhead as the railroaded boyfriend. (Apart from Bancroft, the film is left to the supporting players to bring alive.) The pacing is slow and the dialogue is delivered in the annoyingly halting style characteristic of so many early sound films. Imperfections and all, however, *Thunderbolt* is light-years ahead of Warner Brothers' *Lights of New York*, the cinema's first "100% all-talking picture" (and first talkie gangster movie, as well), released the year before.

A tale (accurately described by one reviewer) of "bootleggers and gunmen, cops and muggs, the latter a couple of simps falling for con men back home in a hotel twice the size of the town—from the looks of the set," *Lights of New York* suggests nothing of the rat-a-tat style of Warner Brothers gangster films to come in just a few short years, and, in terms of excitement and realistic acting, shows little kinship with most silent gangster films, either. Savaged by the critics, who cautioned exhibitors to put off wiring their theaters for sound if "this is the best the talkers can offer," *Lights of New York* remains a crudity even by early talkie standards, a film whose major claim to fame, apart from its pioneer status as the first all-talkie, is its classic use of the mobster's foreboding order (delivered here in hilariously slow motion by Wheeler Oakman) to "Take . . . them . . . for . . . a . . . ride."

More akin to *Thunderbolt*, but executed in much faster style, was Rouben Mamoulian's *City Streets* (1931), in which Sylvia Sidney and Gary Cooper play a nice young couple who get in over their heads with mobster Paul Lukas and his gang. Sidney urges Cooper to give up his dead-end job in a shooting gallery and get rich by joining the mob. When she lands in prison, Sidney realizes gangland is endsville, too, but by this time Cooper has taken her initial advice and become a big-time beer baron targeted for murder by rival Lukas.

Practically forgotten today, *City Streets* is a remarkable early gangster film, noted early sound-film historian Ken Hanke:

> The story, penned by Dashiell Hammett, is rather typical stuff, but the presentation is anything but typical. Frequently, it is very violent. Guy Kibbee's cold-blooded murder of his mentor, Stanley Fields, is a nasty bit of goods, while a scene in which one of Lukas' henchmen skewers a man's hand with a fork for daring to talk back is as sadistic as anything in the Warner catalogue. [But] the best thing about *City Streets* is Mamoulian's handling of his leads. The image of Cooper and Sidney trying to touch each other and kiss through the wire grating in the visitors' room at the prison remains etched in the mind.

"I'll be waiting for you when you come out." Gary Cooper and Sylvia Sidney in Rouben Mamoulian's City Streets *(1931).*

Splendid, too, as Hanke noted, is a sequence where mobsters cruelly arrange for a released female convict to be met at the prison gates by the corpse of her lover. Similarly strong in this underrated Roaring Twenties melodrama is the exciting finale, where Cooper outwits the mobsters holding him and Sidney captive by taking them on a perilous high-speed drive across mountain roads until they cry uncle and agree to toss out their weapons. Then he makes them take off on foot, and drives away with Sidney to begin a new life.

THE ROARING TWENTIES REVISITED

Though long gone, the lawless decade of the Roaring Twenties remains one of the most vivid periods in our nation's history—an era as familiar to those of us who didn't live through it as to those who did. And the gangster movie is largely responsible.

The earliest gangster movies of the silent era—especially those shot on location or those that included on-location footage mixed with studio scenes—did much to keep the era alive by providing us with an enduring pictorial record. By the time the talkies arrived, the decade itself had become as much of an unstated topic in gangster movies as the bootleggers and mouthpieces, mobsters and molls who figured in their plots. And for the next sixty years, moviemakers sought to recapture the glamour, excitement, and violence of that era in one period gangster film after another.

Still the most ambitious of these period pieces is Raoul Walsh's expansively titled *The Roaring Twenties* (1939), which attempted not just to recapture the look and sound of the era but to chronicle its rise and fall from Prohibition through to the 1929 Crash. In fact, the film begins even earlier, during World War I, when stars James Cagney, Humphrey Bogart, and Jeffrey Lynn meet up in France, become pals, and discuss what they intend to do with their lives once the war is over. Garage mechanic Cagney intends to get his old job back and marry Priscilla Lane, a girl who has been writing to him throughout the war, although they've never met. Lynn plans to study law. Only the vicious Bogart seems destined for a life of crime, as suggested by his shooting of an enemy soldier seconds after the armistice has been announced.

Stateside, unemployment for returning vets is running high, and Cagney fails to get his old job back. Ultimately, he is spurned by Lane, as well, even though he helps her realize her own ambitions as a singer. With the financial backing of speakeasy owner Gladys George, he establishes a successful taxi business used as a front for an even more lucrative bootleg operation and hires Lynn as his mouthpiece. Bogart becomes a big-time crook and bootlegger, also, and as the lawless decade rolls on, he and Cagney become business associates and eventually fierce rivals.

The upright Lynn decides to go straight, joins the district attorney's staff, and earns Cagney's enmity by marrying Lane. The Crash wipes Cagney out and he finds himself down-and-out again, driving a cab. Coincidentally, he picks up Lane as a passenger; she asks for his help when Bogart threatens to kill Lynn for using his knowledge of Bogart's gangland activities to bring the mobster to justice. Out of a rewnewed sense of loyalty—and feeling he has nothing more to lose— the basically decent Cagney goes to bat for his wartime buddy and kills Bogart, but he is later gunned down himself and dies on the steps of a church as the bells symbolically ring an end to the era and to the archetypal Roaring Twenties character he personified.

The Roaring Twenties was a troubled production from the start: Three writers were required to turn columnist/reporter Mark Hellinger's kaleidoscopic original story into a concise and workable screenplay; Walsh stepped in late as director when producer Hal B. Wallis dropped Anatole Litvak; and there were several last-minute casting changes, as well. Yet none of these problems show on screen. The film is energetically and believably acted (particularly by Cagney, Gladys George, and Frank McHugh), and convincingly directed by Walsh. It remains one of the great gangster films of the thirties—the genre's true golden age—and a noteworthy recreation of the tumultuous era it strived to sum up.

The same studio, Warner Brothers, sought to recapture the gaudiness and gunplay of the era for a new generation of moviegoers—this time in spectacular CinemaScope and sumptuous Warnercolor—in *Pete Kelly's Blues* (1955), directed

by and starring Jack Webb as the jazz bandleader of the title. Rather than chronicling the rise and fall of big-city bootleggers, Richard L. Breen's screenplay focused instead on fictional mobster Frank McCarg's (Edmond O'Brien) efforts to take over the Midwest music business on behalf of his boss, the real-life Big Jim Colosimo, by shaking down speakeasy bandleaders and musicians during the period historically known as the Band Wars.

Webb refuses to knuckle under at first, but after his hotheaded drummer (Martin Milner) is shot down on the streets of Kansas City in reprisal, he gives in to O'Brien's demands for a 25 percent kickback on the band's earnings. In return, the gangster gets Webb and his band more exposure and better play dates. O'Brien also provides the band with a bluesey lead singer, Peggy Lee, an alcoholic girlfriend of the gangster's, whose fading career O'Brien wants to revive.* Lee winds up in a mental asylum due to O'Brien's pressure and abuse, and when the pacifist Webb finally decides to fight back, it is she who provides the bandleader with the information he needs to bring O'Brien down.

Colorfuly photographed by Hal Rosson and studded with great original musical numbers and songs drawn from the Roaring Twenties itself, *Pete Kelly's Blues* does a nice job of giving modern audiences a feeling of the era. But its weak script, full of trite situations and paper-thin characters; generally bland performances (except for O'Brien, who shamelessly chews up the scenery); and especially Jack Webb's turgid, "Dragnet"-like direction (narration included) turn the film into an exercise in campy nostalgia. Webb's stiff-necked, just-the-facts performance as

Above, left: *Mobster Edmond O'Brien muscles band leader Jack Webb into giving singer Peggy Lee a job in actor-director Webb's stiff-necked but tuneful saga of the Roaring Twenties band wars,* Pete Kelly's Blues *(1955). (Copyright © 1955 Warner Bros.)*

Right: *Cynical mob attorney Robert Taylor finally confronts his boss (Lee J. Cobb) in Nicholas Ray's campy but stylish* Party Girl *(1958). With John Ireland and Cyd Charisse. (Copyright © 1958 Metro-Goldwyn-Mayer)*

---

*The scene where O'Brien bullies the drunken Lee into singing and she humiliates both of them when her voice fails is almost a replay of a scene in John Huston's 1948 gangster film *Key Largo*, which costarred Edward G. Robinson and Claire Trevor in very similar roles.

Kelly is egregious. We're supposed to care about Kelly and worry about his plight; except for an occasional face-cracking upward turn of the lips suggesting a smile (and possible human warmth), however, Webb's Kelly is such a dour ramrod that we never give a damn about him.

The film captured audience interest, though, and even won some acclaim for its Roaring Twenties musical sequences. Peggy Lee earned an Oscar nomination for her performance (she lost to Jo Van Fleet in *East of Eden*). Webb later reworked the material into a television series for NBC that was also produced by Warner Brothers. William Reynolds played Kelly in the short-lived series, which ran on NBC for less than a season. (Warner Brothers also produced a television series called "The Roaring Twenties" around the same time. More successful than the TV version of *Pete Kelly's Blues,* it ran on ABC for two seasons. Except for its title and period setting, however, it had nothing to do with the 1939 Walsh film.)

Campier even than *Pete Kelly's Blues,* but intentionally (and more stylishly) so, is Nicholas Ray's *Party Girl* (1958). Although it left audiences and critics cold when it was released, *Party Girl* has since become a cult favorite due to director Ray's vaunted maverick reputation, Cyd Charisse's showy dance numbers, and a flamboyant visual style that's more characteristic of MGM's musical extravaganzas of the fifties than your typical gangster film.

The film stars Robert Taylor in the clichéd role of the cynical defense attorney who devotes his skills to keeping mobsters out of jail. Taylor is even more cynical about the law then Warren William in *The Mouthpiece,* but his motivations are very different. William's character subverted the legal system on behalf of his guilty clients because he'd once been a prosecutor and sent an innocent man to the chair; Taylor, on the other hand, suffers from overriding ambition coupled with a strong inferiority complex. He has a clubfoot, and the ugly affliction drives him to debase himself by working the wrong side of the law as mobster Lee J. Cobb's highly paid puppet.

Taylor's outlook changes when he reluctantly falls for a beautiful nightclub dancer (Charisse) whose services Cobb enlists for several mob galas, inadvertently giving the honest young woman an inside look at the workings of his underworld activities. Charisse falls for Taylor in return and pushes him to go straight—which he does by turning state's evidence when Cobb targets Charisse for murder.

George Wells's script employs the entire catalog of Roaring Twenties gangster-film ingredients. But the script is secondary to the film's look, which is full of Roaring Twenties razzle-dazzle and really quite stunning. *Party Girl* is not a great film by any means, but it does offer a feast for the eyes.

Superior to *Pete Kelly's Blues* and *Party Girl* both as a musical and as an evocation of the Jazz Age is MGM's biographical drama *Love Me or Leave Me* (1955), the story of show-business legend Ruth Etting (Doris Day), who rose from the ranks of Chicago's show girls to become one of the most highly paid singers of the Roaring Twenties with the help of her cutthroat, crippled mobster husband, Marty "the Gimp" Snyder (James Cagney), whose obsession with the singer eventually drove her to drink.

When Day finally hits the big leagues, she swears off the booze and dumps Cagney for her accompanist, John Alderman (Cameron Mitchell), whom Cagney shoots in a jealous rage. Mitchell survives his wounds, keeping Cagney out of jail, but the mobster's life with Day is over. He has nothing left but the splashy new Los Angeles nightclub he's sunk all his money into, which now promises to be a bust after all the negative publicity surrounding the shooting. The grateful Day publicly acknowledges her debt to Cagney, however, by appearing as headliner on opening night, making the club's debut a smashing success.

Ruth Etting, Marty Snyder, and John Alderman were all living when *Love Me or Leave Me* was produced; they not only gave the filmmakers permission to screen their story but were consulted as technical advisers, as well—which is probably why the film has such a strong sense of authenticity despite all its MGM gloss. Daniel Fuchs and Isobel Lennart's incisive and often biting script doesn't skirt around the unattractive nature of the stormy Etting/Snyder relationship—namely, that is is he, the brutish gangster, who, for all his faults, loves Etting and does everything he can to help her realize her ambitions. And that if Etting is a victim,

James Cagney gave a lacerating performance as real-life mobster Marty "The Gimp" Snyder in Love Me or Leave Me *(1955). With Doris Day and Robert Keith. (Copyright © 1955 Metro-Goldwyn-Mayer)*

she's an all too willing one, who takes everything Snyder dishes out in order to get what she wants.

Doris Day is a little whiny during the emotional scenes, but she knows how to belt out a song, and the film lets her shine with twelve of them, many of them Roaring Twenties hits made famous by Etting herself. Yet the film really belongs to Cagney, who gives a lacerating performance as the monstrous (yet oddly endearing) Snyder—the actor's last great gangster role. The climactic moment where Day comes to the aid of the jailed mobster and offers him money and he pridefully throws the offer back in her face has powerful impact.

More recent films attempting to recreate the mood, music, and mayhem of the Roaring Twenties—with varying degrees of seriousness and success—include the following.

Robin and the Seven Hoods (1964), in which Frank Sinatra and fellow Rat Packers Sammy Davis, Jr., Dean Martin, et al., transplanted the legend of Sherwood Forest's most famous outlaw to Prohibition-era Chicago. A reasonably funny and tuneful romp featuring mostly new songs (including the debut of the Sinatra classic "My Kind of Town") rather than Roaring Twenties standards, the film's highlight is an in-joke cameo by Edward G. Robinson as a Little Caesar–type mobster who's bumped off at his own birthday party in the film's amusing opening scene.

The Sting (1973), starring Paul Newman and Robert Redford as a pair of Roaring Twenties down-and-outers who pull off an intricate con game on big-time Irish mobster Robert Shaw. The setting is Chicago once again, but the contemporary ragtime score featuring the tunes of Scott Joplin is much more evocative of the era than the Sammy Cahn and James Van Heusen pastiches created for *Robin and the Seven Hoods.*

Bugsy Malone (1976), Alan Parker's offbeat and bizarre musical salute to the classic Roaring Twenties gangster films, featuring kids toting whipped-cream ma-

Below, left: The Sting (1973), starring Paul Newman, Robert Redford, and Robert Shaw, recaptured the Roaring Twenties era quite well. Richard Bakalyan is the hood on the right. (Copyright © 1973 Universal Pictures)

Right: David Janssen as rackets czar Arnold Rothstein, the King of the Roaring '20s (1961). (Copyright © 1961 Allied Artists Pictures)

chine guns (including a teenaged Jodie Foster) in the roles of the cigar-chomping mobsters and their molls. Composer Paul Williams supplied the lively but decidedly un-Twenties score.

The Cotton Club (1984), Francis Ford Coppola's megabuck musical period piece about the famous Harlem nightclub (*Thunderbolt's* Dreamland Cafe was modeled on the same establishment) whose clientele included not only movie gangsters such as James Cagney (played in a cameo by look-alike Vincent Jerosa) but some of the era's most infamous mobsters, as well, like Dutch Schultz and Lucky Luciano. Even the club's owner, Irishman Owney Madden, was a gangster. Spectacularly staged by Coppola in a style reminiscent of his *Godfather* films, *The Cotton Club* does a great job of recreating the look, the music, and the gunplay of the era, but it suffers from an inadequate script (by William Kennedy and Coppola) that focuses too much attention on the banal lives and loves of its two lackluster fictional heroes (Richard Gere and Gregory Hines), when the background story of the real-life gangsters surrounding them is implicitly more colorful and interesting. In the end, neither Gere nor Hines but, rather, supporting players James Remar (as Dutch Schultz) and Bob Hoskins (as Owney Madden) steal the film.

Hollywood had another go at the Dutch Schultz story in *Billy Bathgate* (1991). Faithfully adapted by playwright Tom Stoppard from E. L. Doctorow's semifictional *Ragtime*–style gangster novel, the $45 million production starred Dustin Hoffman in a very Cagneyesque performance as the vicious Schultz, Loren Dean as the callow title character (and titular hero), who befriends Schultz because he wants to become a fearless gangster just like him, and Nicole Kidman as the moll who comes between them. The film ran into trouble, according to some accounts, when perfectionist Hoffman and director Robert Benton clashed over creative control, and the film's original ending had to be scrapped. The film's early 1991 release was delayed several months so that Benton (cowriter of the classic *Bonnie and Clyde*) could get his actors back together and shoot a new ending; the film was then slipped into theaters with little fanfare, and died a quiet death. Like most Roaring Twenties–revisited films, *Billy Bathgate* recaptures the look of its Depression-era setting vividly and is a triumph of the production designer's art. But for all the high-priced talent involved, its plot is singularly uninvolving, its performances professional but uninteresting (with the exception of Steven Hill's), and its pace, unlike its genre forbears of the thirties, slow and remarkably dull.

Influenced more by the hit TV series "The Untouchables" (1959–1963) than by the success of such big-screen Jazz Age spectaculars as *Love Me or Leave Me* and *Party Girl* were Budd Boetticher's *The Rise and Fall of Legs Diamond* (1960) and Joseph M. Newman's *King of the Roaring 20's: The Story of Arnold Rothstein* (1961). Both revisited the lawless decade from the perspective of two non-Italian mobsters whose nefarious careers hadn't received much exposure in films before.

King of the Roaring 20's is the lesser of the two in terms of effectively recreating the era, but it's an absorbing little picture, nonetheless. David Janssen, who had yet to achieve stardom in the title role of TV's "The Fugitive," plays Rothstein, a sharp-dressing gambler who rises to become the era's first big-league racketeer, predating and in some cases bankrolling Lucky Luciano and other, more famous mobsters. Known variously as *The Big Bankroll* (the title of the book upon which the film is based) and *The Fixer* (allegedly it was Rothstein who spearheaded the infamous Black Sox scandal of 1919, netting a small fortune in the process), Rothstein is held in high esteem by his mobster partners because of his willingness to share the wealth. As the decade wanes, however, he becomes more extravagant in his losses and gains and is finally targeted by his former cronies for the big rubout, which he receives in his hotel room following a high-stakes poker game.

A well-acted and exciting Jazz Age crime thriller, *King of the Roaring 20's* offers an intriguing behind-the scenes look at the mob politics of the time, even if it does play a bit fast and loose with the real story of Rothstein's life.

Though it, too, runs roughshod over the facts, *The Rise and Fall of Legs Diamond* is much more successful in recapturing the era and personality of its gangster hero. Director Boetticher and cameraman Lucien Ballard blended genuine newsreel footage of the era with a grainy photographic style so seamlessly that the film actually looks like a bona fide gangster picture of the twenties.

Arrogant, charismatic, ambitious, and well-armed. Ray Danton as the doomed title character in The Rise and Fall of Legs Diamond *(1960), with Karen Sharpe. (Copyright © 1960 Warner Bros.)*

Ray Danton plays the title character, who earned his celebrated nickname as a teenager when he scored packages off the backs of delivery trucks, always managing to outrun the police who pursued him. After his mentor, Arnold Rothstein (Robert Lowery), is murdered, Legs, a charismatic dandy on the surface and a cold-blooded killer underneath, sets out on his own, destroying anyone who stands in the way of his rise to the top, including his own brother, played by Warren Oates, his wife (Karen Steele), and a flapper girlfriend (Elaine Stewart). The arrogance and death-dealing ways of the ambitious lone wolf earn Legs the enmity of every other gangster in New York City, but they repeatedly fail in their attempts to kill the scoundrel, who thereafter laughingly pronounces himself "unkillable." Following a European vacation, during which he sees some newsreels depicting the end of his style of lone-wolf gangsterism, Legs returns home, to find that the big organized crime syndicates have taken over. Arrogant to the last, he announces that he's taking over the syndicate's operations; shortly thereafter, he is proven killable, after all, when he's murdered in a hotel room where he's hiding out. (The real mobster who successfully brought off the hit isn't known, though it's presumed to have been Legs's chief nemesis, Dutch Schultz, whose presence is oddly omitted from the film. Boetticher fictionalizes Legs's demise instead by having him set up by scorned ex-girlfriend Stewart.)

After reprising his role as Legs Diamond in *Portrait of a Mobster* (1961), the story of Schultz himself, Danton took on the title role of *The George Raft Story*, released the same year. The film offered a highly fictionalized account of Raft's rise from the dance halls of Chicago and New York to the top of the Warner Brothers gangster-movie heap in the 1930s, then to his fall from the box-office pinnacle in the 1940s, when his style of screen tough guy was eclipsed by the more versatile performances of fellow movie gangsters Robinson, Cagney, and Bogart.

Below, left: *Dutch Schultz (Vic Morrow) narrowly escapes a mob-ordered hit in* Portrait of a Mobster *(1961). (Copyright © 1961 Warner Bros.)*

Right: *Mobster Spats Colombo (George Raft) orders the infamous St. Valentine's Day Massacre in Billy Wilder's classic gangland farce* Some Like It Hot *(1959). (Copyright © 1958 United Artists Corp.)*

Raft, a reported acquaintance and admirer of many actual Roaring Twenties mobsters—including Legs Diamond—made one of the most interesting movies of his career when he returned to the type of role he'd made famous during the thirties and forties in Billy Wilder's gangland farce *Some Like It Hot* (1959). The film remains the definitive treatment of the familiar tale of rubes on the run from the mob—a comic subgenre of the gangster film that extends as far back as *Lights of New York* and *Broadway* (in which Raft had starred) and *The Gang Buster* (1931) and that endures today in such recent variations as Jonathan Demme's *Married to the Mob* (1988); Charles Lane's *True Identity* (1991); *Nuns on the Run* (1990), with Eric Idle and Robbie Coltrane as two British gangsters who pose as nuns to escape the wrath of their unforgiving boss after blowing a robbery; and Whoopi Goldberg's distaff version of the same change-of-identity plot, *Sister Act* (1992).

Perhaps the funniest gangster movie ever made, *Some Like It Hot* was loosely based on a 1932 German musical about two unemployed Depression-era musicians who don disguises to get work in various all-gypsy, all-female, and all-Negro bands. Wilder and I. A. L. Diamond's script transposes the story to gangland Chicago during the least years of the Roaring Twenties. Down-and-out musicians Tony Curtis and Jack Lemmon witness the St. Valentine's Day Massacre by the Capone-like Raft and his coterie of comic thugs, who act like characters out of a Preston Sturges movie. To avoid being rubbed out themselves, they lam it to Florida disguised as Josephine and Daphne, members of an all-girl jazz band hired to play at a resort full of aging millionaires. Curtis falls for the band's lead singer, Sugar Kane (Marilyn Monroe), and assumes a second bogus identity (a Cary Grant–like millionaire yachtsman) in order to court her. Meanwhile, Lemmon's Daphne is pursued by real millionaire Osgood Fielding III (Joe E. Brown), an oft-married eccentric who is not only blind to Lemmon's charade but doesn't care much ("Nobody's perfect!") even when he does find out she's a man.

Raft and his mob show up for a gangland convention at the same resort where Curtis and Lemmon are hiding out, and the hapless boys witness yet another gangland slaying—this time of Raft and his thugs. Forced to take it on the lam again, they make out much better this time around, when the obliging Brown spirits them (and Monroe) to his waiting yacht.

Some Like It Hot includes many satiric nods to the classic gangster films of the genre's golden age—as when Raft stops a young mobster from irritatingly flipping a coin in his face, growling, "Where did you learn that stupid trick?"—a coy reference to Raft's own star-making turn in *Scarface*, where the same annoying habit was one of his identifying traits. Later, the irascible Raft threatens to let another annoying mobster have it in the face with a grapefruit, à la James Cagney in *The Public Enemy*.

A top-notch gangster comedy from start to finish, *Some Like It Hot* also succeeds in evoking the heady Roaring Twenties milieu in which it's set—or at least two-thirds of it does. During the middle section of the film, Wilder loses the Roaring Twenties atmosphere a bit as the film's attention drifts inevitably to the play among Lemmon, Curtis, and Monroe. But, as Joe E. Brown says, "Nobody's perfect!"

James Cagney walks the last mile in Angels with Dirty
Faces *(1938). (Copyright © 1938 Warner Bros.)*

CHAPTER 3

AL CAPONE:

SCARFACE

At the height of his criminal career during the closing years of the Roaring Twenties, Al Capone was the most famous gangster in America, and with the combined influence of books, films, and television, he retains that status to this day. He ranks alongside Jesse James and Billy the Kid as one of the legendary criminal figures in American history and culture.

More than just the best-known American gangster, however, Capone has become a symbol of the phenomenon of gangsterism itself. Even today, almost fifty years after Capone's death, contemporary mob kingpins such as John Gotti are referred to in the press as "gangsters in the Capone tradition." By virtue of their association with Capone, as either confederates or adversaries, other gangsters of the period have achieved a degree of immortality, as well. In all likelihood, the names Frank Nitti, Johnny Torrio, Dion O'Banion, and George "Bugs" Moran would be much less familiar to the public today were it not for the enduring legend of Scarface.

Capone was so well-known, notorious, and even popular a figure that books and movies began mythologizing his career and exploits during the gangster's reign. Capone enjoyed seeing himself represented on the screen. Before considering the numerous films that have been made about this American icon in the past sixty years, however, it's worth taking a look at the real Capone first.

Alphonse Capone long maintained that he'd been born in Italy and that his family had emigrated to the United States shortly after his birth in 1899. Actually, he was the youngest of four brothers, all of them born in Brooklyn. Capone also maintained that he'd received the infamous slash on his left cheek from an enemy bayonet on the battlefields of France during World War I, when, in fact, the only combat Capone ever saw was on the gang-ridden streets of New York and Chicago. Capone got the scar early in his career in a knife fight over a girl with a rival hoodlum named Frank Galluccio. Capone later hired Galluccio as his bodyguard when he became Chicago's top mobster, an act that bolstered his power and prestige in the underworld because it showed what a generous guy he was even with former adversaries who joined him.

Capone began his criminal career as a minor hoodlum on the streets of New York. Known and feared for his brutality, he quickly rose to a position as one of the top killers in the notorious Five Points Gang, the city's last great pre-Prohibition terrorist mob. The gang's members also included Johnny Torrio and Charles "Lucky" Luciano. When Prohibition came in, Torrio moved to Chicago to assist his uncle, Big Jim Colosimo, one of the city's top crime bosses, and imported Capone as his bodyguard and partner. But Colosimo was challenged by Torrio, who wanted to expand profits from South Side prostitution, gambling, and bootlegging activities to the lucrative North Side, the off-limits turf of the city's other top gangster, Irishman Dion O'Banion. Uninterested in a gang war that would threaten to kill each mob's golden goose, Colosimo instructed Torrio to put the brakes on his greed. Refusing to be thwarted, Torrio and his pal Capone orchestrated their boss's assassination and took control of the South Side mob themselves. They then engineered the murder of O'Banion, who was gunned down in the flower shop that served as his headquarters, and moved against O'Banion's North Side associates. Gang war erupted as Colosimo had anticipated, and the streets of Chicago rang with gunfire until Torrio decided he'd had enough: After being severely wounded in an assassination attempt by the North Siders, he handed control of the South Side mob to Capone and went back to New York, where he lived in wealthy retirement until his death in 1957.

A wily organizer and businessman as well as a degenerate killer, Capone became gangland's first equal-opportunity employer by opening up his organization to Irish, Jewish, Polish, black, and other ethnic gang members. The result was not only a growing operation but a stronger one poised to take over the North Side, now the dominion of O'Banion associate George "Bugs" Moran. Repeatedly frustrated in his efforts to kill Moran, Capone finally made the biggest mistake of his criminal career by setting the wheels in motion for an all-out attack on the North Side mob. Capone missed his main target, but the slaughter of seven members of Moran's gang on February 14, 1929—the notorious St. Valentine's Day Massacre—was headlined coast to coast, resulting in a chorus of public outrage against the bootleg wars and an official crackdown (by federal agent Eliot Ness and his Untouchables, along with many others) on mob activities. Fearing that two of the murderers — John Scalise and Alberto Anselmi — might knuckle under and reveal who had ordered the massacre, Capone personally beat them to death with a baseball bat and had their bodies dumped in an Indiana field as an object lesson to anyone in the organization who might be thinking of turning state's evidence. As a result, federal agents were unable to pin the massacre on Capone, and no one was ever brought to justice for the crime.

Capone never did get Moran, who died of cancer in 1957, his power in the underworld long gone. But the feds finally did get Capone, who was convicted on a tax-evasion charge in 1931 and given an eleven-year sentence. Although the powerful underworld organization he'd set up remained intact (and would flourish as the years wore on), Capone's power over it evaporated while he was in prison. Released in 1939, he retired to his private estate in Florida, where he died in 1947 from the ravages of syphilis, a disease he'd contracted many years earlier in a New York City brothel.

LITTLE CAESARS

Although the character of the murderous mobster chieftain had become a gangster-movie staple by the close of the 1920s, very few such screen characters were boldly suggestive of the real Capone. Even *Underworld*'s Bull Weed is not a particularly Capone-like character except in the broadest sense, although the underworld milieu in which von Sternberg sets the character is clearly modeled on Capone's Chicago. There are indications, however, that before von Sternberg revised and generalized it, Ben Hecht's original story may have offered fewer veiled references to Capone and his murderous activities, and one of them actually survives in the finished film: The scene where Weed tracks down and shoots his rival, Irish mobster Buck Mulligan, in Mulligan's flower-shop headquarters bears more than a passing resemblance to the Capone-ordered hit of Dion O'Banion.

The character of Nick Scarsi in *The Racket* was more openly suggestive of Capone, although the film version soft-pedaled the analogy far more than Bartlett Cormack's original stage play, in which the playwright not only mentioned Chicago by name but even referred to such authentic Capone cronies as the corrupt mayor Big Bill Thompson. More to the point, the actor who created the part of Scarsi on stage, Edward G. Robinson, physically resembled Capone, while his screen counterpart, Louis Wolheim, looked more like central casting's idea of a typical movie thug.

A year later, Universal's gangland musical, *Broadway*, featured a minor mob character named Scar Edwards (Leslie Fenton). But it wasn't until Warner Brothers' *Little Caesar* (1930) that the screen finally tackled the brutal story of Chicago's infamous gang leader head-on.

Some revisionist film historians have written that Edward G. Robinson was not director Mervyn LeRoy's first choice to play Capone figure Rico Bandello in *Little Caesar*. They say that LeRoy sought Robinson for the part of one of the film's minor mobster characters (Otero, eventually played by George E. Stone) instead, and that Robinson refused to have anything to do with the film unless LeRoy gave him the lead role. In his autobiography, *Take One*, LeRoy firmly disputed this assertion. But even if he hadn't, it seems unlikely that the actor who had risen to fame on Broadway as the Capone-like Nick Scarsi, who had played several lead roles in previous gangster films and even looked like the homicidal gang chieftain, would be offered a supporting role in what was to be the most realistic depiction of the Capone saga yet screened.

Based on a 1929 best-seller by thriller specialist W. R. Burnett, *Little Caesar* offered moviegoers a more brutal gangster antihero than they'd ever seen before. His Rico Bandello is no gentleman mobster or decent guy gone temporarily bad until regenerated in the end by the love of an honest woman. Rico seems to have no interest in women at all: He's an ungentlemanly, avaricious, homicidal punk who kills people because they stand in the way of his rise to power—or just because he covets some jewelry they're wearing. And, like Chaney's Blackbird, he goes to his death unrepentant of his violent criminal ways.

While eating in a luncheonette, the down-and-out Rico and his pal Joe Massara (Douglas Fairbanks, Jr.) see a newspaper article about wealthy Chicago racketeer Diamond Pete Montana (the film's Big Jim Colosimo character, played by Ralph Ince) and head for the Windy City to change their luck. Rico falls in with Montana's

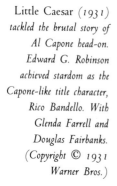

Little Caesar (1931) tackled the brutal story of Al Capone head-on. Edward G. Robinson achieved stardom as the Capone-like title character, Rico Bandello. With Glenda Farrell and Douglas Fairbanks. (Copyright © 1931 Warner Bros.)

right-hand man, Sam Vettori (Stanley Fields), the film's Torrio, and soon makes his mark as one of the South Side mob's most brutal enforcers. Meanwhile, Rico's pal Massara, an aspiring entertainer, becomes a successful dancer at a nightclub run by North Side mob boss Arnie Lorch (Maurice Black), the film's O'Banion character, and turns his back on his criminal past when he falls for his glamorous and honest dance partner, Olga (Glenda Farrell).

Although Rico has been ordered by Vettori to "keep out of the North Side," his ambitions overwhelm him and he coerces Massara into being his front man in a daring robbery of Lorch's club. During the robbery, Rico cold-bloodedly murders one of the customers, the head of the crime commission (Landers Stevens) investigating gangland activities in the city, and Massara witnesses the shooting, although he keeps silent to all but Olga.

Lorch strikes back at Rico and is killed. As a result of his boldness, Rico becomes boss of the North and South Side mobs and pushes Massara to join him. To get Rico out of their lives, Olga tries to convince Massara to turn state's evidence, but he refuses after Rico threatens both their lives. So she calls the cops herself and identifies Rico as the crime commissioner's killer (Massara says nothing). Rico attempts to go through with his threat but goes soft for the first time in his life and is unable to kill his former pal. The cops round up Vettori and several other gang members, and Rico becomes a hunted man. Reduced to poverty and forced to hide out in a flophouse where fellow down-and-outers, unaware of who he is, snicker over newspaper articles recounting the gangster's fall from wealth and power, the frustrated Rico goes berserk with egocentric rage, emerges from hiding at last, and is fatally shot down by police ("Mother of Mercy, is this the end of Rico?") beneath a billboard advertising Olga and Massara's successful engagement at the Tipsy, Topsy, Turvy Theater.

Reviewers applauded *Little Caesar* as a realistic portrait of the world of gangsterism, but they generally failed to comment upon the many parallels between the exploits of the fictional Rico Bandello and those of Capone, whose name was even then a household word. What they did point out were the similarities in character and performance between Robinson's Rico and *The Racket*'s Nick Scarsi, the role that had catapulted Robinson to fame on Broadway three years earlier and with which he was still strongly identified despite his absence from the controversial film version. Writing in *The New Yorker*, for example, critic John Mosher noted: "Since his appearance on the stage in *The Racket*, Edward G. Robinson has grown to be the leading authority on the behavior and mannerisms of those gunmen and gangsters whose doings often occupy the attention of the press. Evidently all his experiences and research work in such a field are now employed in the study of Rico Bandello, the central figure of this movie." And in the *New York Herald Tribune*, Richard Watts, Jr., said: "Not even in *The Racket* was he [Robinson] more effective. Taking one of the most familiar roles in the universe,

Scarface (1932) dealt with the Capone saga even more overtly . . . and violently. With Osgood Perkins and Paul Muni. (Copyright © 1932 United Artists Corp.)

he makes it seem fresh and real. By a hundred details of characterization, he transforms a stock figure into a human being. And, heaven knows, he doesn't make Little Caesar human by suggesting any softness in him. Never does he cease being a savage and terrifying killer, a man who is all the more sinister because of his reality."

Indeed, *Little Caesar* is Robinson's film all the way. Its power and enduring status as a classic gangster film stem almost exclusively from his performance, for Mervyn LeRoy's reticent direction offers him very little support. Although it was criticized for being excessively brutal, *Little Caesar* is infinitely more subdued in its violence than many of the silent gangster melodramas that preceded it. This is probably why *Little Caesar,* unlike the bolder and more graphic *The Public Enemy* (1931), seems like such an antique today.*

LeRoy averts the camera's eye from Rico's brutal behavior at virtually every point. He shows us Rico's robbery of Lorch's nightclub and murder of the crime commissioner in a series of arty, fast-paced dissolves designed to obscure the gory details of the mobster's character; he keeps the key murder of Lorch, Rico's North Side rival, offscreen entirely. (We see Rico coveting Lorch's expensive stickpin, then proudly wearing it—the implication being that he murdered Lorch for the pin during an intervening dissolve.) As a result, the task of putting across the violence of the man and the primitive instincts that drive him falls almost entirely upon Robinson's fortunately capable shoulders.

As its title suggests, *Scarface* (1932) is more direct in dealing with the Capone saga than even *Little Caesar* had been. Reportedly, Capone was aware that the film was to be modeled very closely after him, and it is said that he sent George Raft, a Capone favorite, to audition as an extra so that he could keep an eye on things and report back to the mobster.† Raft caught the eye of director Howard Hawks, landed a much bigger part, and left the mob to pursue a movie career instead.

The Capone figure in *Scarface* is Tony Camonte (Paul Muni), a former member of New York City's Five Points Gang who has come to Chicago to work for Johnny Lovo (Osgood Perkins), a lieutenant of South Side mob boss Big Louis Costillo (Harry J. Vejar). Camonte becomes Costillo's bodyguard and kills him so that he and Lovo can take over the South Side themselves. Pulled in for

---

*Even then, the influential *New York Times* termed the production "ordinary" and "just one more gangster film" save for Robinson's performance.

†Conceivably, Raft might have served as the inspiration for the Joe Massara character in Burnett's novel *Little Caesar.*

questioning by the police, the arrogant Camonte lights a match for his cigarette on an officer's badge (a bit of business the Coen brothers would reuse in their 1990 gangster film homage *Miller's Crossing*) and smugly denies everything. When asked where he received the ugly scar on his face, he echoes Capone's own smug reply: "Got in the war," he says.

Over Lovo's objections, the ambitious Camonte sets his sights on a North Side takeover and has the Irish leader of the rival mob gunned down in a flower shop. Another mobster named Gaffney, played by Boris Karloff, replaces the dead chieftain and orders his North Siders to assassinate Camonte in a restaurant. But the attempt fails and an all-out gang war ensues between the North and South Side gangs. Feeling the pinch, Lovo tries to pacify the other side by having his impetuous partner rubbed out. But Camonte survives the attack, and his loyal henchman, Guido (George Raft), kills Lovo in reprisal.

With Lovo out of the way, Camonte assumes control of the South Side mob and wins the affections of the dead man's moll, Poppy (Karen Morley), as well.*

Camonte (Paul Muni) suggests expanding operations into the North Side. From Scarface *(1932). With George Raft and Osgood Perkins. (Copyright © 1932 United Artists Corp.)*

*Ben Hecht was one of five writers who contributed to the screenplay of *Scarface*, and so it's difficult to know who wrote what. But one scene so closely echoes a scene from the earlier *Underworld* that it seems a likely Hecht contribution. Boasting about what he has planned for Poppy if she sticks with him, Camonte shows her a billboard for Cook's Tours with the symbolic headline THE WORLD IS YOURS. In *Underworld*, ambitious mobster George Bancroft had impressed moll Evelyn Brent about what her future held by pointing to a billboard for the ABC Investment Company bearing the identical headline.

Feeling his oats, Camonte launches a vicious St. Valentine's Day strike against the North Siders by luring several key mob members to a garage, where his men line them up against a wall and strafe them with tommy-gun bullets. By a twist of fate, Gaffney escapes the massacre, but he's later gunned down in a bowling alley, and Camonte takes control of the North Side, as well.

The film's most significant departure from the Capone story—the real Scarface was already in jail for tax evasion when the movie was released—is its perverse finale. The overprotective Camonte discovers that his sister Cesca (Ann Dvorak), his affection for whom exceeds the brotherly, is living with his pal Guido; he kills the man in a rage, only to learn that the two are legally man and wife. With his sister turning against him and the police hunting him for Guido's murder, Camonte loses his grip altogether and (like Bull Weed in *Underworld*) seeks refuge in his steel-shuttered hideout. Cesca sneaks in with a gun to revenge herself, but is unable to shoot her brother when she realizes she's suppressing incestuous feelings of her own. Forgiving Camonte, she takes up arms with him against the police as the street is cordoned off and the hideout is pelted with gunfire and tear gas. She takes the first bullet and dies in the forlorn gangster's arms. With nothing to live for, Camonte makes a suicidal run for it and the cops shoot him down in the street, where he expires beneath the Cook's Tours sign advertising THE WORLD IS YOURS.

Scarface was so overt in its depiction of gangland morals and mayhem that it drew heavy fire from state censor boards all over the land. They accused producer Howard Hughes of glamorizing the world of gangsterism by dealing with it not just realistically but much too objectively, and they demanded that *Scarface* be held from release until their criticisms were addressed. Hughes complied by adding several scenes (directed by Richard Rosson) to make the film more blatantly denunciating. In one of the added scenes, a newspaper publisher (Purnell Pratt) accused of giving too many headlines to the city's bad men looks straight into the camera, decries the problem of gangsterism, and admonishes the government and the public for their own lack of responsibility in countering mob violence ("You can end it. Fight!"). In another, the city's chief of detectives (Edwin Maxwell) denounces the glorification of gangsters, echoing the very cries of the censors who ordered the changes. A foreword demanding a solution to the problem of gangsterism was added, as well. And the film was released with a subtitle designed to appease the censors: *Scarface: The Shame of a Nation*.

Hughes's efforts to salvage his investment didn't work, however. Unfavorably reviewed by much of the press and still denounced by censor boards and citizens' watchdog groups as the most vicious and demoralizing gangster picture ever made, it died at the box office; the petulant Hughes withdrew it from circulation for almost fifty years. Following Hughes's death, the controversial film was finally rereleased to television and on home video, and it is now hailed as one of the genre's pioneer efforts—a tough, no-nonsense portrayal of a Capone-style mobster that delivers almost as much of a punch today as when it was made.

Director Brian De Palma remade the Hawks classic in 1983 under the same title. Dedicated to Ben Hecht, the script by Oliver Stone updated the saga to the early 1980s, when Castro's Cuba exiled boatloads of political prisoners, criminals, and other "undesirables" to U.S. shores. One of them is Al Pacino's Tony Montana, a scar-faced punk with an unhealthy (and unsavory) attachment to his sister (Mary Elizabeth Mastrantonio). Montana rises to become a kingpin in Florida's flourishing drug trade, only to be brought down by his own brutal and deranged excesses. Like the original *Scarface*, the remake ran into trouble with censors: Its over-the-top violence—torture by chain saw, nonstop shoot-outs, and a concluding bloodbath designed to top (as well as parody) Sam Peckinpah's ferocious finale to *The Wild Bunch* (1969)—almost earned the film an X rating, but the film's distributor, Universal, resubmitted it with minor cuts, and the MPAA was finally persuaded to give it the coveted R rating.

Like most De Palma movies, *Scarface* starts out looking as if it might amount to something, just to become a send-up of itself. Sporting a Frito Bandito accent, Pacino chews up the scenery so broadly that his scar-faced Tony Montana comes across less as a gangland monster (a primitive man dressed in street clothes like Muni's Camonte) than a sort of ultraviolent buffoon. And despite all the spectacular firepower and gruesome bloodletting, the finale, wherein he drowns his sorrows—and his entire face—in a plate full of cocaine as his mansion and bodyguards are reduced to ruins, isn't anywhere near as powerful as the less graphic but equally violent (and disturbingly incest-laden) conclusion to Howard Hawks's 1932 original—even if it *is* a lot funnier.

Throughout the thirties, forties, and fifties, gangster-movie makers continued to draw on the life and legend of Al Capone for inspiration, even though the "Big Fellow" himself had faded from the scene. One of the more interesting later Capone films was *The Gangster* (1947), an unrelentingly grim film noir about the final days of a scar-faced Capone-type mobster named Shubunka (Barry Sullivan), whose independent operation has been targeted for hostile takeover by a big-time syndicate. A cynical, paranoid tough guy who has built up his criminal empire by trusting no one and eschewing all human contact, Shubunka becomes infatuated with an aspiring show girl (Belita); as he lowers his guard for the first time in his life to win her over, he pays less and less attention to his rackets, leaving the door open for a better-organized, more powerful mob to horn in. When the squeeze comes, he seeks help from the connections and underlings he'd always despised but finds they've all turned their backs on him and joined the rival mob. In a surprise twist, even the girl he loves turns out to be a puppet for the other side. As the gangsters close in for the kill, Shubunka plays his last card and seeks temporary shelter from a teenage girl (Joan Lorring). But she despises him for

The Gangster (1947)
grimly portrayed the final
days of a Capone-like
mobster named Shubunka
(Barry Sullivan, center).
With Belita and Sheldon
Leonard.

the way he's always treated people and turns him out into the rain with the admonition that it's time to pay for his sins. Bitterly admitting that his real error was in allowing himself to soften while other gangsters even more rotten successfully encroached on his turf, he surrenders to the hit men on his trail and is shot down in the street. A chilling character study marred only by some unfunny sequences of comic relief, *The Gangster* is the *High Noon* of mob movies.

The 1944 *Roger Touhy, Gangster* — directed by Robert Florey — focused not on Capone but on one of his most successful and feared rivals. In fact, Capone never appears in the film, but his presence is clearly felt as Touhy (Preston Foster) and his gang of Terrible Touhys find themselves muscled out of business by rival mobsters who engineer Touhy's conviction on a kidnapping charge. Touhy escapes from prison to prove his innocence but is recaptured and walled up for life as the warden (Joseph Crehan) delivers the film's "crime doesn't pay" message. It especially doesn't pay if you're innocent — as the real Touhy in fact was, for the kidnapping that sent him to prison for life (plus an additional ninety-nine years for his escape attempt) never even occurred. Some crime historians believe that the FBI may even have been involved with the mob in the frame-up. Paroled for good behavior in 1959, Touhy was murdered on a Chicago street three weeks later by a onetime Capone enforcer, and he departed the world with an even more potent message for future would-be criminals and racketeers. "I've been expecting this," Touhy gasped. "The bastards never forget."

Other Capone films merely traded on the image of the legendary gangster for marquee value and were not necessarily about the real Capone at all. For

example, the 1949 *The Undercover Man*, based on a magazine article titled "Undercover Man: He Trapped Capone" by Frank J. Wilson, focused on Treasury agent Glenn Ford's efforts to nail a fictional mobster (Ken Harvey), nicknamed the "Big Fellow," on a tax-evasion charge. In *Lady Scarface* (1941), Judith Anderson played a distaff version of Capone, complete with an ugly slash on her cheek, who heads a successful robbery gang operating out of Chicago that is felled by Treasury agent Dennis O'Keefe and detective magazine reporter Ann Rogers.

Brighton Rock (1947), directed by John Boulting from a novel by Graham Greene, offered moviegoers a British variation on the peculiarly American type of the Caponesque gangster. Richard Attenborough plays a smarmy, again scar-faced killer and small-time racketeer named Pinky. He marries the witness to one of his rubouts in order to silence her but gets what he deserves anyway in a nicely handled (and bitterly ironic) twist. The film was released in the United States with the more promotable title *Young Scarface*.

It was the medium of television, however, that stirred nationwide interest once more in the life and times of the real Al Capone.

THE UNTOUCHABLES

Today, Eliot Ness is an American folk hero. But in 1928, when he got the job of putting together an elite task force of crime busters "to pry some seams in the Capone organization," he was just another faceless Prohibition agent working for the Justice Department. Ness was keenly aware of the value of publicity, however, and he used it not only to advance his own career but to gain public support for attacking the mob, as well.

Ness poured through hundreds of personnel files to find ten men whose law-enforcement skills and reputations for honesty were unmatched in the department, then invited the press along to observe his special squad in action as it began knocking over Capone's stills throughout Chicago. Losing income from the raids, Capone repeatedly attempted to bribe Ness and his men to lay off. When these attempts failed, the Capone gang dubbed Ness's squad the Untouchables; before long the name was picked up by the press. Buoyed by the notoriety, Ness and his Untouchables got bolder and more aggressive. They infiltrated Capone's head-quarters and placed a tap on his phone to learn the locations of Capone's vital breweries throughout the city and the Midwest. They then constructed a heavy-duty ramming truck that enabled them to break through the breweries' steel-enforced doors and catch Capone's men by surprise. After almost two years on the job, they'd succeeded in putting scores of Capone stills and breweries out of business and confiscated literally hundreds of Capone's delivery trucks—which they drove past the mobster's headquarters one morning on the way to the government warehouse just to rub it in. Capone flew into a rage and ordered that efforts be stepped up to get Ness. They failed, and Capone never did get his man. But then again, neither did Eliot Ness.

Ness and his Untouchables did cost the gangster's bootlegging rackets dearly, but Capone's other rackets—gambling, prostitution, and so on—continued to flourish, and he was finally nailed by the Treasury Department for the relatively unexceptional crime of holding out on his taxes.

With the fall of Capone, the Untouchables disbanded and went their separate ways, not to be heard from again until 1957. During the intervening years, Ness continued in law enforcement for a time, then took a stab at politics. When that career move proved unsuccessful, he went into private business, floundering there, as well. By 1956, he was both a forgotten man and heavily in debt—until a chance encounter with a UPI sports reporter named Oscar Fraley that same year changed his life. A mutual friend encouraged Ness to talk to Fraley about his experiences during the Capone years, and the conversations turned into a book. Published in 1957, *The Untouchables* shot onto the best-seller list and transformed the obscure former Prohibition agent into the most famous American lawman since Wyatt Earp. Unfortunately, Ness never lived to see his rediscovery. He died from a massive heart attack at age fifty-six, just a few months shy of the book's debut.

Producer/actor Desi Arnaz bought the rights to the book and turned it into a two-parter for his dramatic anthology series *Desilu Playhouse*. Titled *The Scarface Mob*, the show aired on ABC during the spring of 1959; it was such a big hit that Arnaz and his producer, Quinn Martin, spliced the two episodes together and released them in Europe as a feature film.

The Scarface Mob is a fairly faithful rendering of Ness's autobiographical account of his years battling the Capone mob (although for some reason the credits for the telefilm list it as being based on Ness and Fraley's "novel"). The book doesn't suggest that Ness and his Untouchables were solely responsible for bringing down Capone, although it's possible to come away with that opinion, since the book focuses only on their activities. The telefilm doesn't suggest such a conclusion, either, but it does play looser with the historical record by giving Ness's main

Below, left: Neville Brand, one of the most decorated heroes of WWII, played the notorious Chicago gangster in The Scarface Mob *(1962).*

Right: Robert Stack as crime-busting folk hero Eliot Ness in The Scarface Mob *(1962), the two-hour telefeature that spawned the hit TV series* The Untouchables.

adversary, mobster Frank Nitti (indelibly portrayed by Bruce Gordon), a bit more power and prominence in the Capone organization than Nitti in fact had. It also provides Capone (Neville Brand) with an Italian accent (of the comic "Whatsa-u-name?" variety) even though the speech patterns of the real Capone were thoroughly Brooklynese. However, compared to the later TV series "The Untouchables"—which had Ness and his men nailing everyone from Jake "Greasy Thumb" Guzik, Capone's chief accountant, to Machine Gun Jack McGurn to hit man Mad Dog Coll—*The Scarface Mob,* narrated in tabloid-headline style by columnist Walter Winchell, is practically a model of documentary realism.

Although *The Scarface Mob* was not intended to be a series pilot, it was such a ratings winner that ABC persuaded Arnaz and Martin to develop it into a series for the fall schedule. Under the title "The Untouchables," the series premiered in October and ran for 111 episodes over four successful years.

The series was controversial from the beginning—not just for its violence, heavy-duty for television back then, but for its ethnicity. In his autobiography *Straight Shooting,* star Robert Stack (who took the role of Eliot Ness after Van Johnson and Van Heflin turned it down), wrote: "*The Untouchables* managed to get in more trouble in a shorter time than any show on TV. One of our biggest problems was the charge of ethnic bias in our scripts. Many of the villains, from Capone and Nitti to the least important, small-time thugs, had Italian names.* No one ever suggested even remotely that the Italian people as a whole had a leaning toward violent crime. But the controversy began. Together with Senator John Pastore, the powerful chairman of the Senate Communications Subcommittee, Frank Sinatra and Cardinal Spellman objected to the large number of Italian gangsters on the program. . . . Eventually, we did stop using Italian names." By the final season, virtually all ethnic groups were well represented, including the Russians, in the form of a slavic hood with the improbable name of Joe Vodka.

The show drew fire from other quarters, as well. The U.S. Bureau of Prisons objected to specific episodes that, true to life, showed Capone living a rather more lavish lifestyle in prison than cons are expected to enjoy. J. Edgar Hoover objected to the show because of its "inaccurate depiction" of T-men. Another Senate subcommittee assailed the show for promoting juvenile delinquency. The FCC skewered it for being too violent. And Al Capone's son threatened to sue the producers for "defaming" the character of his late father, a suit that never materialized.

A popular but seldom top-rated series, despite all the controversy surrounding

---

*No one seemed to care that one of Ness's closest lieutenants, Enrico Rossi (Nicholas Georgiade), was also Italian. The series' other Untouchables, a much smaller group than Ness's actual squad, included Jerry Paris, Abel Fernandez, Anthony George, Steve London, and Paul Picerni (who ironically debuted in the original two-parter not as an Untouchable but as one of Capone's henchmen).

it, "The Untouchables" finally shut down on September 10, 1963. Ness and his men had killed or put away most of the mob by then, and the show was running out of steam. It went into syndication, but because of the furor it had caused, the series soon disappeared from U.S. airwaves almost entirely, finding continued success only in Europe.

The spectacular success of Francis Ford Coppola's *Godfather* films in the early seventies revived public interest in all things gangster, however, and a few local stations began running the old series again, usually at night. There was some discussion at the time about resurrecting "The Untouchables" in network prime time in a new format with a younger actor as Eliot Ness.* But these plans failed to materialize, and it fell to the movies to rescue the property from limbo.

Writer David Mamet and director Brian De Palma faced the same problem in adapting *The Untouchables* (1987) to the big screen that scriptwriter Paul Monash encountered when he turned Ness and Fraley's book into *The Scarface Mob* — namely that the story of the Ness/Capone feud lacked a satisfying third act. Although Ness struggled mightily to put Capone out of business and behind bars, it was the Treasury boys who got the job done. Monash dealt with this structural problem by having the usually tight-lipped Ness fly into a rage when he hears that the murderous mobster is going to prison for a crime that paled in comparison to his other offences. Mamet and De Palma took a different approach. They ignored the facts altogether and concocted an entirely fictional finale in which Ness (Kevin Costner) and his Untouchables come up with the idea of nailing Capone (Robert

Kevin Costner as Eliot Ness in the "Odessa Steps" sequence of Brian De Palma's The Untouchables *(1987). (Copyright © 1987 Paramount Pictures)*

*Robert Stack reprised his most famous role once more in a fictional 1991 telefilm, *The Return of Eliot Ness*, in which the redoubtable lawman emerges from retirement just after World War II to clear the sullied name of one of his former Untouchables.

De Niro, who snatched the part away at the last minute from the already-cast Bob Hoskins) on tax evasion and provide the Treasury boys with the evidence they need to do so. This sets the stage for an elaborately mounted confrontation between Ness and his adversaries toward the end of the film. Ness and his sole surviving Untouchable (in reality, only one of Ness's original ten-man squad was killed by the Capone mob), played by Andy Garcia, stake out a Chicago train station to nab Capone's bookkeeper for the tax boys and are faced with the dilemma of protecting a woman with a baby carriage, as well as themselves and the bookkeeper, from the gunfire of Capone's hit men. De Palma modeled the highly touted scene, which was not in Mamet's script, after Sergei Eisenstein's classic Odessa Steps sequence in *The Battleship Potemkin* (1925), which the director admitted not having looked at in several years. Maybe he should have; shot in languorous slow motion (unlike Eisenstein's fast-paced prototype), the scene seems to go on forever and is more showy than suspenseful.

Taking their cue from the TV series, and topping it many times over, De Palma and Mamet turned the dramatic, if unspectacular, saga of Eliot Ness and his Untouchables into an epic historical cartoon drenched in blood. Not only does the unsmiling, morally upright Ness—who is even given a wholly fabricated family in the film—get Capone, he also gets Frank Nitti (Billy Drago), whose body is hurled from a building and pulverized as it crashes through the roof of a car. (The real Nitti committed suicide in 1943.) There are a few isolated moments of fact in the film, however; the brewery raids are fairly accurately portrayed, and, just as he had in real life, this Capone bashes in the head of a conniving henchman with a baseball bat.

The commercial success of the De Palma film showed there was still a lot of commerical life left in the Ness/Capone saga. When several other big-budget gangster movies such as *GoodFellas* and *The Godfather, Part III* struck box-office gold as well, Paramount decided the time was right to revive the TV series idea, and in 1993 an all-new version of "The Untouchables" reached the airwaves as a weekly program over the independent Fox Television Network. Art Linson, the producer of the De Palma film, served as executive producer of the series, which writer-creator Christopher Crowe fashioned into a pastiche of the De Palma film, the classic Stack series, and the historical record. Jimmy Stewart–like newcomer Tom Amandes took the role of Ness, William Forsythe played Capone, and Welsh actor John Rhys-Davies stepped into a facsimile of the Sean Connery role in the De Palma film. In keeping with our age of political correctness, a Native American (played by Michael Horse) was finally added to the multiethnic team of venerable crime fighters whose graphically violent confrontations with the Capone mob each week were more reminiscent of the R-rated De Palma bloodbath than the controversial television series that had spawned it.

MORE CAPONES

The revival of interest in Capone and his times sparked by the success of *The Scarface Mob* at home and abroad prompted Allied Artists to cast Rod Steiger in the first big-screen biography of the legendary gangster.

Narrated in Winchell style by James Gregory's Sergeant Schaeffer, a fictional Chicago cop patterned after *The Racket*'s Captain McQuigg and *The Scarface Mob*'s Eliot Ness, *Al Capone* (1959) takes up the gangster's story with his arrival in Chicago in 1919 to help out his mentor, Johnny Torrio (Nehemiah Persoff). Its account of Capone's rise to the top of the Chicago underworld is, on the whole, fairly accurate. The ambitious Capone rubs out Big Jim Colosimo (Joe De Santis), then he and Torrio move against O'Banion (Robert Gist). Things get too hot and Torrio retires, handing control of the mob over to Capone, who quickly locks horns with Bugs Moran (Murvyn Vye). Capone orders the St. Valentine's Day Massacre to dispatch Moran, gets massive amounts of adverse publicity and a police crackdown instead, and is convicted on tax evasion. At this point, the film departs wildly from the facts, however, by having Capone sent to prison and beaten to death by his fellow inmates, presumably on Moran's orders. There are also a number of fictionalized scenes dealing with the gangster's womanizing private life: He presses his attentions on an upstanding widow (Fay Spain) whose husband was rubbed out by Capone's men because he had witnessed the murder of Colosimo.

On the left, the real Al Capone (a.k.a. Scarface and Snorkey). On the right, Rod Steiger, a.k.a. Al Capone (1959). (Copyright © 1959 Allied Artists Pictures)

They don't add up to much, but they do provide a welcome respite from the film's bursts of gunfire and Steiger's monotonous ravings. The low-budget feature lacks tension and excitement. It looks more like a television show than a theatrical film.

Director Roger Corman offered another blow-by-blow account of the Capone/O'Banion/Moran power struggle in his 1967 Twentieth Century–Fox film *The St. Valentine's Day Massacre*, starring Jason Robards, Jr., as Scarface. Though shot on a relatively low budget as well, the film looks like a million because Corman was able to make use of several standing sets left over from other, more expensive Fox films: An ornate ballroom from *The Sound of Music* (1965) used for Capone's mansion and an elaborate bar/brothel from *The Sand Pebbles* (1966) used for a speakeasy give the film a very rich period look. Howard Browne's kaleidoscopic script is quite factual and does a good job of dramatizing the events leading up to and following the massacre without playing undue havoc with the truth. As in *The Untouchables*, a Walter Winchell–type narrator (actor Paul Frees) is used to heighten the drama and keep the flow of events and characters clear for the viewer. Browne even provides some interesting bits of gangland lore along the way—such as the reason why the powerful Capone wasn't able to assume leadership of the Mafia. He wasn't Sicilian.

There are a few departures from the film's otherwise-documentary approach. For example, the roughhouse scenes between George Segal's Cagney-like Peter Gusenberg and his blond bombshell moll (Jean Hale), which culminate in his letting her have it with a sandwich in the face, are tossed in simply as references to gangster films like *The Public Enemy*. But on the whole, this is probably the most accurate Capone film ever made—even in spite of the physical miscasting of the

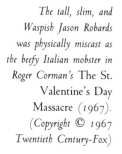

The tall, slim, and Waspish Jason Robards was physically miscast as the beefy Italian mobster in Roger Corman's The St. Valentine's Day Massacre *(1967). (Copyright © 1967 Twentieth Century-Fox)*

tall, slim, and Waspish Robards as the beefy Italian mobster. (Corman had wanted Orson Welles for the part.)

Known mostly for his output of horror and science fiction pictures during the fifties and sixties, the prolific Corman had made several stylish, low-budget gangster films before *The St. Valentine's Day Massacre*, such as *Machine-Gun Kelly* and *I, Mobster* (both 1958). The former was a highly fictionalized look at the career of the Depression-era bank robber (Charles Bronson) who gave the feds their enduring label of G-men. The latter was a gritty portrayal of a Caponesque gangster (Steve Cochran) who rises to the top of the underworld by murdering a syndicate chieftain named Moran (Grant Withers), then falls precipitously when he's called to testify before a Senate committee, and finally has to be rubbed out because he knows too much. Corman returned to the gangster genre again in *Bloody Mama* (1970), a mostly fictional account of the exploits of Kate "Ma" Barker (Shelley Winters) and her murderous, bank-robbing offspring (Don Stroud, Clint Kimbrough, Robert De Niro, Robert Walden, and Alex Nicol) who plagued the South and the West during the Depression years. Imitative of *Bonnie and Clyde* (1967) throughout, and mostly just an exploitative potboiler, *Bloody Mama* does include one inspired, surrealistic moment when the gang is surrounded in a cabin by federal agents and dozens of locals set up bleachers across the road from the shoot-out to cheer and jeer the opposing sides as if watching a hometown football game.

In 1975, Corman essentially remade *The St. Valentine's Day Massacre* as *Capone*. Directed by Steve Carver, with Ben Gazzara playing a cross between Rod Steiger and Marlon Brando's puffy-faced Godfather in the title role, the film relied heavily for most of its action scenes on stock footage from the earlier film. And a too-

Shelly Winters as Ma and Robert Walden, Robert De Niro, Clint Kimbrough, and Don Stroud as her boys in Bloody Mama *(1970), director Roger Corman's version of the Ma Barker story. (Copyright © 1970 American International Pictures)*

thin Ray Sharkey reprised the role yet again in a 1989 telefilm titled *Capone*, which added little in terms of fact or fiction to understanding the venerable gangster's life and times.

The trend continued: Veteran movie villain Jack Palance donned the legendary gangster's cheeky trademark in *Mr. Scarface* (a.k.a. *Rulers of the City*, 1977), an Italian-made bloodbath set in America about a contemporary Caponesque mobster whose gambling empire is being encroached upon by ambitious rival Edmund Purdom.

Director Larry Cohen and football player turned actor Fred "The Hammer" Williamson offered moviegoers an African-American variation on the enduring saga in *Black Caesar* (1973), one of the many popular black-oriented crime movies that followed on the successful heels of *Shaft* (1971) and *Superfly* (1972). Inspired in part by the success of *The Godfather* as well, *Black Caesar* chronicled the bloody rise and fall of a shoe-shine boy turned mobster named Tony Gibbs (Williamson), who becomes the Godfather of Harlem. "Nobody had ever made a black gangster movie with an Edward G. Robinson type character. Suit and tie, hat, a real Edward G. Robinson guy," notes Williamson, who provided director Cohen with the money-making idea. The low-budget film earned $2 million in North America alone — and spawned such other black gangster films as *Hell Up in Harlem* (1973, also starring Williamson) — during the golden age of what has become known as the black exploitation (a.k.a. blaxploitation) film, a seventies phenomenon whose modern descendants include *I'm Gonna Git You Sucka!* (1988), a very funny satire of the entire blaxploitation cycle, and Mario Van Peebles's *New Jack City* (1991).

In the atmospheric but factually dubious 1988 telefilm *Nitti*, Capone (Vincent Guastaferro) received a fair amount of screen time but took an overall backseat to his more famous (thanks to TV and the movies) enforcer, whom writer/producer

Fred Williamson played an Afro-American version of Capone in Larry Cohen's Black Caesar *(1973). (Copyright © 1975 American International Pictures)*

Lee David Zlotoff has federal agent Michael Moriarty declare "bigger" than the legendary Scarface himself. The real Nitti was never bigger than Capone, although, much to the syndicate's irritation, he often acted that way. As Nitti, Anthony LaPaglia does a remarkable job of imitating Robert De Niro's performance as the young Vito Corleone in *The Godfather, Part II.* The film begins with the mobster's death by gunshot wound in a Chicago train yard in 1943, then flashes back to show the events, beginning with Nitti's arrival from Sicily in 1913, that led up to it. In keeping with its grandiose view of Nitti, the film suggests he may have been murdered, but the facts are that he probably killed himself in an effort to escape a fate even worse than death: the syndicate's revenge for not doing what he was told.

The made-for-cable telefilm *The Lost Capone* (1990) told the little-known story of Scarface's nonmobster brother James Capone (1887–1952), played by Adrian Pasdar. Bullied by his younger brother Al (Eric Roberts) for not being tough enough, and sought by police for a murder that Al actually committed, James leaves the family fold and disappears for several years, resurfacing in Nebraska during the 1920s under the name Richard Hart. During the bootleg wars, he becomes sheriff and earns the name Two Gun Hart when he goes head-to-head with Brother Al's mobsters as they try to transport liquor through the state and sell booze to the Indians. Al sends brother Ralph (Titus Welliver, who looks enough like the real Capone to *be* his brother) to kill the troublesome lawman. Ralph discovers the man's true identity, which the honest and upright James has kept secret not only from the townspeople but his own wife (Ally Sheedy). James has a brief reunion in Chicago with brother Al. There, he informs Al that he wants no part of the Capone empire and that he will do everything in his power to keep his state free of mob infiltration. Furious, Al orders that James be killed, but James is saved in the nick of time by members of the Indian tribe he has sworn to help and protect.

The Lost Capone deserves high marks for offering a different take on the Capone saga, but, like so many Capone films, it places the emphasis more on fiction than on fact. The actual James Capone/Two Gun Hart was indeed a lawman, but he used the power of his office to beat up on Indians in his territory rather than to protect them. During one such fracas, he lost an eye. He also stole from the businessmen and shopkeepers he was elected to serve. Drummed out of office, he eventually became so destitute that he was forced to turn to his mobster brothers for help, and Ralph (1893–1974) sent him and his family monthly support checks for the rest of James's life.

The press dubbed James Capone the "white sheep" of the family. The film turns him into a white-knight pillar of the community. In reality, says crime historian Carl Sifakis, "James Capone was not precisely a model citizen—except in comparison [to his siblings]."

Robinson went undercover to nail mobsters Barton MacLane
and Humphrey Bogart in Bullets or Ballots *(1936).*
(Copyright © 1936 Warner Bros.)

CHAPTER 4

KINGS OF THE
UNDERWORLD

ROBINSON, CAGNEY, AND BOGART

During the gangster film's golden age, when the studio system was grinding out one underworld drama after another on a regular basis, virtually every up-and-coming young actor in Hollywood played a mobster at one time or another. Spencer Tracy, Paul Muni, Clark Gable, Robert Taylor — the list goes on and on. Most didn't stick with such roles, however, and became stars only when they broke out of them. Other actors of limited range, such as George Raft, managed to achieve stardom playing one-note gangster parts, then found their careers in decline when the genre went into one of its periodic slumps. Only Edward G. Robinson, James Cagney, and Humphrey Bogart succeeded in making their mark (and screen history) in gangster roles — roles they continued playing, off and on, well into their careers and with which they are still strongly identified — yet had the versatility to transcend their genre identification and avoid typecasting.

Individually, Robinson, Cagney, and Bogart made more gangster films throughout their careers than anyone else before or since. Of the eighty-nine feature films Edward G. Robinson appeared in during his six-decade career as a movie actor, thirty were gangster movies. Cagney, whose movie career also spanned six decades, made sixty-four feature films in his lifetime — a third of them gangster movies. And Bogart's total is thirty-two gangster movies out of a total of seventy-nine feature films. Unlike Robinson and Cagney, however, whose final screen appearances were not in gangster films, Bogart movingly bowed out the way he'd come in, for the last two films he made before his untimely death of cancer in 1957—*The Desperate Hours* (1955) and *The Harder They Fall* (1956)—were *both* gangster films. The former had a special feeling of closure to it; in the film, Bogart played an on-the-run gangster not unlike Duke Mantee in *The Petrified Forest* (1936), the gangster part that had brought him to the attention of Hollywood and moviegoers around the world twenty years earlier.

The remarkable achievement of these three actors is that while many of the films they made in the genre (quite a few for the same studio, Warner Brothers) seem quite similar and tend to overlap in our minds, the type of mobster character each created—and continued to play from film to film—remains separate and distinct. Many of the films themselves may seem interchangeable, but the personae these actors created are not. The murderously envious mobster Robinson introduced in *Little Caesar* is as different from the violence-loving tough guy Cagney introduced in *The Public Enemy* as the existentialist loner sketched by Bogart in *The Petrified Forest* (and more fully developed by him in *High Sierra*) is from each of them. And every movie mobster since has been a variation on the three types of gangster characters created, molded, and immortalized by Robinson, Cagney, and Bogart during their long reigns as the undisputed kings of Hollywood Gangland.

MANNY

Edward G. Robinson was born Emanuel Goldenberg in Bucharest, Romania, in 1893. His family emigrated to the United States in 1902 and settled in New York City. After attending City College of New York and the American Academy of Dramatic Arts, Manny (as his friends called him and would continue to do so to the end of his days) legally changed his name to the more Anglo-Saxon-sounding Edward G. Robinson in order to pursue a career in the theater. He made his Broadway debut in 1915 in a play called *Under Fire,* where he had a small role as a French soldier. A year later, he made his film debut with a walk-on as a Hungarian émigré in the silent five-reeler *Arms and the Woman* (1916), prints of which no longer survive. Scores of stage appearances in a variety of ethnic roles and another minor film part opposite Richard Barthelmess and Dorothy Gish in the 1923 silent *The Bright Shawl* followed before Robinson finally hit the big time as gangster Nick Scarsi in Bartlett Cormack's controversial play *The Racket.* The play was a smash hit and so was Robinson, whose performance as the dapper Italian mobster modeled after Al Capone—the only gangster role Robinson ever played onstage—was singled out by reviewers as "a marvelous creation of character."

Although Robinson failed to get the plum part of Scarsi in the film version of the play, movie producers were soon knocking on his door to play other gangster roles for them. In *The Hole in the Wall* (1929), his first talkie, Robinson played the Fox, the dapper Scarsi-like ringleader of a gang of thieves and con artists posing as spiritualists. In *Night Ride* (1930), he played another racketeer in the Scarsi mold, nailed by a crusading reporter (Joseph Schildkraut). Then Tod Browning cast him as the Chinese-American Cobra Collins in the remake of his popular Lon Chaney silent gangster film *Outside the Law* (1930).*

Robinson shifted to a new studio, Warner Brothers, for his next gangster film, *The Widow from Chicago* (1930), in which he played a dapper Italian mobster with an even stronger resemblance to *The Racket's* Nick Scarsi. Reviewers were quick to take notice of this, calling his performance "... in the best Nick Scarsi manner ... a vivid and striking portrait of a coldly malignant killer." Robinson termed the film awful, but it's likely that his strong supporting performance was what prompted the Warner Brothers and director Mervyn LeRoy to give him the starring role in his next film, the influential *Little Caesar*, wherein he finally cast off the shadow of Nick Scarsi. Wrote Robinson in his autobiography: "Rico Bandello was not at all like Nick Scarsi. Bandello was very naive, while Scarsi was an extremely sophisticated character."

The scene in *Little Caesar* where Rico meets mob boss Diamond Pete for the first time — and examines the well-heeled big shot from head to toe the way some men eye a woman — neatly summed up the difference between Nick Scarsi and Rico Bandello and firmly established Robinson's gangster persona. The hungry look on the ambitious young gangster's face expresses admiration for the man, yet contempt at the same time. It is a look of unbridled envy coupled with hatred and mistrust ("He ain't so much!"); deep down, Rico *knows* that Diamond Pete is a false god. When Rico overthrows Diamond Pete and dons his trappings, believing they will turn him into a true god, he finds they are only as illusory on him as on Diamond Pete, and just as easily snatched away. The film's celebrated close finds him wondering incredulously just what the hell happened: "Mother of Mercy, is this the end of Rico?"

Critic John Mosher noted in his contemporary review of the film in *The New Yorker*:

> Mr. Robinson's diagnosis [of Rico] is so articulate as to be the outstanding characterization of the kind at the moment. The most naive vanity seems to be the moving spirit of Little Caesar. His eyes glitter at the sight of a scarfpin in the tie of his superior, and nothing will stop him until he

---

*Robinson's image is pure Nick Scarsi. Whatever the reason for his Chinese identity — again, his character is totally Western in appearance — it was probably determined by Browning himself; Robinson obviously had no problem wearing Asian makeup if the role called for it (as it certainly does here). He'd already played a Japanese role on Broadway, and for his next film, the comedy *East Is West* (1930), he would don Oriental makeup to play a character called Charlie Yong, the "chop suey king of San Francisco's Chinatown." And he wore it again in a later gangster film, *The Hatchet Man* (1932), where he played a Tong chieftain. Makeup or not, Robinson earned good reviews for his performance in *Outside the Law*, even though he considered the film itself "agony" — which, to sit through, it certainly is.

Edward G. Robinson's performance as the murderously envious Rico Bandello in Little Caesar *(1931) firmly eastablished his gangster film persona. With Douglas Fairbanks, Jr., Glenda Farrell, and George Stone. (Copyright © 1931 Warner Bros.)*

has then disposed of that gentleman and assumed his leadership and his jewels. When he reaches high pinnacles where he must don a dinner coat, with spats, he is fearful that he looks a fool yet is fascinated by the elegance of his own appearance. Mr. Robinson makes this more sensitive side of his character amusing, yet hardly poignant. He is doubtless correct in the suggestion of a stupidity behind this slick and adroit gunplay which is this Caesar's solution to all problems.

This is the key to what separates Robinson's gangster film character from those of Cagney and Bogart. He's a killer to be sure, but he's not a clever, homicidal crazy like Cagney or a desperate loner looking for a way out like Bogart. He's a fool guided by stupidity—and thus an essentially *comic* figure. This may be why many of Robinson's best gangster films following *Little Caesar* were, in fact, outright comedies in which he not only poked fun at the distinctive gangster film character he'd created but further defined that character in a way that some of his gangster dramas failed to do.

In the first of these mob comedies, *The Little Giant* (1933), Robinson plays Chicago beer baron Bugs Ahearn, a kinder, gentler version of his snappily dressed, cigar-smoking Rico Bandello character but with just as many rough edges. When FDR is elected President and Prohibition is repealed, Bugs decides to close down shop and pursue a more genteel life as a millionaire gentleman. His pal Al Daniels (Russell Hopton), who has been with Bugs since their days in reform school, is skeptical about Bugs's plans to go straight and mingle with the upper classes. ("What are you gonna talk to them about? Tommy-guns and stickups?") But Bugs has already begun preparing himself by reading Plato (whom he calls Pluto) and steeping himself in music and art. "I'm just crawlin' with culture," he tells Al as he points out the lack of perspective in an abstract painting he's just bought.

After liquidating the mob's assets ("We sold our ammunition to an Army-Navy store and the machine guns to some guy in Mexico," his cronies assure him), Bugs pays the gang off and he and Al head for the West Coast, where Bugs rents a Santa Barbara mansion complete with servants for entertaining his high-society guests. He hires Ruth Wayburn (Mary Astor), the woman who leased him the house, to be his personal secretary, unaware that Ruth is the rightful owner of the house and that she'd been forced to put it on the market to climb out from under a mountain of debt incurred by her late father in a phony stock deal. A svelte high-society dame, Polly Cass (Helen Vinson) catches the eye of the former gangster and he sets his sights on marrying her. But Polly and her effete family consider the posturing ruffian to be a joke—worse still, a joke with no money—and she ignores him until her brother (Donald Dillaway) discovers that Bugs is a millionare. Unaware that Polly and her family are frauds and that it was old man Cass (Berton Churchill) who was behind the phony stock deal that bilked Ruth's father and many others out of a fortune, Bugs proposes marriage. Polly accepts, with the intention of divorcing him imme-diately afterward and collecting a hefty settlement.

Robinson played a kinder, gentler version of Rico (but with just as many rough edges) in the mob comedy The Little Giant *(1933). With Mary Astor. (Copyright © 1933 Warner Bros.)*

Ruth knows the Casses for what they are but says nothing because she's fallen for Bugs herself and doesn't want to hurt him by revealing that the woman he loves is a gold digger. Reality comes crashing in, however, when Bugs's prospective father-in-law sets him up in business by unloading the family's fraud-ulent investment company on him on the eve of the nuptials and Bugs finds *himself* in hot water with the law for selling the bad bonds. Realizing he's been had, Bugs persuades the district attorney (John Mar-ston) to give him twenty-four hours to set everything to rights. He rings up his old gang and they fly to California (polishing their machine guns on the plane) to help him out. "I got in over my head," Bugs tells them in a moment of self-reflection that might have profited Rico Bandello; and he enlists them as en-forcers to sell the phony bonds back to old man Cass, the investment company's chiseling board of directors, and everyone else involved in the swindle. (In a sur-

prising departure from the film's otherwise-comic tone, one of the gang members gruesomely tortures a recalcitrant board director into buying back some bonds by holding a lighted cigar to the man's foot!) The money that flows in puts Bugs's company in the black, and he pays back everyone who was bilked by the Casses, including Ruth, whom he subsequently marries when he realizes it was her he loved all along.

An amusing satire of the evolving Warner Brothers–style gangster film in general and the almost eponymous *Little Caesar* in particular, *The Little Giant* is at its funniest in the beginning, as the crude mob boss with pretensions to culture and respectability lays out his plans for storming high society. It falls a bit flat, however, when the scene shifts to California and the former gangster finds himself being taken for a ride. And some scenes intended as farce, such as Bugs's attempts to play polo, which send him again and again falling off his horse, don't work at all. Even when playing it for laughs, however, Robinson sharply retains his grasp of the character; particulary in his scenes with the warmhearted Astor (who sees him for what he is, and loves him), he adds greater resonance to it. Like Rico, Bugs is a fool guided by stupidity. But he's also human and not altogether incapable of doing the right thing. Some of Robinson's later, more serious gangster films make the same point, notably *The Last Gangster* (1937), in which he plays a mobster named Joe Krozac. Krozac loses his criminal empire as well as his wife and son when he's sent to prison for a ten-year stretch on an income-tax charge. When he gets out, he finds that his wife has remarried and he vows revenge. A former cronie (Lionel Stander) persuades him to reunite the old gang, but this is merely a ruse to get Joe to reveal the whereabouts of some long-hidden loot. When the gang gets their hands on the money, they leave Joe holding the bag and he vows revenge on them, too. In the somewhat syrupy conclusion, Joe sees the error of his ways, however, and does the right thing by leaving his happily resettled wife and child in peace and giving up his quest for revenge against the gang—though he is subsequently killed in a shoot-out with a former rival who's out to settle an old score.

More consistently entertaining, even though writers Jo Swerling and Robert Riskin tend to telegraph many of their jokes and plot twists ahead of time, is John Ford's *The Whole Town's Talking* (1935). Robinson plays two roles: Arthur Jones, a meek office clerk with dreams of making it big as a writer and marrying his attractive coworker Miss Clark (Jean Arthur), and his look-alike, Killer Mannion, a top mobster recently escaped from prison and on the lam from the law. Almost fired from his job for being late, Jones calms himself with Miss Clark (who has been fired) over a cup of coffee at a nearby café. Another patron, named Hoyt (Donald Meek), mistakes Jones for the escaped mobster and calls the police to turn him in and collect the reward. The cops swarm the café and arrest the confused and terrified Jones, as well as Miss Clark, whom they mistake for his moll. Jones's office supervisor, Seaver (Etienne Giradot), clears up the mistake and Jones is given a "passport letter" signed by the DA (Arthur Byron) to prove his real identity in case he's mistakenly picked up again.

An ambitious newspaperman named Healy (Wallace Ford) sees a good story in the case of mistaken identity and cooks up a scheme to have Jones byline a series of derogatory articles about his villainous look-alike. Jones's publicity-loving boss (Paul Harvey) goes along with the scheme and calls the timid clerk into his office (Jones's shoes squeak when he enters) to celebrate the deal over whiskey and cigars. Robinson amusingly plays on his hard drinking, cigar-chomping gangster image by choking on the booze and tobacco. Significantly, as he gets progressively drunker and more used to the alcohol and cigar smoke, he starts to look and behave more like his character Rico or Bugs.

Jones goes home drunk, finds Mannion waiting for him in his room, and the wily gangster coerces his look-alike into handing over the DA's passport letter so that he can move about the city freely, posing as Jones, robbing banks to fund his escape plans.* One hilarious (and occasionally suspenseful) situation piles on another until the timid Jones finally realizes he must take matters into his own hands to bring the gangster's charade to an end. Consistent with the film's theme,

---

*The split-screen photography allowing the two Robinsons to interact with each other in the same frame constantly reinforces the alter-ego aspect of the two characters and, for the time, is technically superb. In one amazing scene, one Robinson (as Mannion) intimidates the other by blowing cigar smoke into his face. The effect is utterly seamless.

he does this by tricking the mobster's gang into thinking *he's* Mannion and ordering them to shoot the real Mannion (whom they believe to be Jones) on sight. In the end, the gang is rounded up and Jones gets the reward and the girl.

In his autobiography, Robinson suggested that "If Rico had expended his energies in another way, he might have been a great, great fellow." To illuminate his point, he made *The Little Giant*'s Bugs Ahearn, for all his Rico-like foolishness and stupidity, succeed in doing just that. In *The Whole Town's Talking*, Robinson reversed the process, and gave more power to his gangster film persona, by showing that there's a bit of Rico and Bugs in all of us. He carried this theme into two of his best serious gangster films, *Bullets or Ballots* (1936) and *The Amazing Dr. Clitterhouse* (1938). In the former, he plays not a good guy *and* a bad guy but a good guy who has enough of the bad guy in him to pose as one convincingly in order to get the goods on the city's top mobster (Barton MacLane). And in the latter (coscripted by John Huston), he plays the good guy, a respected doctor researching the criminal mind, who gets so caught up in the milieu he is studying that the criminal in him rises to the fore and he *becomes* the bad guy.

In *The Whole Town's Talking*, Robinson provided an amusing visual cue to his respective good guy/bad guy characterizations. Killer Mannion, like Rico, Bugs, Cobra Collins, et al., is immediately identifiable as a Robinson-style gangster due to his flashy, immaculately fitted suits and stylish headgear, which he always wears with the brims pulled sharply down over his forehead. As good guy Jones, however, the actor's clothing is ill-fitting and rumpled and his hats, which he wears brim-

Robinson played a respected doctor turned gangland mastermind in The Amazing Dr. Clitterhouse *(1938) opposite Claire Trevor and Humphrey Bogart. (Copyright © 1938 Warner Bros.)*

up, follow suit. Robinson sustained this clever signal in most of the gangster, crime, and film noir (*Double Indemnity,* et al.) roles he played from then on. In *Bullets or Ballots,* for example, he's the complete fashion plate, with the brim of his expensive-looking hat pulled down when he poses as a mobster to infiltrate the city's rackets; his clothing is bedraggled and the brim of his dumpy department-store fedora is worn up when he's his real self, good-guy cop Johnny Blake. In the gangland comedy *A Slight Case of Murder* (1938), based on a play by Damon Runyon and Howard Lindsay, he pushed this amusing visual identification of his character even further.

The film opens similarly to *The Little Giant:* Prohibition has ended and Robinson's beer-baron character, here named Remy Marko, is faced with the challenge of what to do next. Unlike Bugs Ahearn, Marko sees the repeal of Prohibition as an opportunity to expand his business, since the legalization of drinking will surely bring more customers. So he tells his mob they'll be selling the beer from now on rather than pushing it at gunpoint, and he becomes a legitimate businessman—albeit one who can't entirely toss off all of his past methods. Robinson's Marko may dress to the nines like Rico, Bugs, and Mannion, but he wears his hat brim *straight.*

Complications arise for Marko when sales of his beer plummet (the stuff tastes dreadful; now that customers aren't being forced to buy it, they don't). The bank threatens to foreclose on Marko's brewery. His daughter falls for a state trooper. "The old days is gone—I been polite to my last cop," snarls Marko in anticipation of the marriage. And an armored-car robbery Marko had nothing to do with results in the stashing of a half million dollars and several corpses in his plush summer home while he's entertaining various bank representatives and high-society guests. How the harried, put-upon former gangster gets out of these various situations—sometimes using his wits, sometimes accidentally—and comes out on top is the core of this very funny gangland farce. Robinson made several more classic gangster comedies, including *Brother Orchid* (1940) and *Larceny, Inc.* (1942), in the years ahead, but *A Slight Case of Murder* (which was remade in 1952 as *Stop, You're Killing Me,* with Broderick Crawford) remains the funniest of the bunch.

Robinson's definitive portrait of the well-dressed tough guy with aspirations to greatness inspired numerous imitations throughout the thirties and forties—notably those of George Raft. Although Raft maintained that he modeled his gangster roles on actual mobsters he'd encountered in his early years as a dancer (particularly Bugsy Siegel, who remained a close friend), it's fairly obvious that Raft was heavily influenced by Robinson's gangster film persona, as well—although Raft's well-dressed tough guy lacks the ebullience and charm of Robinson's. Robinson's influence on Raft is especially apparent in Raft's last gangster movie role, as Spats Colombo in the Billy Wilder farce *Some Like It Hot,* a role with Edward G. Robinson written all over it. In amusing acknowledgment of this, Wilder has the usurper Raft mowed down in the end by a machine gun–wielding hood played by Edward G. Robinson, Jr.

JIMMY

James Francis Cagney was born in 1899 on the tough Lower East Side of New York City. After graduating from high school, he enrolled at Columbia University to study art but later had to drop out of school and take a variety of odd jobs to help support his family. He got his first taste of show business when he joined a local drama club sponsored by the Lenox Hill Settlement Society and graduated to vaudeville shortly thereafter as a dancer.

Below, left: In an amusing in-joke, George Raft's Robinson-like Spats Colombo was mowed down by Edward G. Robinson, Jr. (off-screen), in the Billy Wilder farce Some Like It Hot *(1959). (Copyright © 1958 United Artists)*

Cagney made his Broadway debut appearing in the chorus of the 1920 musical *Pitter Patter.* He then toured the vaudeville circuit for several years before returning to Broadway in 1925 to play a hobo nicknamed Little Red in the Maxwell Anderson play *Outside Looking In,* an adaptation of the novel *Beggars of Life* by the "poet laureate of the hobos," Jim Tully. (Tully's novel was filmed under its own title in 1928 by director William Wellman, sans Cagney and anyone else connected with the Broadway version.) Larger roles in a variety of comedies, revues, and musicals followed until Cagney made a splash in the 1930 slice-of-life drama *Penny Arcade,* playing a tough young rumrunner who frames his sister's boyfriend for murder. The play was sold to Warner Brothers with the stipulation that Cagney recreate his role on screen (his *Penny Arcade* costar, Joan Blondell, came along, as well) and the film was made in 1930 under the title *Sinner's Holiday.* Cagney went from there into his first full-fledged gangster film for Warner Brothers, *Doorway to Hell* (1930), based on the Rowland Brown story "A Handful of Clouds" ("The kind that come out at the end of a .38 automatic," explains Cagney's character in the film), whose plot was loosely inspired by the career of the Chicago mobster

Right: Cagney's first full-fledged gangster picture for Warner Brothers, Doorway to Hell *(1930). (Copyright © 1930 Warner Bros.)*

Johnny Torrio. Cagney plays Steve Mileaway, the chief lieutenant of top mobster Louis Ricarno (Lew Ayres). When Ricarno decides to go straight, he turns his empire over to Mileaway (as Torrio did to Al Capone, although there is nothing in Cagney's performance that suggests it was modeled on Capone). Ricarno's redemptive plans are thwarted, however, when his wife and Mileaway betray him and his brother is murdered by former gang rivals. Ricarno returns to the rackets to exact his revenge and ultimately seals his doom in pursuit of that goal.

Critics of the time called *Doorway to Hell* "an excellent gangster film . . . fast, colorful and exciting" and singled out Ayres and Cagney for their credible performances. In light of Cagney's later superstardom in gangster roles, revisionist critics now tend to believe the film would have been more compelling if Ayres and Cagney had switched roles. Wrote early talkie historian Ken Hanke, however: "It is unfortunate that *Doorway to Hell* has been neglected due to its lack of a seminal gangster star. It is possible that the film would have been livelier with [the roughneck] Cagney in the lead rather than in a supporting role. [But Ayres] is not supposed to be a roughneck, [rather] a kind of organizational whiz. Ayres isn't so much wrong for the role as he is simply too young—and the fact that he's not Cagney is a poor reason to dismiss the film out of hand."

Ironically, Cagney's next gangster film would benefit greatly—indeed become a classic—from his switching roles with another actor. When *The Public Enemy* (1931) began production, it was the established Edward Woods who'd been signed to play the film's vicious title character, and the virtually unknown Cagney who had been given the part of Woods's underworld pal. When the first rushes were screened, though, director William Wellman discovered that Cagney was eating Woods alive on the screen. So he scrapped the early footage and resumed shooting with Cagney in Woods's role, and vice versa; the decision paid off with Cagney's starmaking performance as the amoral, violence-for-violence's-sake Tom Powers sustaining the film and giving it its enduring punch.

The script by Kubec Glasmon, John Bright, and Harvey Thew, based on Bright's unpublished novel *Beer and Blood,* picks up Powers's saga in 1909, when he and his pal Matt (Frank Coghlan, Jr., and Frankie Darro, respectively) are kids living in the slums of an unnamed city (presumably Chicago), where they deliver beer in buckets to neighborhood saloons. Under the tutelage of a Shylock-type character named Putty Nose (Murray Kinnell), they get involved in petty thievery, then graduate to more ambitious armed robbery. When they grow up, they fall in with top mobsters Paddy Ryan (Robert Emmett O'Connor) and Nails Nathan (Leslie Fenton) and become successful rumrunners. At the height of the bootleg wars, Matt (Woods) is killed by a rival gang, and Powers goes on a vengeful rampage, killing Matt's murderers in a saloon shoot-out during which he, too, is wounded. While Powers is recuperating in the hospital, his upstanding older brother Mike (Donald Cook), a World War I vet and night-school student, encourages him to get out of the rackets. Powers agrees to return home and think about it. Several days later, Mike receives a phone call letting him know that his brother is on the way. But when Powers fails to show up, Mike begins to suspect that something may have happened to him. His suspicions prove horrifyingly correct. As Ma Powers (Beryl Mercer) euphorically prepares a room for her "baby boy's" return home to the accompaniment of "I'm Forever Blowing Bubbles" on the family Victrola, there's a knock at the front door, and when Mike opens it, Powers's bullet-riddled corpse, deposited on the doorstep by his mob murderers, pitches headlong into the room.

Although the film realistically details the environmental conditions that can give rise to criminality, it's fairly clear that the particular criminal at the center of the story, Tom Powers, was born, not made. He is portrayed from the beginning as a fundamentally bad lot who treats everyone (with the exception of Woods) cruelly and opportunistically. Practically as soon as the film begins, he is seen tripping a female playmate with string as she tries out a pair of roller skates he's just given her—and which he'd stolen from someone else. When his policeman father (Purnell Pratt) takes a belt to him for his thievery, the young tough refuses to utter a cry as his face fills with hatred and contempt for the old man and for the authority he represents—an authority that seeks only to suppress Powers's natural instincts. Freed to unleash those instincts under the lawless conditions of Prohibition, the adult Tom Powers exuberantly does just that and becomes an even more vicious and brutal character—a killer of men and, in the famous scene where he lets his moll (Mae Clarke) have it in the face with a grapefruit, a sadistic abuser of women. The Edward G. Robinson gangster is motivated to murder for reasons of ego and envy. Unlike him, the Cagney gangster robs, fights, and kills mainly because he *likes* to. "No one expresses more clearly in terms of pictorial action the delights of violence, the overtones of a semiconscious sadism, the tendency toward destruction, toward anarchy [than Cagney]," accurately noted the poet and critic Lincoln Kirstein in a 1932 appraisal of Cagney's charming yet deadly gangster persona.

Cagney's performance drew unanimously rave reviews and turned *The Public Enemy*, otherwise a very uneven film, into a major box-office success. Influential *New York Herald Tribune* critic Richard Watts, Jr., called it ". . . the most ruthless, unsentimental appraisal of the meanness of a petty killer that the cinema has yet devised. Its central character is a homicidal little rat, and there is never any effort to show him as anything else. James Cagney plays [the character] with a simple, relentless honesty that should immediately place him among the top personages of the screen. From the time you see him engaged in his first robbery to the moment when he walks out on the girl he is about to win in order to shoot down the horse that had thrown the head of his gang, he is utterly merciless, utterly homicidal, and utterly real." Critic James Shelley Hamilton of the *National Board* of *Review* magazine put it even more succinctly: "The real power of *The Public Enemy*—and it has a certain power, of the hit-you-between-the-eyes kind—lies . . . in the stunning—stunning in its literal sense—acting of James Cagney."

Even before the film was released, Warner Brothers realized they had a new money-making gangster star on their hands. So what was more natural than to team him with their other money-making gangster star, Edward G. Robinson, and reap twice the rewards? This they did in *Smart Money* (1931), Cagney's next film, in which he played a soft-edged variation of Tom Powers opposite Robinson's Rico Bandello-like main mobster. The film was a success, but it was clear that Cagney could command the screen on his own and didn't need a partner; neither did Robinson. Neither Warner Brothers nor any other studio ever teamed the two again; Cagney went on to stardom by himself—although for some reason the studio didn't give him another gangster role until the 1933 *The Mayor of Hell.*

Coupled with Robinson's *Little Caesar* and Paul Muni's *Scarface* (which reached the screen a year after *The Public Enemy* but was made at the same time), Cagney's charismatic, thoroughly vicious gangster antihero proved too much for several of the country's most powerful religious and civic groups to take. Protesting the "glorification" of crime and violence in gangster films—Cagney's particularly—they raised the specter of state-by-state censorship with renewed vigor. Will H. Hays, the former U.S. Postmaster General turned movie morals czar who headed up the industry's self-monitoring Motion Picture Producers and Distributors of America (MPPDA), joined the fray when he got wind of a proposed film based on the life of real-life public enemy John Dillinger, whose notorious career had recently come to an abrupt end when he'd been shot outside a Chicago movie theater. Hays quickly fired off a telegram to the heads of the various studios, emphatically stating that "No picture on the life or exploits of John Dillinger will be produced, distributed or exhibited by any member [of the MPPDA]. This decision is based on the belief that the production, distribution or exhibition of such a picture would be detrimental to the best public interest." And to the best interest of the movie industry as well, Hays subtly suggested. In response, the studios agreed to the establishment of a strict set of moral guidelines governing its films, called the Motion Picture Production Code, and allowed they would green-light no project that had not been granted a Code Seal of Approval by the MPPDA.

Insofar as the depiction of crime and violence was concerned, the code strictly

"The most ruthless, unsentimental appraisal of the meanness of a petty killer the cinema has yet devised." Cagney as Tom Powers in The Public Enemy *(1931) opposite Jean Harlow. (Copyright © 1931 Warner Bros.)*

Warner Brothers teamed its two biggest gangster stars for the first and only time in Smart Money *(1931). (Copyright © 1931 Warner Bros.)*

forbade any film that might "make criminals seem heroic or justified," for, the code maintained, this would "inspire potential criminals with a desire for imitation." There were many other stipulations, all aimed squarely at the gangster films that had begun to proliferate on America's movie screens. Whether Robinson's high-living gang leaders and Cagney's pugnacious cutthroats were guilty of inspiring potential criminals with a desire for imitation is open to question. What was not, however, was the fact that the gangsters they played were undeniably these films' heroes — if only because they were the films' central characters. It satisfied neither the code nor the nation's moral crusaders that they got what they deserved in the end. The spotlight, the code insisted, had to be shifted. Gangster movies — especially those with Robinson and Cagney — were big money-makers, however. "The movie industry [began looking] for a loophole," wrote Murray Schumach in his history of screen censorship, *The Face on the Cutting Room Floor.* "[And they] found one. A wave of kidnappings had focused national attention on the Federal Bureau of Investigation. They now made the FBI agents the nominal heroes, but gave the same fat parts to the gangsters."*

---

*The popular stories and plays of Damon Runyon (*Guys and Dolls*), and the success of Robinson's *The Little Giant,* offered producers another ingenious way of outwitting the code: Tone down the violence and make gangsters figures of fun and sentimentality. The huge popularity of Runyon's *Little Miss Marker* (1934), which made a star out of Shirley Temple, cemented the idea, and the gangster comedy quickly became a subgenre all its own.

And so, in their first gangster films following the creation of the code, both Robinson and Cagney put their gats to work for the law instead. In *Bullets or Ballots,* Robinson took the part of an honest New York City cop—although he had it both ways by posing as his standard gangster character, as well. And Cagney, whom the studio had dubbed "Hollywood's Most Famous Bad Man," became a member of the Department of Justice in *G-Men* (1935)—albeit one fairly indistinguishable from Tom Powers. He plays Brick Davis, a former slum kid and associate of racketeers seeking revenge for the gangland murder of his best friend, who lands a job as a G-man because the Justice Department realizes he has just the right connections to infiltrate the mob and bring it to its knees.

In *Great Guy* (1936), Cagney pulled off a similar trick playing a prizefighter turned racketbuster for the Bureau of Weights and Measures. *Angels with Dirty Faces* (1938), on the other hand, found Cagney back on the wrong side of the law, where he belonged and where he would stay in his gangster films from then on. *Angels* offered a sop to the code, however, by giving Cagney's vicious lead character, Rocky Sullivan, an upstanding counterpart in the form of Pat O'Brien's Jerry Connelly, a childhood pal of Rocky's who'd chosen religion over gangsterism and grown up to be a priest. Sentenced to death in the end of the film for his life of crime, Rocky is urged by Father Jerry to do a good deed for the first time in his life and destroy the heroic image a gang of slum kids has of him by going to the chair acting like a sniveling coward. Rocky does go to his death a sniveling coward, but the genius of Cagney's performance—the best thing in this fast-moving but sometimes mawkish film—is that we're not sure whether his hysterical breakdown (which he recreates even more chillingly in *White Heat*) is being faked or not.

As popular as his gangster films were, and as convincing as he was in such roles, Cagney never really cared for the genre. He won his only Oscar playing legendary song-and-dance man George M. Cohan in *Yankee Doodle Dandy* (1942),

Below, left: Cagney put his gat to work for the law as a member of the Department of Justice in G-Men *(1934). (Copyright © 1934 Warner Bros.)*

Right: Angels with Dirty Faces (1938). *(Copyright © 1938 Warner Bros.)*

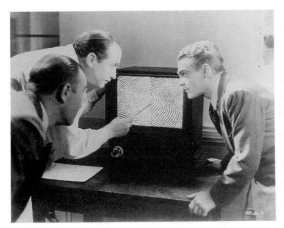

the type of picture he much preferred. Following *Yankee Doodle Dandy*, he decided to shed his Tom Powers persona and pursue a variety of parts in a succession of comedies, dramas, and war thrillers, some of them made for the independent company Cagney Productions (headed by his brother, William), into which the actor sunk a substantial amount of his own money. None of the films under the Cagney Productions banner scored very well with the critics or the public, however, and by the late forties the actor desperately needed a hit. So he returned to the genre and the studio that had made him a star in Raoul Walsh's classic *White Heat* (1949), the actor's best gangster film since *The Roaring Twenties* and the capstone of his (and Walsh's) gangster-film career, in which Cagney gives an absolutely towering performance as the movie "mug to end all mugs," Cody Jarrett.

In this landmark American gangster film, Cagney's character evolves from a Depression-spawned train robber to a remorseless killer with grandiose dreams of making it "to the top of the world." And as he does so, the style of *White Heat* itself shifts from an early thirties-type gangster film to the kind of men-behind-bars prison picture characteristic of the late thirties or early forties, then to a frosty, urban heist film, to a film noir study in amorality and duplicity, to a psychological gangster film about a very contemporary type of desperado: the pathological nobody who longs to be a somebody and achieves that goal in an almost-apocalyptic manner.

During a railroad heist at the beginning of the film, Jarrett cold-bloodedly murders the train's engineers because they overheard his name mentioned and would be able to identify him to the police. To further throw the cops off his trail, he confesses to a robbery committed in another state at the same time as the railroad job. The police put undercover cop Hank Fallon (Edmond O'Brien) in Jarrett's cell to befriend the gangster and lure him out into the open by helping him escape. Fallon, posing as a convicted felon named Vic Pardo, carries out his assignment with equal cold-bloodedness. When Jarrett discovers that Fallon, the only person besides his mother the paranoid gangster has ever allowed to get close to him, is a fraud, he goes berserk. For the repugnant Fallon, however, it's not enough to have succeeded in spritually crippling his prey; he also volunteers to be the one to shoot Jarrett down. Wounded, Jarrett triumphantly shouts, "Made it, Ma! Top of the world!" as he suicidally fires bullets into the petroleum tanks atop which he's been trapped. He is blown into eternity in a classic cinematic moment that also stands as an unsettling metaphor of the derangement of our nuclear age.

Cagney's powerful performance in *White Heat* commands the screen throughout, and sears it in many individual scenes, such as the remarkable one in prison when he learns of his mother's death and goes wild with anger and grief and starts slugging guards right and left and has to be carried away, screaming all the while like some mortally wounded animal. And he's just as powerful in quieter moments, such as the scene where he discovers that his close pal Fallon is really an undercover cop out to destroy him. The look of astonishment, pain, despair, then vengeful

Cagney as Cody Jarrett,
the "mug to end all
mugs," in the classic
White Heat *(1949).*
(Copyright © 1949
Warner Bros.)

rage that fleets across the actor's face is an example of screen acting at its best.

Cagney's distinctive tough-guy persona influenced many other actors as well, notably Richard Widmark, who made his screen debut in the 1947 gangster film *Kiss of Death,* playing a violence-loving psychopath very much in the Cagney mold. Widmark's wiry mob hit man, Tommy Udo, whose skeletal features suggest a grinning death's-head at times, lacks the Cagney gangster's streetwise cleverness but not his viciousness. In the film's most famous scene, he manages to top even Cagney in the brutality department when, partly out of anger but mostly for pleasure, he kills the elderly, wheelchair-bound mother (Mildred Dunnock) of a suspected stoolie by pushing her down a flight of stairs after she lies to him concerning her son's whereabouts. Like Cagney's gangsters, Widmark's maniacally grinning Udo has a real appetite for violence and is motivated mainly by the need to have that appetite fed—even during off-hours, such as when he attends a boxing match and flies out of his seat, screaming at the fighters to stop dancing and start tearing one another up. Widmark even uses a variation on the line of dialogue most associated with the Cagney gangster when, much in the Cagney manner, he calls a pal who has fallen out of favor with him "a dirty little rat!"

Mickey Rooney also acquitted himself well in the equally Cagneyesque role of the notorious thirties gunman and bank robber in *Baby Face Nelson* (1957). An absorbing, well-crafted B film directed on an extremely low budget by action specialist Don Siegel, *Baby Face Nelson* picks up the story of the diminutive, psychotic killer (a real man whose name was Lester Gillis) shortly after he's released from prison. After carrying out a murder contract, Nelson finds himself on the run from the law. He joins the Dillinger gang and assumes leadership after Dillinger (Leo Gordon) is killed. Hunted by the FBI, the dangerously unstable gangster refuses to lie low, committing a series of daring bank robberies and murders that result in the gang's being squeezed by the law even harder. When the FBI begins to close in, Nelson engineers his escape by throwing in his associates. But the authorities track him and his moll (Carolyn Jones) to their hideout, where the killer gleefully takes on all comers in a furious shoot-out. (Like Cagney's gangsters, Rooney's Nelson is turned on by violence; it's clear from the outset that he can't get enough of it.) Wounded in the gun battle, Nelson manages to escape once more, but he gets no farther than the local cemetery, where, blood spewing from his mouth, he persuades his moll to finish him off before the law arrives.

"What gave the picture its vitality . . . [was that] we made no apologies for Nelson," Don Siegel told his biographer, Stuart M. Kaminsky. "If you felt anything for him, it was because of his size and his rebellious attitude towards society." The same could be said of many of Cagney's gangster characters.

Rooney won the César, the French film industry's equivalent of the Oscar, for his charismatic, emotionally charged performance as Nelson, and the film itself was a big hit throughout Europe. In the United States, however, *Baby Face Nelson* was dismissed as just another low-rent gangster film, and it is seldom revived today. But it remains one of Siegel's best, along with *The Lineup* (1958), a taut, well-paced thriller inspired by the popular fifties TV series of the same name (and later syndicated under the title *San Francisco Beat*). The character of Dancer, the brutal hit man played by Eli Wallach, has more than a trace of the Cagney gangster in him, as well. Dancer's mobster boss, Julian (Robert Keith), describes him as a "wonderfully pure pathological study. A psychopath with no inhibitions." During the course of the film, Dancer lives up to this description by gleefully executing a number of people, including the syndicate's wheelchair-bound head man (Vaughan Williams), whom he pushes to his death from a platform overlooking an ice-skating rink in a scene that recalls Tommy Udo's vicious murder of Ma Rossi in *Kiss of Death*.

Bob Hoskins turned in a vintage Cagney performance as the pit-bull leader of a gang of London mobsters in John Mackenzie's compelling British gangster film *The Long Good Friday* (1980)—intriguingly mixing in a bit of the Robinson gangster, as well. Hoskins plays Harold Shand, the pugnacious, fashionably attired, fiercely patriotic head of London's East End mob, who is negotiating a deal with the American Mafia to convert London's slummy harbor area into a money-making enterprise and the "jewel" of Europe and the Common Market. During negotiations, however, Shand's turf erupts in violence that threatens his power and position and the fate of the project. Shand's limousine is blown up and the driver killed. An unexploded bomb is found in one of the gangster's nightclubs. Another of his clubs is blown up. And one of his henchmen is found murdered in a public bath.

As his dreams of power and glory collapse around him, Shand finally uncovers the root of his trouble. His right-hand man, Jeff (Derek Thompson), and a politician (Bryan Marshall) in his pocket have been making payoffs to the Irish Republican Army for years to prevent the terrorist organization from fomenting strikes among the predominantly Irish laborers working on Shand's various construction projects. When some of the terrorists were coincidentally arrested shortly after being short-changed by Shand's payoff man, the IRA ringleaders began to suspect Shand of pulling a double cross and had mounted a violent campaign to destroy the gangster's power and prestige. Stunned by the realization that he's been unknowingly funding the hated IRA—and, worse still, that their muscle may be more far-reaching than his—Shand goes berserk, and, in the film's most horrific scene, reveals his Cagneyesque appetite for sadistic violence by stabbing Jeff to death with a broken bottle. Overcome with grief for killing the boy, who had been like a son to him, Shand sets out to get even with the IRA and reestablish his power and position. But his plans to awry and, at the film's harrowing conclusion, he's kidnapped at gunpoint by two of the terrorists, and the beleagured gangster, who truly didn't comprehend what he was up against, realizes he's a goner.

Hoskins is superb as Shand, especially in the final scene when he realizes he's been had and his face (like Cagney's in *White Heat*) fills with a range of emotions, from rage, frustration, and despair to grim acceptance of his situation and fate. He deservedly won top honors at the British equivalent of the Academy Awards for his powerful performance in this complex, politically overtoned gangster film, which was almost denied release in its native Britain due to the sensitive IRA subject matter.

Even more recently, actor Joe Pesci has sought to assume the Cagney mantle with his series of cocksure, tough-guy performances in such films as Martin Scorsese's *GoodFellas*, and *The Public Eye* (1992), wherein which he plays a tabloid photographer similar to Cagney's character in the 1933 *Picture Snatcher*.

BOGEY

Like Cagney, Humphrey Bogart was born in 1899. Like Robinson *and* Cagney, he grew up in New York City. Unlike his fellow kings of the underworld, however, Bogart's parents were fairly well off; the young Bogart grew up surrounded by the rich and sometimes famous rather than the low-life thugs he would eventually play on the screen.

The son of an eminent surgeon, Dr. Belmont DeForest Bogart, and a successful commercial artist, Maud Humphrey Bogart (legend has it that she used her toddler son as the model for the first series of Gerber baby-food ads), Bogart attended the prestigious Trinity School in New York and prep school at Phillips Academy in Andover, Massachusetts. His parents intended him to go to Yale, but he was

Spencer Tracy played the gangster and Humphrey Bogart the railroaded good guy in Up the River *(1930), directed by John Ford.*

expelled from prep school before graduation and joined the navy instead. While serving in World War I, he received the scar on his lip that caused the distinctive lisp that became his screen trademark later on.

After the war, Bogart returned to New York and went to work for stage and film impresario William A. Brady, a close family friend. It was Brady who suggested that he go into acting, and Bogart made his Broadway debut playing a small part in the 1922 drama *Drifting*. A larger role followed the same year in *Swifty*, for which the aspiring actor earned the worst reviews of his career. Bogart nevertheless persevered in his chosen occupation and won parts in a succession of Broadway dramas and comedies over the next few years. The image he created in them couldn't have been more removed from the one he established on the screen, however. Wrote Clifford McCarty in *The Films of Humphrey Bogart:* "He usually was cast as romantic juveniles, his stage equipment a tennis racquet and a pair of flannels."

Bogart journeyed to Hollywood in the early thirties to pursue a film career. Though he got work, his film roles were fairly minor; he went back to Broadway, where in 1934 he got the part that would dramatically change his image with casting agents from then on and finally launch him on the road to movie stardom. In Robert E. Sherwood's tense drama *The Petrified Forest*, Bogart was perfectly cast as Duke Mantee, a gangster escaped from prison and on the run from the law who holds a number of people hostage at a roadside café in the Arizona desert

Humphrey Bogart as the hostage-taking Duke Mantee, the first of his desperate loner gangsters, in The Petrified Forest *(1936). With Joe Sawyer (brandishing rifle). (Copyright © 1936 Warner Bros.)*

while waiting for his moll to arrive with the money he needs to finance his getaway into Mexico. Although Bogart's role was a supporting one, he used it to good effect, and his performance as Mantee all but stole the show out from under its heavyweight star, Leslie Howard. The play was a substantial hit and Warner Brothers quickly purchased it for filming. Howard was signed to re-create his starring role in the film version, but the studio passed over Bogart and assigned its more established gangster star Edward G. Robinson to play the part of Mantee. Upon learning of this, Howard used his clout to oust Robinson by refusing to appear in the film unless Bogart was given the part of Mantee. The studio relented and Bogart returned once more to Hollywood — this time for good.

Sherwood wrote *The Petrified Forest* to express his changing views on pacifism and isolationism and the need for violent sacrifice if evil is to be thwarted and future generations are to be given a chance. The story's pacifist character is Alan Squier (Howard). While wandering, physically and spiritually, through the arid Arizona landscape, Squier, a failed poet, stops at a roadside café in the desert and befriends a young waitress named Gabrielle Maple (Bette Davis), a kindred spirit who longs to better her life by pursuing the artistic ambitions Squier himself has given up. Escaped convict Duke Mantee arrives and he and his gang hold Squier, Gabrielle, and everyone else in the café hostage while waiting for Mantee's moll to show up with getaway money. Squier and Gabrielle grow closer during this forced confinement; as the police close in and the desperate Mantee prepares to flee to Mexico, Squier sees a way to help the girl achieve her dreams by sacrificing his own life. He signs his life-insurance policy over to her and manipulates Mantee into shooting him before the police arrive and bring the gangster down.

A stagebound, talky, and somewhat improbable drama—unless you swallow its heavy-handed symbolism whole—*The Petrified Forest* endures as a classic mainly because of Bogart's defining performance as the sad-eyed but vicious Mantee, the first of the actor's desperate loner gangsters—characters who seem fated almost from birth to be outsiders. Unlike the Robinson and Cagney gangster, the Bogart gangster isn't so much motivated by greed, envy, and the thrill of violence as by the need to survive in a world he perceives as totally hostile. Whether he's an underling or the mob's top man, the Bogart gangster always looks and acts *cornered.* (To some degree, Bogart's good guy characters, among them Rick in *Casablanca,* share this quality.) Somewhat out of step with the dynamic, hell-bent gangster characters of the thirties as personified by Robinson and Cagney, Bogart's desperate loner was much closer in essence to the heroes and antiheroes of forties films noir—the milieu, not coincidentally, in which the actor would finally come into his own.

Bogart's scene-stealing performance as Duke Mantee notwithstanding, *The Petrified Forest* failed to catapult him into the big leagues as Warner Brothers' next great gangster star. Robinson and Cagney still reigned supreme as the studio's two most popular movie gangsters. Their films were drawing heavy fire from the MPPDA and civics groups for excessive violence and brutality, however. Not

Leslie Howard was the star, but Humphrey Bogart stole the show in The Petrified Forest *(1936) opposite Bette Davis. (Copyright © 1936 Warner Bros.)*

oblivious to Bogart's value as a charismatic movie villain, the studio signed the actor to a long-term contract and took some of the heat off its two major gangster stars by casting Bogart opposite them as the bad guy—or worse guy—in a series of underworld dramas.

Even before *The Petrified Forest* was released, the studio cast Bogart as top mobster Barton MacLane's strongarm lieutenant, Bugs Fenner, the chief nemesis of Robinson's good-guy undercover racketbuster in *Bullets or Ballots*. The 1938 *Angels with Dirty Faces* softened the Cagney gangster a bit by pitting him against an even worse character (an unscrupulous lawyer and racketeer) played by Bogart— a duel they would repeat a year later in the classic *The Roaring Twenties*. Occasionally, the Bogart gangster took center stage all by himself, as in William Wyler's social drama *Dead End* (1937), where Bogart, similar to Cagney in *Angels,* played the gangster idol of a bunch of slum kids. In between, Bogart sometimes got the opportunity to play the lesser of two gangster evils, as well—and occasionally even the hero. In *Marked Woman* (1937), for example, he played a crusading district attorney who brings down mob kingpin Eduardo Cianelli by persuading Bette Davis, a victimized "hostess" (polite word for prostitute) in one of Cianelli's "nightclubs" (polite word for brothel), to turn state's evidence against her murderous, double-dealing boss. Bogart's character, David Graham, was loosely based on Thomas E. Dewey, the crusading special prosecutor and future governor of New York State who nailed mob chieftain Lucky Luciano on prostitution charges that year with the help of testimony from several disgruntled "hostesses" in Luciano's employ.

"Bogart had yet to hit it big and was playing supporting roles. . . . [His] performance [in *High Sierra*] made Bogart a star," exaggerated *Sierra* director Raoul Walsh in his autobiography. Bogart's costarring role in *Marked Woman* opposite Bette Davis, the studio's most popular female star, could hardly be termed supporting; he had already played leads in several of the studio's B pictures. *High Sierra* was an A picture, however, and it gave Bogart his meatiest gangster role since Duke Mantee. It was his performance in the John Huston/W. R. Burnett–scripted film (adapted from Burnett's novel of the same title) that led to his being cast as private eye Sam Spade in Huston's directorial debut, *The Maltese Falcon,* released the same year (1941). And it was *Falcon* that made the veteran actor a star.

Ironically, Bogart was almost shut out of both roles. The studio wanted to star George Raft in *High Sierra* and *Falcon,* but, to Bogart's good fortune, Raft turned the studio down flat. He declined *High Sierra* because the role called for him to die once again at the end of the picture, and Raft felt his rising star status had earned him the right to play heroes who would be left standing come the final fade. The part of Sam Spade in *The Maltese Falcon* would have allowed him to do just that, but Raft let the part slip to Bogart because he feared putting his fate—and mediocre talents?—in the hands of a fledgling director like Huston. In a double note of irony, Bogart triumphed in both parts and very soon eclipsed Raft as one of the studio's shining stars.

Bogart's "Mad Dog" Roy Earle in *High Sierra* is an older, more world-weary version of Duke Mantee—a man who carries doom with him like a backpack. He is also a chronic self-deceiver in the mold of many later Huston protagonists, notably the Dix Handley character in Huston's 1950 gangster film *The Asphalt Jungle*, also based on a novel by W. R. Burnett. A notorious bank robber (the character was loosely based on John Dillinger), Earle is sprung from prison by a mob crony, Big Mac (Donald MacBride), to mastermind the stickup of a deluxe hotel in a California resort town. On the way to his rendezvous with the holdup men Big Mac has lined up to work with him, Earle helps out an old man with car trouble, Pa Goodhue (Henry Travers), and falls for his crippled daughter, Velma (Joan Leslie). Having no idea who Earle really is and grateful for his kindness and generosity toward them, the Goodhues readily accept Earle into their home and treat him like one of the family. Earle deceives himself into believing that he can erase his past and settle down to a normal life with Velma after he pulls off the big heist. He finances the operation to repair Velma's clubfoot in the belief that the grateful girl will come to love him in return—even though the worlds they're from, not to mention their ages, are so different that they are clearly incompatible.

The robbery goes off without a hitch, but two of Earle's confederates (Arthur

Below, left: Bogart's desperate loner Roy "Mad Dog" Earle in Raoul Walsh's High Sierra *(1941). (Copyright © 1941 Warner Bros.)*

Right: Jack Palance *played "Mad Dog" Earle in the 1955 remake* I Died a Thousand Times *opposite Shelley Winters. (Copyright © 1955 Warner Bros.)*

Kennedy and Alan Curtis) are accidentally killed when their car crashes and burns during the getaway from the hotel. The cops force a confession from Mendoza (Cornel Wilde), the inside man on the job, and Earle becomes a hunted man. The operation on Velma is a success, but when Earle shows up to propose to her, he finds she's become engaged to her childhood sweetheart. His bogus dream gone sour, Earle goes to hell fast. Blowing a last chance for happiness, however short-lived, with the girl (Ida Lupino) who genuinely loves him, he winds up trapped in the Sierra mountains, where the police shoot him down like a dog.

Fully recognizing that the gangster film was, in many ways, a modern-day variation of the Western, director Walsh took the plot of *High Sierra*, one of his most successful films, and refashioned it into an outright Western just eight years later. Retitled *Colorado Territory* (1949), it featured Joel McCrea in the Bogart role, Dorothy Malone in the Joan Leslie role and Virginia Mayo in the Ida Lupino part. And in 1955, Warner Brothers returned the durable property to its gangster milieu and remade it once more (this time in WarnerColor and CinemaScope) as *I Died a Thousand Times*, directed by Stuart Heisler and starring Jack Palance as the doomed "Mad Dog" Roy Earle.

Despite his potent performance in *High Sierra*, Bogart didn't appear in another gangster film until the 1942 *The Big Shot*. (John Huston's intervening *The Maltese Falcon* was only marginally a gangster film and Bogart played not a crook but the hero — albeit a hero with many shady tendencies.) *The Big Shot* was a weak variation on *High Sierra*. Bogart starred as ex-con Duke Berne, another loser in the Duke Mantee/Roy Earle mold. Recently released from prison, Bogart is pushed into engineering an armored-car robbery that goes fatally wrong. Due to the duplicity of one of his accomplices (Stanley Ridges), he winds up back in prison, but he escapes and heads for the mountains with his moll (Irene Manning) to elude capture. Manning is killed and the vengeful Bogart later goes to his own death after getting even with the double-dealing Ridges. Bogart starred in a number of gangster (or quasigangster films) after *The Big Shot,* but not until *The Desperate Hours* (1955), his penultimate film, was he once again cast in the role of bad guy.

The Desperate Hours drew Bogart's movie career almost full circle; its plot, once again, recalls *The Petrified Forest*, and Bogart's role as the hostage-taking escaped convict Glenn Griffin is not unlike that of Duke Mantee in many ways. The setting this time around was not the Arizona desert, however, but a quiet Indianapolis suburb.

After Griffin, his brother Hal (Dewey Martin), and a brutal thug named Kobish (Robert Middleton) break out of jail, they head for nearby Indianapolis to rendezvous with Griffin's moll, who is to arrive at midnight with cash to aid them in their getaway. They pick a suburban house at random and hold the family — the Hilliards — hostage while Griffin relays the gang's whereabouts to his moll by telephone. The police and the FBI mount roadblocks and put a tail on

Bogart's hostage-taking gangster Glenn Griffin in The Desperate Hours *(1955) brought the actor's career full circle. With Martha Scott. (Copyright © 1955 Paramount Pictures)*

Griffin's moll. When she realizes she's being followed, she ditches her car and calls Griffin to alter plans. Griffin tells her to put the money in an envelope and mail it to Mr. Hilliard's (Fredric March) office instead. Forced to hole up longer than he'd anticipated, Griffin instructs the Hilliards to go about their daily routine. Hilliard is allowed to go to work so that he can be there to pick up the envelope when it arrives in the mail, and his daughter, Cindy (Mary Murphy), is permitted to keep a date with her boyfriend (Gig Young). As the cops tighten their net around the area, the gang members start arguing among themselves. Hal decides to make a break for it while he still can, runs into the police, and gets killed, and the cops find the Hilliards' address in his pocket. As Hilliard returns home with the envelope full of cash, the police waylay him and tell him they plan to mount an assault on his home to recapture Griffin. Realizing that his family could be killed in the shoot-out, Hilliard asks for time to get Griffin out of the house on his own, and the cops give him ten minutes. His nerves stretched to breaking, Hilliard goes back into the house, cleverly gains the upper hand on Griffin with an unloaded gun, orders Griffin out of the house, and the gangster is shot down on the front lawn by the police.

Like *The Petrified Forest*, *The Desperate Hours* was also based on a successful Broadway play (by Joseph Hayes, who adapted it from his own best-selling novel). The play starred Paul Newman as a much younger and less world-weary version of Griffin. Newman's name as yet meant nothing to moviegoers, however, so when director William Wyler purchased the screen rights, he had Hayes age the character twenty years and gave the part to veteran screen gangster Bogart. For the role of

Hilliard, Wyler wanted Spencer Tracy, but Bogart and Tracy disagreed over who was to get top billing, Tracy bowed out, and the part went to March instead. The tense byplay between the rough, school-of-hard-knocks Griffin and the dignified and likable Hilliard echoes many similar sequences between Duke Mantee and Alan Squier in *The Petrified Forest*. Like Mantee, Griffin exhibits a grudging respect for his hostage and a bitter contempt for him at the same time. He envies and hates Hilliard for the same reasons, for everything about Hilliard—his strength in the face of adversity, his reciprocated love for his family, his comfortable middle-class background—points up just how much of a loner and loser in life the desperate gangster really is.

The Harder They Fall (1956) returned Bogart once more to the role of hero, albeit a flawed one like Sam Spade, who discovers his sense of decency and morality in the final reel. Bogart plays Eddie Willis, a down-on-his-luck ex-sportswriter hired by gangster/fight promoter Nick Benko (Rod Steiger) to ballyhoo a strapping young boxer with a glass jaw, Toro Moreno (Mike Lane), as the next heavyweight champ while Benko fixes fight after fight to ensure Moreno's continued victory in the ring. (Lane's character was loosely based on heavyweight fighter Primo Carnera.) Through Willis, the gentle Moreno discovers his bouts have all been rigged. Out of pride (and the need for more money to support his parents in Argentina), Moreno decides to go through with the big heavyweight title fight, which has not been fixed. (Knowing Moreno will lose, Benko and his gang have bet the ranch on the fighter's odds-against opponent so that they'll collect a fortune.) In one of

Bogart played the hero, albeit a flawed one, in The Harder They Fall *(1956), his final film. With Rod Steiger, Nehemiah Persoff, and Mike Lane. (Copyright © 1956 Columbia Pictures)*

the most harrowing fight scenes ever staged, Moreno gives his all in the ring and is beaten to a bloody pulp. The reprehensible Benko makes a bundle but pays the savagely beaten Moreno a pittance. This pushes the morally embattled Willis over the edge; he gives Moreno his far more substantial share of the winnings and puts the fighter on the next plane home to Argentina. Then he tells Benko of his intentions to write a scathing exposé of gangland influence on the fight game — for the benefit of "every bum who ever got his brains knocked loose in the ring" — and get the sport outlawed "even if it takes an act of Congress."

The Bogart gangster had an enormous influence on the underworld dramas of forties film noir. Shades of his existential loners can be seen in most of the heroes and antiheroes populating the films of this period. Alan Ladd's cold-blooded hit man in *This Gun for Hire* (1942) is just one example of a now-iconographic antihero of the period, for whom the Bogart gangster clearly paved the way. Diminutive, tight-lipped and unsmiling, motivated to violence simply to survive, and looking perpetually cornered and trapped, Philip Raven, the role that made Ladd a star, is spiritual kin to Duke Mantee and Roy Earle — as are many of the troubled underworld heroes and antiheroes played by Robert Ryan, a very different type of actor from Ladd, throughout the forties and fifties in films ranging from *Queen of the Mob* (1940) and *The Racket* (1951) to *On Dangerous Ground* (1952) and the relatively late film noir *Odds Against Tomorrow* (1959).

The Bogart influence pervaded many foreign-made gangster films as well, particularly in France. It was the French, of course, who first celebrated film noir, and for many film noir–inspired French filmmakers, Bogey's loner character served

Many of Robert Ryan's anti-hero gangsters shared characteristics with Bogart's desperate loner gangster also. From Odds Against Tomorrow *(1959). (Copyright © 1959 United Artists)*

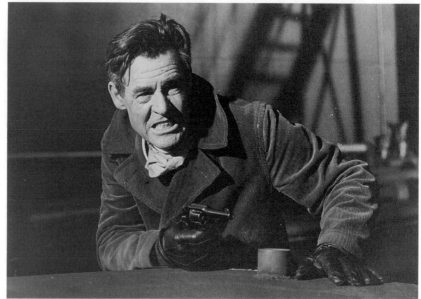

as the doom-laden genre's most representative symbol. For example, although he looks more like a dissolute version of the actor Paul Henried, Carl Mohner's heavy-lidded, world-weary thief in the classic French gangster film *Rififi* (1955), directed by the American Jules Dassin, is a direct descendant of Bogart's doomed Roy Earle. Both characters are inveterate underworlders and loners who assume leadership of a carefully planned and executed robbery in an effort to dig themselves out from under, but who wind up digging themselves even deeper—and rush headlong toward death for final release. Jean-Luc Godard's *A Bout de Souffle* (a.k.a. *Breathless*, 1959) reveals the Bogart influence even more overtly. "[The film] is dedicated to Monogram Pictures, a sign of Godard's devotion to the American B-movies," wrote David Shipman in *The Story of Cinema*. "[Godard's] young thug hero (Jean-Paul Belmondo) tote[s] a gun, steal[s] money from his girlfriend's handbag, mutter[s] 'Bogey' affectionately before a poster of Humphrey Bogart, [and] face[s] death—as everything else—with a shrug."* Cigarette dangling from his lips in the Bogart style, Belmondo went on to play other Bogey-inspired tough guys and gangsters in Claude Sautet's *Classe Tous Risques* (a.k.a. *The Big Risk*, 1960) and *Le Doulos* (a.k.a. *Doulos the Finger Man*, 1962), directed by film-critic-turned-filmmaker Jean-Pierre Melville, France's most prolific and important director of French-style films noir. Melville's most widely released entries in the genre include: *Le Deuxième Souffle* (a.k.a. *Second Breath*, 1966), in which Lino Ventura, playing a veteran criminal not unlike Bogart's Roy Earle, escapes from prison to spearhead one final caper that ultimately leads to his death. And *Le Samouraï* (1967), the story of the last desperate days of a cold-blooded hit man (Alain Delon, whose character in the film is a combination of the Bogart gangster and Alan Ladd in *This Gun for Hire*). Released in the United States five years later under the title *The Godson* in an effort to capitalize on the success of *The Godfather*, the film was favorably reviewed by *Newsweek* as "a first-rate thriller of uncompromising simplicity, time-bomb pacing, and an acuteness about the world of the professional criminal that puts *The Godfather* near to *Cheaper by the Dozen.*" In an accurate summation of the Bogart gangster himself, the reviewer concluded: "In Melville's vision, prison is no answer to the criminal; he is already there."

---

*Like Belmondo's thug in *A Bout de Souffle*, Albert Finney's down-at-the-heels private eye in Stephen Frears's British-made *Gumshoe* (1972) is not only inspired by Bogart's screen persona; he's obsessed with it—an obsession the character acknowledges to the audience repeatedly throughout the film.

Godard dabbled with the gangster genre once more in his futuristic thriller satire *Alphaville* (1965). The film starred Eddie Constantine as a trench-coated private eye in the Bogart manner named Lemmy Caution, a character Constantine had made famous in a series of B films made in France during the early sixties.

"We rob banks." Warren Beatty and Faye Dunaway in Arthur Penn's controversial Bonnie and Clyde *(1967). (Copyright © 1967 Warner Bros.)*

CHAPTER 5

PUBLIC

ENEMIES

When we think of outlaws, our image is of the Old West—of the cowpoke, guns blazing, astride his horse as he flees the law, the spectacular scenery of the great outdoors his backdrop. When we think of gangsters, however, our image is more contemporary and distinctly urban: that of the well-dressed hood in a fedora, gat in hand or tommy gun in his arms, blazing away at the coppers from a speeding car, its tires screeching across some nameless city's mean streets.

The historical record is not so clear-cut, however. For, in fact, many of history's most famous gangsters were also outlaws, descendants in spirit, if not by blood, from their Old West forbears, who preyed on America's rural towns and communities during the years of the Great Depression with a ferocity that put many of their nineteenth-century counterparts to shame. The only difference was their method of getaway . . . horsepower rather than horseflesh.

The movies have not ignored them. Largely because of the silver screen, in fact, their bloody exploits have taken on the characteristics of myth, and their colorful names are as famous to us today as they were during those long-ago times when they lived and killed. Ma Barker, Baby Face Nelson, Pretty Boy Floyd, Verne Miller, Homer Van Meter, Machine Gun Kelly, Alvin "Creepy" Karpis—the list goes on and on. All have had at least one movie made about them, most more than one.

But the immortals in this corner of Gangland—immortal in that they've come to symbolize the era of the outlaw/gangster more than anyone else — are Bonnie and Clyde and John Dillinger.

BONNIE AND CLYDE

The relationship between Bonnie Parker and Clyde Barrow has been heavily romanticized in the media. Bonnie herself gave it melodramatic shadings with the various poems and pictures about her life with Clyde that she sent to the press for publication. But there remains some confusion as to how romantic their affair actually was. Some accounts say Clyde was a homosexual who recruited other males into the gang to service his sexually voracious partner, and himself, as well. Others say he was bisexual, even impotent. In any case, theirs was without a doubt a distinctly unusual relationship.

Bonnie was nineteen and married (her husband was in prison) when she met Clyde; Clyde was twenty-one and just out of prison. He was arrested shortly thereafter on seven counts of car theft and burglary and returned to the slammer for another two-year stretch. Bonnie, who maintained that she'd been "bored crapless" before she met Clyde, smuggled him a gun, and he escaped. But he was recaptured after commiting another robbery and was given a fourteen-year sentence. While in prison, he chopped off two of his toes to get off a work detail, and his handicap won him an early parole. He rejoined Bonnie in 1932 a hardened criminal. The pair formed the Barrow Gang and went on a spree of robberies, kidnappings, and murder throughout the Southwest that landed them quickly on the government's Most Wanted list.

Others were recruited into the gang off and on, including an escaped convict and gunman named Ray Hamilton; a filling station attendant named William Daniel Jones, whom the pair kidnapped then persuaded to join them; and a petty thief named Henry Methvin, whose recruitment would spell doom to the pair. But the most lasting recruit was Clyde's brother Buck, who'd also done time in prison, and Buck's wife, Blanche, who went along, she later told the police, because it was "a wife's duty to stay with her husband."

Tracked by police to a tourist camp in Missouri, the gang was surrounded and their cabins sprayed with machine-gun fire. Buck was severely wounded and Blanche partially blinded in one eye, but Bonnie and Clyde were unhurt and the gang managed to elude capture and escape across the border into Iowa, where a two-hundred-man posse descended on the gang's hideout in the woods and opened fire from every direction. Buck was hit again and he and Blanche were captured. Bonnie, Clyde, and gang member William Daniel Jones were wounded as well but waded into the nearby river and succeeded in escaping in a stolen car.

After recuperating, the gang stepped up its campaign of robberies, kidnappings, and murder throughout Louisiana and Texas. Jones was captured, and Bonnie and

Clyde recruited Henry Methvin to take his place. Wanted on robbery charges in both states, Methvin made a deal with the law to escape prosecution by helping to set a trap for the duo. The year was 1934.

Methvin scheduled a rendezvous with the pair at a secluded spot on a country road near the Louisiana-Texas border. But the Texas Highway Authority, under the command of ex-Texas Ranger Frank Hamer, met them instead. The lawmen hid in the bushes alongside the road and when Bonnie and Clyde pulled up in their white Ford V-8 sedan, the lawmen opened fire. Almost two hundred rounds of ammunition were fired at the car and its trapped occupants, killing Bonnie and Clyde almost instantly. In one of the eerie ironies of the case, Clyde's body was riddled with twenty-five rounds, Bonnie's with twenty-three—their exact ages at the time of their deaths.

Bonnie had romanticized the pair's finish in a poem she'd sent to the newspapers just prior to the ambush. Titled "The Ballad of Bonnie and Clyde," it prophetically served as their epitaph, its concluding lines reading: "Some day they will go down together, and they will be buried side by side. To a few it means grief, to the law it's relief. But it's death to Bonnie and Clyde."

John Dillinger, fellow public enemy number one, who followed them in death the same year, offered a different send-off. His memorial to Bonnie and Clyde: "They were kill-crazy punks and clodhoppers, bad news to decent bank robbers. They gave us a bad name."

Three years after their deaths, the story of Bonnie and Clyde received its first

Henry Fonda and Sylvia Sydney as the doomed lovers on the run from the law in Fritz Lang's You Only Live Once *(1937), the first screen treatment of the Bonnie and Clyde saga.*

screen treatment in producer Walter Wanger's *You Only Live Once* (1937), the second American film by expatriate director Fritz Lang. Lang had made several underworld dramas in his native Germany before fleeing the Nazis in 1933 — notably his series of quasigangster films about the master criminal Dr. Mabuse and the classic *M* (1931), the story of a child murderer (Peter Lorre) who is hunted down and tried for his inhuman crimes by Berlin's gangsters and underworlders when the cops' far-reaching manhunt for the killer threatens their criminal activities. Lang's first American film, *Fury* (1936) was a crime drama as well, with overtones of social criticism about the specter of Nazi-style mob violence in America.

You Only Live Once centers on Eddie Taylor (Henry Fonda), a "three-time loser" (the film's original title) who attempts to go straight but is railroaded back to prison for an armed robbery he didn't commit. Eddie is sentenced to death. As his date with the executioner draws near, he boldly breaks out of prison with the help of his wife, Jo (Sylvia Sidney), who has smuggled him a gun, and kills a priest — the only man who had ever been kind to him and had faith in him — during the escape. He and Jo flee to Canada, the newspapers filled with sensational stories of Eddie's daring escape and the pair's subsequent criminal deeds — most of which have been committed by others. Eventually, they're trapped and shot by police. But they manage to get across the Canadian border to "freedom," where they die in each other's arms.

Apart from the "young lovers on the run" angle, there is little of the real Bonnie and Clyde in the film. Unlike the hard case Clyde Barrow, Eddie Taylor is an inherently decent chap who seems condemned to a life of crime due to the callousness of others and an implacable fate. As Jo's sister Bonnie (Jean Dixon) says of him: "Eddie Taylor's been pounding on the door of the execution chamber since he was born."

Jo, on the other hand, is a complete innocent — at least as the film begins — who believes in the fairness of society's institutions and the willingness of others to give Eddie a square deal. Her belief system is sorely put to the test (a favorite Lang theme) and ultimately shattered when her innocent husband is sentenced to death, and she becomes a criminal herself.

What *You Only Live Once* lacks as an authentic recounting of the Bonnie and Clyde saga, it more than makes up for in excitement and atmosphere. Lang's staging of the bank robbery for which Eddie is framed is especially taut, as well as ominous. Portions of the sequence were later used as stock footage for a bank robbery scene in the low-budget *Dillinger* (1945).

Though not as artfully done as Lang's fictionalized take on the Bonnie and Clyde saga, the 1939 *Persons in Hiding* inched much nearer to the truth of it. J. Carrol Naish plays the Clyde character, a brutish petty thief named Gunner Martin who graduates to bigger crimes when he meets and falls for the attractive and ambitious Dorothy Bronson (Patricia Morison). A scheming parcel of greedy goods,

Bronson pushes the no-brain hoodlum into a spree of robberies, kidnappings, and, ultimately, murder that lands the deadly duo on the FBI's Most Wanted list. G-man Pete Griswold (Lynne Overman) picks up their bloody trail and at one point gets captured by them. But he manages to turn the tables and he and his fellow agents finally bring the pair down.

Unlike the Lang film (and many other Bonnie and Clyde–inspired films to come), *Persons in Hiding* doesn't portray the deadly couple as innocent victims or castoffs of an indifferent society. They're venal and brutal, and they get what they deserve—from each other and from the law. This is particularly true of Morison's Bonnie character, for unlike many other screen Bonnies, Morison makes no attempt to invite our sympathy. Noted B movie historian Don Miller of the actress's performance (her screen debut): "Attractive, but not in the manufactured Hollywood way, Miss Morison possessed an insight into her character far in excess of her tender years, and gave her part a cold viciousness that was chillingly effective. It contrasted with Naish's evocation of brute force uncompensated by brain power, so that by the fateful conclusion one could almost, but not quite, sympathize with him."

A gritty, fast-paced little B movie (the film runs barely over an hour), *Persons in Hiding* was adapted from a book of the same name by FBI chief J. Edgar Hoover (ghosted for him by professional writer Courtney Riley Cooper). A calculated attempt by Hoover to promote the image of his beloved Bureau by chronicling its more challenging cases for a sensation-hungry public, the book was an immediate

Scheming Dorothy Bronson (Patricia Morison) urges her petty-thief boyfriend "Gunner" Martin (J. Carrol Naish) to graduate to bigger crimes in Persons in Hiding *(1938), based on the book by J. Edgar Hoover. (Copyright © 1938 Paramount Pictures)*

best-seller. Paramount snapped it up and enlisted various writers and directors in its B picture unit to turn the material into a series of quickie feature films. Combining elements of the Bonnie and Clyde saga with material in the book about other killer couples on the run whom the FBI did run to ground, *Persons in Hiding* was the first and best of the series. It was followed in rapid succession by *Undercover Doctor* (1939), *Parole Fixer* (1940), directed by Robert Florey, and *Queen of the Mob* (1940), the concluding (and second-best) installment in the series. A fictionalized account of the career of Ma Barker and her killer brood, *Queen of the Mob* featured veteran actress Blanche Yurka as the murderous matriarch (renamed Ma Webster in the film) and Paul Kelly, William Henry, Richard Denning, and James Seay as her sons. J. Carrol Naish also appeared in the cast, which starred Ralph Bellamy as the FBI man who nails Bloody Mama and her boys. Forties film noir antihero Robert Ryan also made his cinematic debut in a small role.

Often confused with *You Only Live Once* is Nicholas Ray's *They Live by Night* (1948), another reworking of the Bonnie and Clyde tale, based on the novel *Thieves Like Us* by Edward Anderson, which was published the same year the Lang film was released. Like the earlier film, the focus of Anderson's Depression-era period piece and Ray's film version is doomed innocence.

Two hardened criminals, T-Dub (Jay C. Flippen) and Chickamaw (Howard de Silva), and one youthful offender, Bowie (Farley Granger), break out of a southern prison farm and kidnap a farmer and his battered Model T to make their getaway. The two hard cases beat up the farmer and dump him, then brutally browbeat the reluctant Bowie into helping them commit several more crimes that prompt a large-scale police manhunt. While hiding out with T-Dub's no-good brother, Dee Mobley (Will Wright), and Mobley's duplicitous wife, Mattie (Helen Craig), Bowie meets a young girl named Keechie (Cathy O'Donnell) and the two fall in love. But their impassioned affair proves short-lived when Mattie tips the cops to the gang's whereabouts in exchange for her husband's freedom. As the cops close in, one of the gang is killed, the other recaptured. The young lovers manage to escape. They're hunted down, and, determined to stay together even in death, perish in one another's arms.

Similar to the Lang film, *They Live by Night* connects with the Bonnie and Clyde saga only in terms of its period setting and its story of two young people on the lam from the law. But the connection is there. Impressively staged by first-time director Ray and movingly acted by Granger and O'Donnell (though their doomed affair is a bit oversentimentalized), *They Live by Night* has a strong sense of place (though most of it was shot in Hollywood) and still packs a punch. Shot in 1946 under the title *Thieves Like Us*, under the auspices of RKO studio chief Dory Schary, the film was shelved for two years when Howard Hughes took over as head of the studio. Retitled later and unceremoniously dumped into theaters on the bottom half of a double bill, it received very few reviews (most of which

were good) and virtually no word of mouth. To Ray and producer John Houseman's chagrin, but not their surprise, the film, like Bowie and Keechie, died a quick death. Time has taken its side, however, and today it is unanimously considered one of the classic gangster films noir of the forties.

There must be something in this type of story that appeals strongly to maverick directors. Lang and Ray were well known for repeatedly locking horns with their Hollywood paymasters, as is Robert Altman, who turned his own hand to the familiar tale in 1974 with *Thieves Like Us*, a remake of the Ray film. Shot on location in Mississippi, the film starred Altman regulars John Schuck as Chickamaw and Bert Remsen as T-Dub. Newcomers Keith Carradine and Shelly Duvall were cast as a much less glamorous and much less sentimentalized Bowie and Keechie. Tom Skerritt played Mobley and Louise Fletcher made her film debut as his wife, Mattie, the woman who turns the gang in and triggers the young lovers' fate. Unlike Anderson's novel and the first film made from it, Keechie survives at the conclusion of Altman's version. Explained Altman biographer Patrick McGilligan: "Altman [felt] that if Keechie died the ending would be too much like that of [Arthur Penn's film] *Bonnie and Clyde*. [He] felt very strongly that if you wanted to make a statement at all, it was that that kind of lady survived, that the Matties survived, that the Keechies survived. Keechie turned into Mattie. The boys got shot down, but that kind of hard, put-upon, embittered woman survived and sired a lot of us." Bowie goes to his bloody, slow-motion death nevertheless, in a hail of gunfire that clearly mimics the conclusion of *Bonnie and Clyde*.

Thieves Like Us was a box-office failure, despite many fine reviews. Altman champion Pauline Kael, for example, termed it "a serenely simple film—contained and complete. The scope is small but [the film] is a native work in the same way that *The Godfather* is; we know the genre (Depression, bank robbers, Bonnie and Clyde), and the characters are as archetypal as one's next-door neighbors."

Above, left: Farley Granger, Howard de Silva, and Jay C. Flippen in They Live by Night *(1948), another reworking of the Bonnie and Clyde tale. (Copyright © 1948 RKO)*

Right: Keith Carradine and Shelley Duvall as the Bonnie and Clyde figures, Bowie and Keechie, in Thieves Like Us, *Robert Altman's 1974 remake of* They Live by Night. *(Copyright © 1974 United Artists)*

Like Ray's film, the reputation of *Thieves Like Us* has deservedly grown over the years, and today it is considered one of Altman's best efforts—though my personal favorite of Altman's back-to-back crime films of the seventies is *The Long Goodbye* (1973), his controversial updating of the classic Raymond Chandler detective novel featuring Elliott Gould as a delightfully offbeat Philip Marlowe and the most vicious misuse of a bottle of Coca-Cola ever seen on the screen. (Coca-Cola signs and bottles crop up in *Thieves Like Us*, too, but to much less injurious effect.)

Joseph H. Lewis's cult film *Gun Crazy* (a.k.a. *Deadly Is the Female*, 1949) takes some of the blame for the criminal escapades of its Bonnie and Clyde characters off society and places it on personality. Based on a *Saturday Evening Post* tale by novelist MacKinlay Kantor, the film portrays its lovers on the run from the law— Bart Tare (John Dall) and Annie Laurie Starr (Peggy Cummins)—as victims primarily of themselves. Yet the film doesn't let society completely off the hook; in its opening scenes, it paints a disturbing picture of America's fascination with and tolerance for guns, an issue no other Bonnie and Clyde film (and few other gangster or crime films) has ever bothered to raise.

As the film begins, the juvenile Bart (Rusty Tamblyn) is seen coveting a gun in a hardware-store window, then breaking the glass and taking it. He's caught and brought before the local judge (Morris Carnovsky), who listens to character testimony from Bart's sister (Anabel Shaw), his two closest friends, and his school-teacher before passing sentence. Each describes Bart's fascination with guns as a

Peggy Cummins and John Dall flee the law in director Joseph H. Lewis's almost-a-masterpiece, Gun Crazy *(a.k.a.* Deadly Is the Female, *1949).*

youthful and harmless obsession. They give evidence that while Bart clearly enjoys handling and firing guns, he is a gentle boy who can't even bring himself to kill wild game. Bart confirms this, telling the judge that he just likes to shoot because it makes him "feel good." The ambiguity of this response is disturbing because it hints at a darker need the use of guns fills in Bart, which the boy can neither fathom nor explain. (Many adult hunters and shooters for sport admit the same thing, and they don't know why, either.) The judge is astute enough to realize this and sentences the orphaned Bart to reform school so that he'll receive the guidance and training he needs either to outgrow his obsession with guns or to learn to control it.

After reform school, Bart joins the army (where he trains others to shoot) and after his stint returns to his hometown to take a low-paying job with the Remington firearms company. During a night on the town with his two boyhood pals Clyde (Harry Lewis) and Dave (Nedrick Young), the former now a cop and the latter a newspaperman, Bart encounters Annie Laurie Starr, a sexy blond sharpshooter in a carnival sideshow, and accepts her boss's (Barry Kroeger) challenge to come onstage and test his skill against hers. Bart wins the match, joins the act, and he and Annie become lovers. Following a violent confrontation with Annie's jealous boss, Bart and Annie are fired. Out of money and down on their luck, Bart goes along with Annie's scheme to pull off a robbery or two for some quick cash "just so long as no one is killed." One robbery leads to another, however, and before long the lovers are being hunted by police in several states. They decide to pull off one final job that'll net them enough money to skip to another country, but during the robbery Annie kills two people and the manhunt for them is stepped up.

The two hide out with Bart's sister, who, fearing for her children's safety, wants them gone as soon as possible. Clyde and Dave begin to suspect the wanted couple's whereabouts and go there to ask Bart to give himself up. He refuses. Knowing that they'll have to report him, Bart flees with Annie into the mountains, where they're trapped in a swamp during a thick fog. As the law surrounds them and Clyde and Dave once more urge them to give themselves up, Annie draws her gun and says she'll shoot if anyone comes closer. As Clyde and Dave become more visible, she goes to fire, and Bart is compelled to shoot his lover—the only human being he kills in the film—to save their lives. His shot is mistaken for an attack and Bart himself is killed in a hail of police bullets.

Gun Crazy is an uneven film that veers from being a masterpiece to an average B picture and back again. Parts of it are banal and slow-moving, while others— the opening sequence featuring the young Bart, the sharpshooting contest between Annie and the adult Bart, the two major robbery sequences (both of which are given an amazing feeling of on-the-spot reality through Lewis's single-take, continuously rolling camera technique), and the final showdown in the swamp—are brilliantly executed. In terms of style and much else, Arthur Penn's *Bonnie and Clyde* owes a lot to this film.

The performances of the main leads are quite good, too—particularly Cummins, whose sexy, manipulative, and thoroughly sociopathic Annie makes *Persons in Hiding*'s Patricia Morison look like a dainty flower by comparison. It's her character that's key to the film's message, for as the judge suspects early on, the gentle, peace-loving Bart's love of guns suggests that something is missing in the boy's personality—a missing piece the judge rightly fears the boy might sooner or later find. Annie herself is that missing piece. As Bart says to her at the end: "We go together—like guns and ammunition." The film was loosely remade and updated by director Tamra Davis as *Guncrazy* (1992), starring Drew Barrymore in the Cummins role and James LeGros in the part played by John Dall.

On the lighter side (albeit not intentionally) is *Guns Don't Argue* (1957), a poverty-row exploitation film culled from episodes of the "Gangbusters" television series that ran on NBC for ten months in 1952 and was later syndicated under the title "Captured." Inspired by the long-running "Gangbusters" radio show created by Phillips Lord, the half-hour TV series dramatized historic cases from the files of the FBI. Each episode had an actor playing an FBI man narrate the story of how the Bureau successfully brought an end to the careers of various well-known public enemies of the 1930s. Producer William Faris updated the stories to the early fifties, however, so that he wouldn't have to come up with a lot of expensive period costumes and cars and could keep overall production costs down by shooting on existing locations in and around the city of Los Angeles. Faris's niggardly approach, coupled with the slipshod manner in which the episodes were put together, resulted in some amusing continuity gaffes, as in the episode where FBI men pursue Ma Barker (Jean Harvey) and her boys to Sioux Falls, but the street signs read BEVERLY BLVD and WILSHIRE.

When the TV series died, Faris stitched several episodes together and re-packaged them as feature films, the first of which, *Gangbusters*, was released in 1955 to unanimous critical scorn. The film made money, though, and was followed two years later by another hodgepodge under the title *Guns Don't Argue.** The section of *Guns Don't Argue* dealing with Bonnie and Clyde telescopes the gang's career into a few short, howlingly funny minutes. FBI agent Stewart (Jim Davis) is assigned to the case after the Barrow gang robs and kills the owner of a music store. Gang member Ray Hamilton is captured by police and sent to a prison farm. Clyde (Baynes Baron) and Bonnie (Tamar Cooper), who wears a black beret

---

*In 1960, Faris also cranked out another low-budget gangland feature called *Ma Barker's Killer Brood*, which some film historians maintain was culled from episodes of the short-lived TV series, as well. This doesn't seem to be the case, however, since the series episode dealing with Ma Barker had already been used in *Guns Don't Argue* and featured a wholly different cast, which included, among others, ex-cowboy star Lash Larue.

and is constantly puffing on a cigar (the real Bonnie once posed for a Barrow gang snapshot with these items), break Hamilton out, machine-gunning everyone in their way. "This ruthless massacre of guards and convicts alike horrified even hardened criminals," intones the narrator.

After his breakout from prison, Hamilton mysteriously disappears from the story (prompting the viewer to wonder why Bonnie and Clyde bothered springing him), and FBI agent Stewart closes in. With the help of a farmer who once aided the duo but who is now repulsed by their ruthlessness, Stewart sets up an ambush. In a scene that's strikingly similar to the conclusion of the 1967 Arthur Penn film, the farmer pulls his rattletrap truck off the road to change a tire while Stewart and his men conceal themselves in the bushes across the way. Bonnie and Clyde drive up and Clyde gets out to lend a hand. In a classic example of amateurish acting, Bonnie does a goofy, wide-eyed double take when she hears a noise coming from the bushes (unable to get enough of a bad thing, the filmmakers repeat this shot several other times throughout the film), and she whips out her machine gun as Stewart and his men open fire. Clyde also goes for his gun, but the duo doesn't stand a chance. As FBI bullets rain the car (causing not a scratch), Clyde falls lifelessly to the road, and Bonnie slumps over dead in the car window, her ever-present cigar dangling and then falling from her lips.

Infinitely better-made and even more of a stage-setter for the groundbreaking Penn film was American-International's *The Bonnie Parker Story* (1958), featuring platinum blond TV starlet Dorothy Provine in the title role. (In keeping with Peggy Cummins's deadly female with the blond tresses in *Gun Crazy* and *The Bonnie Parker Story*'s Provine, Arthur Penn turned his Bonnie [Faye Dunaway] into a blonde, as well; Dunaway is actually a brunette, as was Bonnie Parker.)

Set in the proper Depression-era period, *The Bonnie Parker Story* generally plays it straight with the facts of the case, although for some reason all of the characters' names are changed except for Bonnie herself. Clyde Barrow is named Guy Darrow in the film; his brother Buck is renamed Chuck; and so on.

An innocent Texas teenager as the film begins, Bonnie marries hometown boy Duke Jefferson (Richard Bakalyan), not realizing that Duke makes his money robbing banks. Her dreams of marital bliss are cut short when Duke is arrested and imprisoned for life. The frustrated and embittered young woman takes to supporting herself as a waitress in a local greasy spoon, where she's picked up by a young drifter named Guy Darrow (Jack Hogan). Guy rescues her from her boring, poverty-stricken existence by introducing her to a life of crime that she finds increasingly attractive. She joins Darrow's gang, which is led by his brother Chuck (Joseph Turkel), and becomes so skilled at planning and executing bank jobs and holding her own with a tommy gun that when Chuck is killed, she assumes leadership of the gang without protest from her impotent and none-too-bright paramour.

More reminiscent of *Gun Crazy*'s Peggy Cummins than *Bonnie and Clyde*'s Dunaway, Provine's cigar-smoking, pistol-packing Bonnie is clearly the deadlier of the male/female duo—an attractive blond package on the outside but a hardened killer beneath. She pays the price, however, when the Texas Rangers set a trap for her and Guy and blow them and their car to smithereens at the film's fiery conclusion.

The Bonnie Parker Story is an exciting, fast-paced little production with a nice hard edge. Released on a double bill with AIP's even better *Machine-Gun Kelly,* the film made money and even got some good reviews. *Variety,* for example, called it "obviously an exploitation item, but capably constructed and intelligently carried out."

Arthur Penn's *Bonnie and Clyde* (1967) remains the most famous and influential film about the exploits of the notorious couple—and also the most controversial. Youthful audiences of the anarchic antiestablishment sixties loved it and turned it into a major box-office hit that tore down the barriers against graphic onscreen violence.

Critics were of two minds about the film. Many embraced it immediately as a daring and original work, despite its well-worn topic; others slammed it as a senseless bloodbath aimed at the yahoo trade. Still others condemned, *then* embraced it: *Newsweek* critic Joseph Morgenstern at first gave it a scathing review, calling it a decidedly ugly affair in which "some of the most gruesome carnage since Verdun is accompanied by some of the most gleeful off-screen fiddling since the Grand Old Opry. The effect is ear-catching, to say the least. For those who find killing less than hilarious, the effect is also stomach-turning." A week later, he reviewed the film a second time and completely recanted his earlier opinion, calling his initial review "grossly unfair and regrettably inaccurate." Even more surprisingly, when three-decade *New York Times* film critic Bosley Crowther, who had also written a review excoriating the film, failed to make a similar turnabout, he lost his job as the paper's first-string film critic to Vincent Canby for being out of touch with contemporary tastes. The film went on to be nominated for Oscars in all the major categories, a record as yet unbeaten by any other gangster film, including the *Godfather* series. (The only winners, though, were Estelle Parsons in the Best Supporting Actress category for her role as Blanche Barrow and Burnett Guffey for Cinematography.)

The script for *Bonnie and Clyde* had been making the Hollywood rounds for years. Even Arthur Penn had seen and passed on it at one time. Novice screenwriters David Newman and Robert Benton had turned their frustrated sights overseas and tried to interest director Jean-Luc Godard, whose anarchic French gangster film about two young criminals in love and on the run, *A Bout de Souffle*, had strongly

Above: *Charles Bronson as Machine Gun Kelly (1958). With Susan Cabot. (Copyright ©️ 1958 American International Pictures)*

Left: *It's only when violence becomes intimate that it turns brutal and ugly. From* Bonnie and Clyde *(1967). (Copyright ©️ 1967 Warner Bros.)*

influenced the avant-garde style of the writers' script. François Truffaut, who had given Godard the idea for *A Bout de Souffle*, was approached, as well. Both directors were interested, but other commitments intervened and the script fell once more into limbo. It finally crossed the desk of Warren Beatty, then a successful young actor determined to become an equally successful producer, who bought it for his first such project. He again showed it to Penn (with whom the actor had worked in an earlier avant-garde gangster film, *Mickey One* [1965]), and this time Penn agreed to direct.

Primarily a director of Broadway plays and live TV drama, the East Coast–based Penn might have seemed an odd choice for such a violent, action-filled tale of rural romance and robbery; but, in fact, his first Hollywood film, *The Left-Handed Gun* (1958), bears striking similarities to the later film in both theme and style. Both are about historically famous young guns on the run (Billy the Kid in the earlier film) who suffer from neurotic feelings of inadequacy that motivate their acts of violence and lead them into a life of outlawry, coupled with a view of themselves that is pure romanticized fantasy—a fantasy that leads ultimately to their deaths. Both films contain several remarkably similar scenes, as well as the use of slow motion to heighten the drama and horror of some violent set pieces. (The technique of slow-motion violence was by no means a Penn innovation. John Ford had employed it for a brief action scene in *Fort Apache* [1948], and Akira Kurosawa had used it several times in his masterpiece *The Seven Samurai* [1954]. After *Bonnie and Clyde*, however, it became an action-movie staple.)

Bonnie and Clyde has often been accused of stretching the historical truth by transforming the deadly duo into romantic and heroic figures. But this isn't totally the case. For the most part, the film is accurate in its recounting of the case, and authentic-looking, as well; the ambush in the woods that results in Buck Barrow's (Gene Hackman) capture and death looks remarkably like existing crime-scene photos of the actual event. It is true that the real Bonnie and Clyde were far from glamorous. Rather drab in appearance, they looked nothing at all like movie stars Beatty and Faye Dunaway. Yet this is exactly how they viewed *themselves*—not as movie stars, perhaps, but as media stars most certainly, who always kept the family Kodak close by to snap off pictures of themselves with their guns. They sent the photos to the newspapers to help feed their growing legend.

Bonnie and Clyde does romanticize the exploits of the notorious couple—because the film is told from their own self-deluded perspective. Its approach to graphic violence is a subtle illustration of this: It is only when the violence comes close to the pair, or reaches into the ranks of the Barrow gang, that it turns gruesomely ugly and painful. The youthful, self-absorbed couple see everything, even death, as relating only to them. A cop blown away at a distance is merely a bloodless doll. But when one of *them* takes a bullet, reality comes crashing in and things become personal. The film makes this point repeatedly: When Bonnie visits her mother for the last time, it takes on a nostalgic hue that reflects her fantasized view of the family get-together perfectly—and Clyde's, too, for their fantasies are inseparable. They behave like distant relatives who have just dropped by for a visit, not like desperate criminals being hunted by the law. Says Clyde to Bonnie's mother, "Bonnie and I were just talking the other day, Mother Parker, about how she wants to settle down and live no more than three miles from her precious mother." Mama's grasp on reality is a lot stronger: "I don't know, Clyde Barrow. She lives three miles from me, and she won't live very long." Reacting as if they'd been dowsed with ice water—particularly Bonnie, whose face pales as if she'd just glimpsed her own ghost—the two quickly escape back to their world of fantasy, where, self-deluded, self-absorbed, and self-destructive to the end, they meet their inevitable doom. Typically, Bonnie romanticizes even that doom—significantly the most graphic scene in the film, as their bodies are grotesquely shot to pieces in an orgy of gunfire—in the poem "The Ballad of Bonnie and Clyde" that she sends to the newspapers to cement their legend.

Director Sam Peckinpah carried *Bonnie and Clyde*'s technique of stylized, slow-motion violence to new heights (or depths, some have argued) in his powerful Western *The Wild Bunch,* and he subsequently took a crack at an outright Bonnie and Clyde–type story himself in *The Getaway* (1972), based on the novel by Jim Thompson.

Steve McQueen stars in *The Getaway* as convicted bank robber Doc McCoy, who is serving a ten-year stretch in a Texas prison. After the parole board denies Doc's request for an early release, he accepts an offer from crooked board member Jack Benyon (Ben Johnson) to rob an oil-company payroll at a small-town Texas bank in exchange for his freedom. He sends his wife, Carol (Ali MacGraw), to finalize the deal. To accomplish this, Carol must sleep with the corrupt parole official.

As soon as Doc is released, he and Carol (his gun moll and getaway driver) begin planning the heist with Benyon's henchmen, Rudy (Al Lettieri) and Frank (Bo Hopkins), unaware that Benyon and Rudy are planning a double cross and plan to kill Doc and keep the money for themselves after the robbery. During the heist, Frank is killed. Doc smells a rat and shoots Rudy first, while Carol kills Benyon. The outlaw couple flee with the loot with Rudy, who has survived his wounds, Benyon's thugs and the cops hot on their trail. Several wild car chases, a tense sequence involving a garbage truck, and much gunplay ensue as Doc and Carol struggle to stay alive while heading for El Paso and the Mexican border. Unlike other Bonnie and Clyde–inspired films (and Thompson's novel, which ends quite differently), the young lovers on the run kill and/or successfully outwit their pursuers and make it to freedom with the money.

The Getaway is an exciting film filled with many suspenseful and powerfully edited action sequences, Peckinpah-style. Its major flaw is the casting of MacGraw as a gun moll; Peckinpah defended her performance, but MacGraw's svelte "Bloomingdale's Bonnie," with her finishing-school accent, turns the film into a joke.

The legend of Bonnie and Clyde refuses to die. In an amusing and effective gender bending of the infamous saga, Clyde was briefly replaced by two Bonnies in the box-office hit *Thelma & Louise* (1991). But a year later, the notorious outlaw couple were back together again in the Fox Network telefilm *Bonnie and Clyde: The True Story*, a tepid recounting of the saga aimed at the "Beverly Hills 90210" crowd, which starred teen heartthrobs Dana Ashbrook as Clyde and Tracy Needham as yet another blond Bonnie. The title notwithstanding, writer-director Gary Hoffman's take on the overly familiar tale is even less faithful to the historical record than critics accused Penn's film of being. The ending is straight out of the Penn film—as the doomed lovers, their eyes filled with the horrific realization that "this is it," reach longingly for one another in slow motion. The graphic bloodbath is eliminated, however. Hoffman dissolves to a shot of the bullet-riddled car on tour, being picked at by souvenir hunters.

DILLINGER

Variously referred to by the public as "Gentleman Johnny" and "America's Robin Hood," John Dillinger became one of the immortals in the history of American gangsterism as the result of a crime spree that lasted just a little more than one year. His short-lived but eventful criminal career consisted of ten bank robberies, one daring prison break, several shoot-outs with the FBI and other lawmen, and one car hijacking across state lines (his only federal crime). Though he ran with gun-happy crazies like Baby Face Nelson, Dillinger was not especially violent himself. He never killed anyone during any of his notorious escapades—although he was once charged with the killing of a patrolman during an Indiana bank raid, a charge he staunchly denied and that was never proven. Why, then, did the FBI consider him to be the most dangerous criminal in America? The answer has a lot to do with image—Dillinger's and that of the FBI, as well.

Born in 1902, Dillinger grew up in a strict, religious family, against which he rebelled early on. By all accounts a wild kid, he first brushed with the law at age seventeen when he found himself on the receiving end of a speeding ticket. He later joined the navy to escape his strict father and repressive home life, but he found the rigorous discipline of military life equally confining, and deserted in 1923 at age twenty-one. That same year, he committed his first serious crime, the robbery of an Indiana grocery store. He was arrested—and, even though it was his first offense, had the book thrown at him, receiving a ten-to-twenty-year stretch.

The state's governor later termed the sentence "[an] obvious injustice [that] had much to do with the bitterness Dillinger developed." Paroled in 1933, Dillinger was reported to have said, "They stole nine years of my life. Now, I'm going to do some stealing of my own." And that he did—independently at first and later with a gang.

A dapper dresser and ladies' man who was unfailingly courteous to his victims, Dillinger had a specific method for stealing. He cased the banks he targeted meticulously and carefully considered all security measures and means of escape so as to ensure a minimum of gunplay. Reportedly, he never stole from any depositors or bystanders who happened to be on hand during his robberies, only from the banks themselves. This led to the public's mythologizing him as an American version of Robin Hood, who robbed only from the rich (the hated banks), although he failed to carry this image so far as to give any of his ill-gotten gains to the poor.

After his capture, his escape from jail before his trial—using a toy gun whittled from wood and painted with black shoe polish—made him an object of public celebration. Dillinger then escaped in a stolen car across state lines—the federal crime that finally pitted him against the FBI. The Bureau's image suffered miserably, however, when Hoover's agents repeatedly failed to capture the "gentleman bandit" despite seemingly endless opportunities and several very close calls. Its image plummeted even more when, during one attempted capture of the notorious public enemy, FBI agents shot and killed several innocent bystanders while still failing to grab Dillinger. The angry public vilified Hoover's Bureau and the special agent assigned to the job, Melvin Purvis, but not its "darling Johnny," whom the humiliated Hoover declared a "yellow rat" and directed Purvis and his men to shoot on sight.

The opportunity to do so fell into Purvis's lap when Anna Sage, an illegal alien facing deportation to her native Romania, notified the Bureau that Dillinger was staying at her Chicago brothel and made a deal to set a trap for the gangster in exchange for her freedom. She told Purvis she would be accompanying Dillinger and his girlfriend to a movie; since Dillinger had recently undergone plastic surgery, she would wear an orange dress to help the agents identify the trio. Purvis and his men waited for them to come out of the theater. As soon as Purvis spotted Sage in her orange dress (which looked a bit red under the marquee lights, giving rise to her erroneous nickname, the "Lady in Red"), he lighted a cigar, signaling his fellow agents, and they quickly drew their guns. Purvis shouted, "Stick 'em up, Johnny!" Dillinger allegedly drew his own gun and fled into an alley beside the theater, where Purvis and his agents followed Hoover's instructions to the letter by shooting the gangster dead on the spot. The year was 1934.

Several Hollywood studios announced plans for a movie about Dillinger before the dead gangster's body was even cold. But movie morals czar Will H. Hays quickly put the kibosh on this with his famous industry directive (see Chapter 4) and it wasn't until eleven years later that such a film was finally made. Raoul Walsh's *High Sierra* (1941) incorporated elements of the gangster's life and legend — his folk-hero status, his supposed sex appeal, his skill as a master bank robber, his unwarranted reputation among lawmen as a "mad dog" killer — into the character of Roy Earle (Humphrey Bogart). But there was no outright biography until *Dillinger* (1945), featuring newcomer Lawrence Tierney in the title role. In fact, the film is a series of overworked gangster-movie clichés strung together into a simpleminded narrative whose resemblance to the facts of the case is remote to say the least. But it was an attempt — however creatively — to commit the Dillinger story to celluloid.

The film suggests that Dillinger's criminal career stemmed entirely from his fixation on women, who drove him to commit his acts of lawlessness in order to keep them in style. As the film begins, he commits his first crime for just this purpose: the robbery of a grocery store for some cash to buy another round of drinks for an admiring bimbo he's picked up. The act lands him in the slammer, where he befriends a criminal mastermind named Specs Green (Edmund Lowe) and several other lifers, whom he agrees to break out of jail as soon as he's released.

Elements of Dillinger's life and legend found their way into the character of "Mad Dog" Earle (Humphrey Bogart) in High Sierra *(1941). With Ida Lupino. (Copyright © 1941 Warner Bros.)*

Once paroled, Dillinger finances the breakout by robbing a movie theater whose pretty cashier (Anne Jeffreys) he takes up with and who urges him later to commit even bolder criminal acts in order to keep her well dressed and comfortable. Dillinger makes good on his word to Specs, and, with Specs as its leader, the gang successfully pulls off a series of bank jobs and is quickly riding high. Dillinger and Specs soon clash due to Dillinger's propensity for violence ("You're a little too free with the gun, John," Specs admonishes him) and his coveting of Specs's position. Specs sets him up to get him out of the way, but Dillinger evades capture, kill Specs in reprisal, and assumes leadership of the gang. The hot-tempered, gun-happy Dillinger proves to be no criminal mastermind, however, and the gang is soon out of money and on the run. Eventually, it breaks up altogether, and Dillinger goes it alone with his expensive babe in tow. As the law closes in, he and his girl are forced to go into hiding. With money running low and cabin fever running high, his girl finally decides she's had enough and suggests a night out at the movies. To disguise himself, he puts on a pair of sunglasses that make him look like Albert Dekker's mad scientist in *Dr. Cyclops,* and she puts on her red dress so that the cops will have no trouble spotting them. In one of the film's few concessions to historical fact, the gangster is summarily shot down while fleeing into an alley next to the theater after the show. It's hard to believe that the Academy of Motion Picture Arts and Sciences felt Philip Yordan's mishmash of a screenplay deserving of an Oscar nomination, but it did.

Whereas most films inspired by the Bonnie and Clyde legend have tended to portray the vicious couple as better than they actually were, *Dillinger* takes the opposite approach, manufacturing an image of the notorious gangster that's much worse than the truth. The film portrays Dillinger as a dull-brained, dead-eyed, uncharismatic cutthroat given to snatching money from the hands of frightened depositors even after emptying the bank's till, and one who delights in repeated acts of sadism and murder. Apparently, the effect of Will H. Hays's 1934 dictum was still being felt—and would continue to be, as most Dillinger films that followed have tended to cast the legendary folk-hero outlaw in a similar light.

In 1965's redundantly titled *Young Dillinger* (dead at thirty-one, Dillinger scarcely lived long enough to be anything but), the future public enemy number one (Nick Adams) was again driven to a life of crime because of a girl. His teenage sweetheart, Elaine (Mary Ann Mobley), wants him to marry her, but the dirt-poor Dillinger says he can't even afford a marriage license, much less support her. So she pushes him into robbing the safe in her wealthy father's warehouse. He's caught and gets a five-to-twenty-year sentence that embitters him against the world forever after.

While in prison, he makes friends with career criminals Pretty Boy Floyd

Above, left: *Dillinger*
(Nick Adams) is driven to
a life of crime because of a
girl (Mary Ann Mobley)
in Young Dillinger
(1965). (Copyright ©
1965 Allied Artists)

Right: *John Milius's*
Dillinger (1973) is
probably Hollywood's most
accurate portrayal of the
legendary gangster's life and
times. Warren Oates
(center) even looks like
"Gentleman John."
(Copyright © 1973
American International
Pictures)

(Robert Conrad), Baby Face Nelson (John Ashley), and Homer Van Meter (Dan Terranova) and promises to spring them when he gets out. With Elaine's help, he makes a successful break while being transferred to an honor farm and quickly makes good on his bargain. With Elaine along, Dillinger and his fellow escapees pull off several small-time robberies, then fall in with a Specs Green–type criminal mastermind named Professor Harrington (Victor Buono) to commit a daring series of bank jobs. Hunted relentlessly by the law, the gang retreats to a mountain cabin in what looks to be California's scenic Lake Tahoe area and is surrounded. Elaine takes a bullet, but her lover gets away at the end of the film to meet his fate some other day.

Macho director John Milius's *Dillinger* (1973) is probably the closest Hollywood has yet come to painting an accurate picture of the legendary gangster's life and times. The film has an authentic period feel, and for once the actor chosen to play Dillinger (Warren Oates) even looked like him. Milius's Peckinpah-style action film plays with some of the facts of the case as well, but it probes much deeper into the reality of the gangster's legend—and Dillinger's preoccupation with sustaining that legend—than any other Dillinger film has ever done. "Milius shows the effort, the narcissism, that goes into making a legend," wrote film historians Michael Pye and Linda Mayles of the movie. "Dillinger and his girl, the half-Indian Billie Frechette [Michelle Phillips], debate crossing the Mexican border to safety; but they stay in America, knowing that flight would break the legend. Before going out to rob, they ask each other anxiously: 'How do I look?' They are obsessed with public image and newspaper response, but Dillinger wants more. In the bank robbery that opens the film, he announces to the camera that witnessing a Dillinger heist guarantees 'stories to tell your grandchildren.' "

For the first time in a Dillinger film, the symbiotic relationship between Dillinger and his FBI hunters—in the form of agent Melvin Purvis (Ben

Ben Johnson (center) as FBI legend Melvin Purvis, the man who got Dillinger. From Dillinger *(1973). (Copyright © 1973 American International Pictures)*

Johnson)*—and the FBI's need to destroy Dillinger to bolster its own image is also substantively explored. "Hunter and hunted are interdependent," Pyle and Mayles wrote:

> Purvis is as much a mythomaniac as Dillinger himself: the two define each other and give each other stature. [Purvis] clings to rituals that parallel the narcissim of Dillinger; he has a uniform, a formal dressing before each robbery in a bulletproof vest, gloves, and an automatic pistol. He has a habit of smoking a cigar, ritually, after rubbing out some gangster. The circularity is completed [when an end title] tells us that Melvin Purvis shot himself in 1961 with the gun he used to kill Dillinger.

*Capitalizing on the success of the Milius film, its distributors, American-International Pictures, later made two fast-moving and entertaining gangster films centering on Purvis for the ABC Network. The first of them, *Melvin Purvis, G-Man* (1974), restaged a number of scenes involving Purvis and Machine Gun Kelly (Harris Yulin) drawn from the Milius film. It was cowritten by Milius and William F. Nolan. Dale Robertson played the cigar-smoking, mythmaking Purvis. *The Kansas City Massacre*, also starring Robertson as Purvis, followed on the network a year later and brought back the character of Dillinger (William Jordan), although Dillinger does not actually participate in the bloody shoot-out of the title, as he didn't in real life. The network and AIP wanted to turn the Purvis saga into a weekly series reminiscent of "The Untouchables." The telefilms proved too reminiscent of the controversial older series, however, when various groups began protesting the extreme violence (by TV standards) in them. Since the ratings of the two films were not impressive enough to counter the protests, the network scrapped the series idea. Both films were excitingly directed by Dan Curtis, who went on to "bigger" things with the epic-scale but ponderous miniseries *The Winds of War* and *War and Remembrance*, made for the same network.

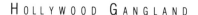
The 1991 made-for-TV movie *Dillinger* returned to form by distorting the truth of the story and manufacturing yet another image for the legendary gangster: Dillinger as matinee idol, played blandly by TV heartthrob Mark Harmon, who, like Tierney and Adams, looks nothing at all like the real Dillinger. (The film ignores Warren Oates's Dillinger altogether, paying homage to the 1945 Tierney film instead by giving the actor a cameo.) In keeping with this eight-by-ten glossy image of Dillinger, the filmmakers are compelled to give him a more spectacular demise than usual. Sure it's okay for a newcomer like Tierney and a roughneck like Oates to be gunned down like a dog in some alley, but Mark Harmon . . . ? So this time around, the legendary bank robber is gunned down *Lethal Weapon*–style in a spectacular shoot-out that takes to the streets and involves not only Purvis (Will Patton) and his handful of FBI agents but seemingly the entire police force of Chicago.

The aforementioned *Guns Don't Argue*, the 1957 feature culled from episodes of the short-lived TV series "Gangbusters," offered a *Reader's Digest* version of the Dillinger story similar to its treatment of the Bonnie and Clyde saga. Updated to the fifties also, the Dillinger story, the longest segment in the film, mixes fact with large doses of fiction by having the legendary gangster pull bank jobs with not only Baby Face Nelson and Homer Van Meter but Ma Barker and her boys, as well. After Ma's taken, Dillinger goes it alone, and the film explores most of the well-known high points of his career: his prison break with the toy gun, the Kansas City Massacre, his efforts to elude capture with plastic surgery, and so on. As in the Tierney film, he's set up not by Anna Sage but by his own girlfriend, who alerts the FBI with her red dress and gets him shot down outside a Chicago theater. B-movie villain Myron Healy plays the notoriously personable gangster with a notable lack of charm.

The legendary bank robber made a much briefer appearance in Mervyn LeRoy's love letter to Hoover and his Bureau, *The FBI Story* (1959), based on the bestseller by Don Whitehead. Written with Hoover's blessing and cooperation, Whitehead's image-polishing book, like Hoover's similar *Persons in Hiding* before it,

Below, left: Dillinger (Myron Healy) tries to evade capture by undergoing plastic surgery and having his fingerprints "removed" in Guns Don't Argue *(1957). (Copyright © Visual Drama Inc.)*

Right: Dillinger (Leo Gordon) strives to put a lid on his psychotic partner's (Mickey Rooney) brutal excesses in Baby Face Nelson *(1957). (Copyright © 1957 United Artists)*

recounted in episodic style the Bureau's history and many adventures in running America's most infamous gangsters, mass killers, and Commie subversives to ground. With the aid of "Dragnet" writer Richard Breen, LeRoy created a fictional agent, Chip Hardesty (James Stewart), through whose eyes we see these events spanning many years unfold. The film alternates numerous real-life FBI cases the fictional Hardesty gets involved in with an insipid domestic drama about the trials and tribulations of Hardesty and his long-suffering wife (Vera Miles) and family over the years, which allows Stewart to give the hokiest performance of his career. The Dillinger story is given fairly short shrift in the 149-minute film. It only covers the FBI's entrapment of the gangster with the help of "Lady in Red" Anna Sage and his being gunned down outside the Biograph Theater.

Surprisingly, LeRoy, the director of the groundbreaking and gritty *Little Caesar*, considered this ponderous string of clichés to be one of his best films. Not surprisingly, Hoover loved it, too. He even allowed LeRoy to film him in his office for a brief prologue.

Don Siegel's B-movie classic *Baby Face Nelson* (1957) gives Dillinger much more screen time, although the film is more concerned, of course, with Nelson's own role within and without the Dillinger mob. Though a bit beefy to play Dillinger, the mustachioed Leo Gordon gives a good account of himself in the part, even bringing some humor to it as he strives to put a lid on the brutal excesses of his diminutive, psychotic partner (Mickey Rooney). In the film, it is Dillinger who gives Nelson his legendary nickname.

When Dillinger is killed in Chicago, Nelson assumes leadership of the gang, and, like Dillinger before him, enlists the aid of a corrupt doctor (Sir Cedric Hardwicke) to alter his features—in this case his fingerprints, since Nelson is determined to keep his trademark baby face. The alcoholic sawbones performs the operation with success, then makes a drunken move on Nelson's wife (Carolyn Jones). In reprisal, the vicious Nelson rows the besotted doc out onto a lake, kills him, and and dumps him into the water. Producer Al Zimbalist apparently liked this scene, for he lifted it virtually in its entirety in his later *Young Dillinger* (1965). In that film, however, it is Dillinger who commits the vengeful deed: After performing plastic surgery on Dillinger, the boozy doctor (John Hoyt) makes the fatal mistake of trying to rape the gangster's wife. In response, the recuperating Dillinger straps the offending medical man into a wheelchair and shoves him into a nearby lake to drown.

The 1979 *The Lady in Red* cast its spotlight not on Dillinger (Robert Conrad), although he appears quite frequently throughout the film, but on the fortunes and misfortunes of the legendary woman (Pamela Sue Martin) who set him up for his fatal fall. John Sayles's screenplay combines the character of Anna Sage with composites of Dillinger's various molls and girlfriends. Other than that, the film offers a realistic view of the gangster's life and times, and, befitting a Roger Corman–produced film, contains enough gunplay to satisfy action movie fans of every age.

The essence of film noir. Jacques Tourneur's Out of the
Past *(1947) with Robert Mitchum and Jane Greer.*
(Copyright © 1947 RKO)

CHAPTER 6

ORGANIZED

CRIMES

When Americans returned from World War II, they found that the values they had been fighting for abroad had suddenly become outmoded at home. The Axis powers had been defeated, but America's underworld figures had not. They had flourished.

While the United States was preoccupied with fighting the enemy overseas, its enemy within, the underworld, had made a strong bid to reclaim some of the ground it had lost in the mob shake-ups by Thomas E. Dewey and others during the late thirties. And America's mobsters had been quite successful. Their power and influence once more were stretched across the country. Various trade unions were now dominated by them, businesses controlled by them, and state and local governments severely compromised or totally corrupted by them.

Countless numbers of vets returned home to find their old jobs or businesses taken over — and they were without the right skills (explosives experts and riflemen need not apply) to replace them. Disillusioned and cynical, they were no longer willing to take up another cause — except that of their own survival. As Humphrey Bogart's returning vet Frank McCloud says to Edward G. Robinson's Lucky Luciano–like gangster Johnny Rocco in John Huston's *Key Largo* (1948), "One more Rocco more or less ain't worth dyin' for." But like so many cynical nonheroes (as opposed to antiheroes) of forties crime and gangster films, McCloud really

*Edward G. Robinson's
Lucky Luciano—modeled
gangster Johnny Rocco in
John Huston's* Key
Largo *(1946).
(Copyright © 1946
Warner Bros.)*

does care whether the Roccos of the world take over or not and he eventually does fight back to regain his lost ideals by killing the gangster.

Some returning vets took advantage of the GI Bill to change their lot in life and move ahead. Others sought opportunities in crime (where explosives experts and riflemen could apply) to achieve the same goals.

With this as a backdrop, it's no wonder that the gangster or crime film, which had dominated movie screens in the thirties but had fallen out of favor with audiences during the patriotic fervor accompanying the war years, made a strong comeback once the war was over.

FILMS NOIR

By the mid-1940s, the romantic gangster melodramas of the Roaring Twenties and the socially conscious "straight from the-headlines" gangster films of the 1930s had been replaced by a new style of gangster film inspired by pulp fiction and the hard-boiled detective novels of Dashiell Hammett, Raymond Chandler, and James M. Cain. The silent-era gangster regenerated by the love of a good woman and the brutal antiheroes and criminal outsiders of the 1930s who always got what they deserved in the end had given way to a new type of gangster-movie protagonist — the disillusioned nonhero who finds himself walking a tightrope through a dark world of greed, cynicism, and corruption, a world of powerful criminals, duplicitous dames, shadowy corners, and rain-slicked mean streets, which threaten to ensnare and destroy him at every turn. Sometimes, he is destroyed. Most of the time, however, he manages to crawl upward toward the light and defeat the dark forces that imperil him morally — even if it means sacrificing his own life.

In most such films, the nonhero was not a gangster himself. He was a shady private eye, disillusioned cop, or some other morally ambivalent and potentially corruptible type who mixes with the world of gangsters and criminals by accident or by profession. This was not always true, of course; the 1947 *The Gangster* makes Barry Sullivan's title character the protagonist, his character and situation basically conforming to the above description. For the most part, however, the screen gangsters and criminals of the 1940s assumed a supporting role, but a very important one, nonetheless: that of Mephistopheles to the nonhero's Faust.

At the time, this new style of gangster or crime film didn't have a name. Most filmmakers, in fact, didn't even recognize that it was a new style — a style that would soon creep into other types of films as well (the Western, the war film) and would finally be viewed by critics a decade later as not just a style but a distinct genre with its own hallmarks and conventions. It was the French who gave the genre its indelible name: film noir.

If there is a definitive noir gangster film, it may well be the 1947 *Out of the Past*. It not only possesses every classic ingredient of the genre but cast many of those ingredients in stone. For example, the sexy, duplicitous dame was already a fixture in *noir* gangster and crime films before *Out of the Past* came along. But none of them — not even *The Maltese Falcon*'s Brigid O'Shaughnessy (Mary Astor) — was a match for Jane Greer's ethereally beautiful deadly manipulator. A large portion of the film's plot also is told in flashback, another classic film noir device that *Out of the Past* employs uncommonly well.

As was typical, the hero is not a gangster. He's a "money doesn't smell" private eye, Jeff Markham (Robert Mitchum), who hires himself out to a gangster, gambling kingpin Whit Sterling (Kirk Douglas), and finds himself ensnared in a black world of double-dealing and murder that threatens his moral and physical existence.

To escape his shady past, Markham adopts an alias, Jeff Bailey, and sets himself up running a garage in a sleepy northern California town, where he falls for a local girl, Ann Miller (Virginia Huston), who knows nothing about him but whose parents suspect there is something a bit too worldly-wise about the man. His past catches up with him as the film begins when one of Sterling's henchmen, Joe Stefanos (Paul Valentine), locates him and says Sterling wants to set up a meeting for old time's sake. Jeff agrees and on a date with Ann that night, he tells her he has to go away for a while. She demands an explanation and the film flashes back as he confesses about himself.

Three years earlier in New York, Sterling had hired Jeff to find the gangster's mistress, who had disappeared with forty thousand dollars of the gangster's money after pumping him with several bullets. Jeff locates the attractive woman, Kathy Moffat (Jane Greer), in Mexico and falls for her when she explains she shot Sterling in order to get away from him but denies having stolen the money. Rather than turn Kathy over to the vindictive gangster, Jeff disappears with her to California. But they're found by Jeff's money-hungry partner (Steve Brodie), who demands a share of the loot Kathy allegedly stole in exchange for his silence. Kathy kills him and Jeff dutifully buries the man's body. Later, he discovers Kathy's bank statement, which shows a deposit of forty thousand dollars, and, realizing he's been had and is now an accomplice to murder, dumps her and heads alone to Lake Tahoe to rebuild his life under an alias.

Back in the present, Ann tells Jeff she still loves him no matter what he's done, still has faith in him, and wants to marry him as soon as his dealings with Sterling are over.

Jeff meets with Sterling and finds that Kathy, having long since run out of the money she stole, has rejoined the gangster, as well. He also finds that his longing for the woman has not cooled over the years. Playing on his feelings for her and his guilt, Kathy explains that she returned to Sterling because she had nowhere else to go. She convinces Jeff she still loves him and always will, and they take up their love affair where it left off, determined this time to get away from Sterling once and for all.

Feeling that Jeff owes him one to settle things, Sterling persuades him to put the squeeze to a crooked accountant (Ken Niles) who saved the gangster a bundle on a tax case and now wants $100,000 of it to keep quiet. When the accountant is murdered, Jeff realizes he's been set up for a frame—a frame that is soon compounded when the conniving Kathy murders Sterling and threatens to pin the rap on Jeff unless he helps her cover her tracks and get away. Filled with self-contempt because he has allowed himself to be used by her again, but unable to spurn her (a dilemma James M. Cain dubbed "the love rack"), Jeff does what she says and they drive straight into a police roadblock. Realizing he's double-crossed her, Kathy shoots him and they die together when she, too, is killed as the police open fire at their onrushing car.

Sublimely directed by Jacques Tourneur, one of the cinema's most under-appreciated stylists, and crackling with cynicism and witty non sequiturs, this moody masterpiece of what one film historian has labeled "the annihilating melodrama" influenced countless other *noir* gangster and crime films of the late 1940s and early 1950s, and continues to influence the genre to this day. For example, Lawrence Kasdan's steamy *Body Heat* (1981), featuring Kathleen Turner as a more explicitly carnal version of Kathy, is an outright homage to *Out of the Past*. And Taylor

Hackford's big budget *Against All Odds* (1984) is not only an homage to Tourneur's film but an outright remake of it. It's even got Jane Greer in a cameo, playing the mother of the character (Rachel Ward) she played in the vastly superior first version.

Robert Siodmak's *The Killers* (1946) is another quintessential *noir* gangster film incorporating all the classic ingredients. The film is based on a short story written by Ernest Hemingway during the closing years of the Roaring Twenties. The action of Hemingway's barely four-thousand-word tale is mostly confined to a lunchroom in some unnamed city (probably Chicago) and is seen through the eyes of Hemingway's fictional alter ego, Nick Adams, who stops into the place late one afternoon for a bite to eat. As night falls, two gangsters, Max and Al, enter the lunchroom. They pull up at the counter for some eats and start asking questions about a prizefighter named Ole Anderson (nicknamed the "Swede") whom they're trying to locate. As the story, told in Hemingway's trademark terse dialogue, unfolds, Nick realizes the two are hit men who have come to kill the Swede for some never-explained past transgression with the mob. The targeted Swede is living in a nearby flophouse. As the killers leave, Nick goes to warn the Swede and finds the man lying in bed, resigned to his fate and waiting for the killers to catch up with him. "I'm through with all that runnin'," the Swede tells Nick. "I got in wrong. There ain't anything to do." Upset by what he's heard and seen,

Insurance investigator Edmond O'Brien probes duplicitous dame Ava Gardner about her boyfriend's gangland murder in The Killers *(1946). (Copyright © Universal Pictures)*

Nick goes back to the lunchroom and announces his intentions to George, the owner, to "get out of this town. I can't stand to think about him waiting in the room and knowing he's going to get it. It's too damn awful." Reflecting the Swede's own sense of fatalism, George tells Nick, "Well, you better not think about it."

Hemingway's story was perfect film noir material, except that it was much too short to sustain a feature-length film. Producer Mark Hellinger challenged screenwriters Anthony Veiller and John Huston (the latter actually wrote most of the script but didn't take a screen credit because he was under contract to another studio) with the task of fleshing the tale out without compromising its style and basic story line. They accomplished this ingeniously by using Hemingway's story as a prologue, then bringing in a new character, an insurance investigator named Riordan (Edmond O'Brien), to delve into the why of it all and bring the contract killers (Charles McGraw and William Conrad) and their sponsors and coconspirators to justice. The character of Nick Adams (Phil Brown) was retained in the film but reduced to minor status. It is Riordan who becomes the film's protagonist, the prototypical noir hero who imperils himself by descending into a world of darkness in order to shed some light, in this case literally as well as figuratively.

Veiller and Huston also added the by-now-requisite film noir character of the sexy, duplicitous dame (Ava Gardner) to their script. It is she who gets the dumb but honest prizefighter (Burt Lancaster, in his film debut) "in wrong" with gangsters and contributes to the double cross that leads the infatuated Swede to his fate. Like most classic films noir, much of *The Killers* unfolds in flashback.

A well-known newspaper columnist and crime reporter of the prewar years, Mark Hellinger gravitated to movies by supplying Warner Brothers with the story for its classic 1939 gangster film *The Roaring Twenties*. He then became associate producer at Warners, where his credits included the George Raft trucker movie *They Drive by Night* (1940), the Edward G. Robinson gangster comedy *Brother Orchid* (1940), and Raoul Walsh's *High Sierra* (1941). In 1945, he moved over to Universal to produce *The Killers* and two other classic crime films, *Brute Force* (1947) and *The Naked City* (1948), the film that inspired the popular ABC TV series (1958–1963) of the same name. Hellinger's producing career proved short-lived, however, when he died suddenly in 1947 at the age of forty-four.

To direct his first solo product, *The Killers*, Hellinger had sought the services of an up-and-coming young filmmaker at Warners named Don Siegel. After years of working as an editor and second-unit director at Warners, Siegel had directed two films for the studio, *Star in the Night* (1945) and *Hitler Lives* (1946), which went on to win Oscars in the Best Short Subject category. The studio decided to give Siegel his first shot at a feature with the film noirish period mystery *The Verdict* (1946), starring Peter Lorre and Sydney Greenstreet. While Siegel was preparing *The Verdict*, Hellinger approached him with the offer to make his feature-film directorial debut with *The Killers*. Siegel was forced to decline the offer due to his prior commitment, however, and the opportunity to direct what would become one of the classic gangster films noir went to the more experienced (and available) German-born filmmaker Robert Siodmak instead. Yet when the same studio, Universal, decided to remake *The Killers* seventeen years later, it turned to Siegel, as well; this time, he was available to accept the job.

Siegel's version of *The Killers* was to have been the first movie made expressly for television. It was scheduled to air in the fall of 1963, but in the wake of the traumatic JFK assassination, Universal decided to temporarily shelve the film, fearing that its brutal subject matter — including a sequence in which a man is shot down by a sniper firing a high-powered rifle from the window of a building — might offend American viewers. In 1964, Universal took the film off the shelf and released it as a theatrical feature in Europe, where it became a sizable hit. The studio's less violent follow-up to *The Killers*, a chase drama titled *See How They Run*, made media history by becoming the first broadcast made-for-TV movie (NBC, October 1964). Siegel still holds second-place honors, however; his next film, *The Hanged Man*, a remake of the 1947 Robert Montgomery gangster film *Ride the Pink Horse*, became the next made-for-TV movie to receive a network airing (NBC, November 1964). His groundbreaking *The Killers* has since aired on television as well, but it never was broadcast on a network.

Siegel's *The Killers* retains many of the 1946 version's *noir* ingredients — the duplicitous dame, the use of flashbacks — but it eschews the atmospheric lighting techniques characteristic of the genre. The remake is in color and much of it takes place outdoors in bright daylight. Befitting the low budgets of most early made-for-TV movies, there is an aura of cheapness to the film, as well. Hemingway's hunted prizefighter, the Swede, is made a race-car driver instead; grainy stock footage is used for the racing scenes and it blends badly with the rest of the film.

Critics have often described Siegel's outlook on life as cynical, when, in fact, it's more sardonic. This is evident in the film's very first scene, when the killers, Charlie (Lee Marvin) and Lee (Clu Gulager), invade a school for the blind and never remove their sunglasses.

The man they've been contracted to kill, Johnny North (John Cassavetes), is working at the school as a therapist under the alias Jerry Nichols. Charlie mercilessly beats up a blind receptionist (Virginia Christine) for information as to North's whereabouts. A janitor discovers the beaten woman, she tells him what happened, and the janitor alerts North over the intercom that two men with guns are coming for him. Long expecting them and resigned to his fate, North makes no attempt to run and is brutally shot to death where he stands.

In Siegel's version, Hemingway's Nick Adams and the Siodmak film's insurance investigator, Riordan, are eliminated. It is the killers, particularly Charlie, who become obsessed with finding out why the victim didn't run — "why he'd rather die." From a former racing partner (Claude Akins) of North's, the killers learn

that North had fallen for an expensive, scheming dame named Sheila Farr (Angie Dickinson), and that North's infatuation with the woman had destroyed the partnership and North's career. Following a racing accident in which he'd almost been blinded, North had fallen on hard times. Through a gangster named Mickey (Norman Fell), Sheila herself, and a polished thug named Jack Browning (Ronald Reagan, in his last movie role before entering politics), Charlie uncovers the rest of the story.

Through Sheila's influence, North had taken the job of driver for a $1 million payroll heist engineered by Browning. But North had double-crossed the gang, dumped Sheila, and absconded with the loot. Charlie suspects otherwise, and his suspicions are confirmed when he beats the truth from the conniving Sheila. It was she and her lover Browning who'd pulled the double cross on the gang. They had taken the money and pinned the blame on North by shooting him and leaving him for dead. North survived, though, and disappeared. It was Browning who'd contracted the hit to make sure North would never talk.

Charlie (his partner, Lee, having been murdered by Browning) demands the stolen $1 million for himself. He kills Browning to get it and is wounded in the process. Sheila uses her sex appeal to try to con the wounded hit man, but he sees through her charade ("Lady, I don't have the time," he says with impatience and disgust) and kills her, too.

He stumbles outside with the suitcaseful of money and tries to make it to his car. But it's no use and he knows it. He is resigned to his fate just as North had been. In a sardonic finish that is pure Don Siegel, he takes aim at a passing police car with his empty gun hand and collapses dead on the grass.

Throughout his career, Siegel directed many other notable gangster and crime movies rooted in film noir, including *The Big Steal* (1949), a fast-paced caper film set in Mexico that reteamed *Out of the Past* costars Robert Mitchum and Jane Greer. The film's production was interrupted when Mitchum was busted for marijuana possession, and Siegel was forced to shoot around him in patchwork style. Recounted the director some years later: "That's why, if you look closely at the film, you see that when Mitchum arrives at a certain place, there are leaves on the trees, and when Bendix [his pursuer] arrives moments later, the leaves are gone."

The Big Steal also teamed Siegel for the first time with Geoffrey Homes, the author of the novel *Build My Gallows High* and of the screenplay for *Out of the Past,* the film adaptation of the novel. In addition to cowriting *The Big Steal,* Homes wrote the scripts for several of Siegel's best B films of the fifties, including the classic sci-fi thriller *Invasion of the Body Snatchers* (1956) and the gangster film *Baby Face Nelson* (1957), both using his real name, Daniel Mainwaring.

In addition to their hard-boiled characters, twisting, turning plots, and other requisite ingredients, 1940s films noir are also recognizable for their expressionistic black-and-white photography, eloquently echoing the genre's pessimistic mood and

William Bendix gets the drop on Robert Mitchum in Don Siegel's The Big Steal *(1949). (Copyright © 1949 RKO)*

themes. Working closely with their talented cinematographers, genre directors created a look to these films that is as much a part of the genre as its other elements and succeeded in lifting black-and-white photography to the level of high art.

Among the most beautiful of all 1940s films noir are those of director Anthony Mann. Today, Mann is better known for the impressive (though still underappreciated) string of scenic, psychological Westerns he made with James Stewart during the 1950s (*Bend of the River, The Naked Spur,* and *The Man from Laramie* among them) and for his visually stunning epics of the 1960s, *El Cid* and *The Fall of the Roman Empire.* But he began his directorial career in the 1940s just as film noir was beginning to evolve, and his contributions to the genre—particularly those made in collaboration with the marvelous cinematographer John Alton—are among the most stylish and visually impressive of the period. In fact, Mann and Alton's delightful Hitchcockian thriller of intrigue and deception set during the times of Robespierre and the French Revolution, *Reign of Terror* (a.k.a. *The Black Book,* 1949), is one of the most painterly films noir of the era.

Of the numerous films noir Mann made before turning to color in the early fifties (with equally impressive results), only a few were outright gangster films. The best of them are his first, *Desperate* (1947), *T-Men* (1947), the film that finally brought him critical and popular acclaim, and *Raw Deal* (1948), the grittiest and most visually striking of the trio. *Desperate* was the only one not photographed by Alton (George E. Diskant was the cinematographer). But its film noirish look, characterized by the big, bold close-ups, dramatic low-angle shots, and intense use of light and shade, strongly hints at the Alton films to come and shows that Mann was a director with an active hand in the lighting and design of his films. The climax of *Desperate,* in which beefy bad guy Raymond Burr takes a bullet from the put-upon hero (Steve Brodie) and plummets from the top of a stairwell, his body

Below, left: Gangster Raymond Burr plots revenge on the man who caused his brother's arrest in Anthony Mann's Desperate *(1947). (Copyright © 1947 RKO)*

Right: Mood and mayhem in Mann's Raw Deal *(1947) with Dennis O'Keefe and Marsha Hunt.*

slamming into the balustrades as it disappears into the dark abyss below, is a prime example of Mann's use of lighting and composition. Burr plays the villain in *Raw Deal*, too, a sadistic mob kingpin who uses fire to torture or intimidate his victims into submission. His fiery death at the conclusion of that film is even more of a visual stunner.

One of the more amusing traditions born of film noir is the use of the name Johnny in gangster movie titles. It's a tradition that continues to this day. Is there something about the name that inherently smacks of illegality? Does it derive from the slang term *john-law*, perhaps? Or the alias John Doe? I, a John, have no idea. But the number of gangster films with the name Johnny in the title practically constitutes a Hollywood Gangland subgenre all to itself.

In Henry Hathway's tense and exciting *Johnny Apollo* (1940), for example, Tyrone Power played the title role, the rebellious scion of an upstanding Wall Street broker (Edward Arnold) who falls head over heels for underworld femme fatale Dorothy Lamour and winds up getting deeply involved with the mob.

Mervyn LeRoy's *Johnny Eager* (1941) offered Robert Taylor and Lana Turner in the somewhat sentimental story of a sociology student (Turner) and daughter of the local district attorney (Edward Arnold again) who takes up with the title racketeer (Taylor) in order to find out what motivates him, and imperils herself (never very seriously) by falling in love with him instead.

Trading on his newfound success as a hard-boiled crime fighter in *Murder My*

Robert Taylor and Lana Turner in Johnny Eager *(1941). (Copyright © 1941 Metro-Goldwyn-Mayer)*

Sweet (1945), ex-singer Dick Powell played the wisecracking partner in a mob-owned gambling casino run by underworld big shot Thomas Gomez. Powell pokes into the murder of a hatcheck girl and a dishonest cop in *Johnny O'Clock* (1947), the directorial debut of noir screenwriter Robert Rossen.

Movie mobster George Raft went straight in *Johnny Allegro* (1949), the story of a hoodlum turned Treasury agent who pursues a top counterfeiter and deranged sportsman (George Macready) to his island hideaway in the Caribbean and gets involved in a tense variation on *The Most Dangerous Game.*

United Artists' well-meaning *Johnny Holiday* (1949) wasn't so much a gangster film as it was a reform-school film in the tradition of MGM's *Boys Town* (1938). Allen Martin, Jr., starred as a troubled youth who turns away from delinquency and on to the straight and narrow when he falls in with bad kid and aspiring gang leader Stanley Clements, then turns on him when Clements tries to kill the school's kindly supervisor (William Bendix).

Future horrormeister William Castle's potboiling *Johnny Stool Pigeon* (1949) teamed narcotics agent Howard Duff with convict Dan Duryea in a scheme to infiltrate and destroy a dope-smuggling ring that has, among other transgressions, turned Duryea's wife (Shelley Winters) into a drug addict.

In *Johnny Rocco* (1958), a loose reworking of the classic film noir *The Window* (1949), a little boy (Richard Eyer) witnesses a gangland shooting and becomes targeted by the mob.

Henry Silva played a dapper, no-nonsense Italian hit man whose Luciano-like boss (gangster movie fixture Marc Lawrence) sends him to the States to rub out some double-crossing former associates in *Johnny Cool* (1963), a moody throwback to the classic films noir but for its hyperactive jazz score.

In the dreary, multinational ganglang comedy *Johnny Banco* (1967), the Walter Mitty–like title character (Horst Buchholz), an impoverished slum kid, absconds with a small fortune in mob funds and heads for Monte Carlo to fulfill his playboy fantasies—with the mob in hot pursuit, of course.

A bit funnier was *Johnny Dangerously* (1984), a Prohibition-era gangland comedy in the tradition of Edward G. Robinson's *The Little Giant* and *A Slight Case of Murder* (though nowhere near as good as either) in which the title character (Michael Keaton), looking for some fast cash to pay his mom's medical bills, gets in over his head with the mob and winds up in the slammer.

On the more serious (albeit bizarre) side, Walter Hill's *Johnny Handsome* (1989) offered the perpetually dissipated Mickey Rourke as a disfigured small-time hood whose pals leave him in the lurch following a robbery. In prison, he undergoes plastic surgery—the doctors believe his ugliness is the root of his criminality. When he's released, he winds up going after the former pals who left him holding the bag and now want him dead.

Least and perhaps last (though I doubt that the "Johnny" genre has yet to be played out) is the cliché-ridden *Johnny Ryan* (1990), a pilot for a proposed TV series that failed to get off the ground. Bruce Abbott headed the cast as a tough but honest cop in the film noir tradition, battling hoods and hookers on the mean streets of Chicago.

Having been a major influence on the genre of film noir with their hard-boiled detective and gangster novels, Hammett, Chandler, Cain, and a host of lesser pulp-fiction writers found themselves in the enviable position of having more and more of their books turned into movies as film noir reached full steam. By the late forties, each had seen some or all of his books adapted to the screen—in some cases more than once. Sometimes, the results were mixed; on other occasions, the film versions proved to be as influential and enduring as the books themselves. For example, Howard Hawks's amusingly convoluted screen version of Chandler's detective/gangster novel *The Big Sleep* (1946), with Humphrey Bogart as private eye Philip Marlowe, continues to cast a spell on audiences and moviemakers to this day. Michael Winner's 1978 remake, which updated Chandler's book to the present day and featured Robert Mitchum in the Bogart role, has its admirers as well, although the film seems more like a send-up of film noir than an attempt at the real thing.

Howard Duff and Dan Duryea in William Castle's Johnny Stool Pidgeon *(1949). (Copyright © 1949 Universal Pictures)*

Cain and the more reluctant Chandler even became screenwriters themselves, turning out a slew of original noir scripts as well as adaptations. Sometimes, they even adapted each other's work, as in Billy Wilder's classic *Double Indemnity* (1944), which Chandler scripted (with Wilder) from Cain's book.

The eldest of the trio, Hammett was already an old hand at seeing his work translated to the big screen.* Two versions of his quasigangster novel *The Maltese Falcon* had already been made in the 1930s before John Huston tackled the job again in 1941 and turned it into a film classic. Hammett's *The Thin Man* had evolved into a successful series at MGM. And his 1931 novel *The Glass Key* was made twice, first in 1935 with George Raft, then again in 1942 with Alan Ladd.

---

*Though his influence on the school of hard-boiled fiction and films remains enormous, Hammett's output was less than prolific. His reputation rests on but five completed novels, only two of which, *Red Harvest* (1929), his first, and *The Dain Curse* (1929), his second, were unfilmed at the time of his death in 1961. *The Dain Curse* was turned into a forgettable TV miniseries in 1978 with James Coburn. But *Red Harvest* has yet to be made into a movie—although director Akira Kurosawa, a big fan of Hammett's work, did borrow the central idea of the book for his satirical Japanese "Western" *Yojimbo* (1961), and Italian director Sergio Leone used it again for his unofficial "Spaghetti" Western remake of the Kurosawa film—*A Fistful of Dollars* (1964).

The story of Ed Beaumont, a wily politician's aide who appears to have turned against his boss but is actually working both sides of the street to help the man, *The Glass Key* was the obvious inspiration for the Coen brothers' 1990 homage to Hammett and gangster films noir, *Miller's Crossing*. The Coens make no attempt to disguise their fondness for Hammett, having borrowed the title of their first film, *Blood Simple* (1984), from a phrase used in Hammett's novel *Red Harvest*.

The Ed Beaumont character in *Miller's Crossing* is Tom Reagan (Gabriel Byrne), the wisecracking Irish brains behind a multiethnic gangland empire run by a brawny Irish mobster named Leo (Albert Finney). Leo falls for Verna (Marcia Gay Harden), the two-timing sister of a homosexual Jewish bookie (John Turturro) who has double-crossed one of the Italian big shots (Jon Polito) in Leo's organization. Reagan knows she's two-timing Leo because he's sleeping with Verna himself. When Leo makes the mistake of shielding Verna's brother from the Italians seeking vengeance, a gang war erupts and he finds his power threatened. The cops and crooked politicians on Leo's payroll sit it out to see who will win. Even the once-loyal Reagan appears to have turned against Leo. Like Ed Beaumont, however, Reagan is working both sides of the street in an effort to keep his boss on top and to improve his own fortunes in the bargain — a deadly game of wits and double-dealing in which Reagan appears to get in over his head and finds his life imperiled.

Gabriel Byrne played the loyal (or is he?) aide to mob boss Albert Finney in Miller's Crossing *(1990), the Coen brothers' loose reworking of Hammett's* The Glass Key. *(Copyright © 1990 Twentieth Century-Fox)*

Reagan conceals his true motivations from Leo until the film's conclusion. The Coens' tricky, sometimes downright baffling script keeps us in the dark about them for almost the same length of time—perhaps too much so, for, unlike Hammett's Ed Beaumont, we never really come to identify with Tom Reagan. Except for isolated scenes, we never even worry very much what will happen to him (or to Leo, for that matter). We spend most of our time wondering what the character is up to: Is he being superclever, superstupid, or something in between?

Miller's Crossing has a vivid period feel to it, though. And some individual sequences are bravura indeed. The attempted murder of Leo, accompanied by Frank Patterson's rendition of "Danny Boy," is a real high point in gangster-film history. In a subtle reference, perhaps, to the classic film noir *The Killers*, the script also includes a memorable character nicknamed the "Dane." Unlike the Siodmak film's Swede, however, he's one of the killers this time.

Coming at the tail end of film noir's heyday, Fritz Lang's *The Big Heat* (1953) was derived from the work of a more contemporary pulp writer—William P. McGivern's *Saturday Evening Post* serial and novel of the same name. Sydney Boehm, a newspaper reporter turned screenwriter in the Mark Hellinger tradition, wrote the script. Glenn Ford was the noir hero Dave Bannion, a tough, incorruptible cop (but gentle family man) who gets embroiled in the case of a fellow officer's suicide. His superiors and the man's widow (Jeanette Nolan) pressure him to ease off the case, but he stubbornly refuses and digs even deeper. He learns that the deceased was on the take from the mob, whose gentlemanly kingpin, Mike Lagana (Alexander Scourby), has many other police officials and politicians on the payroll, too. When Bannion doesn't back off, Lagana orders him hit. Bannion's car is wired to explode on ignition, but his wife (Jocelyn Brando) is mistakenly killed instead. Embittered by the loss of his wife and more determined than ever to nail Lagana, Bannion descends into the perilous noir underworld. Aided only by some war buddies, a few loyal associates, and the brutalized moll (Gloria Grahame) of Lagana's sadistic henchman (Lee Marvin), Bannion finally prevails and brings the gangster and the corrupt officials to justice.

Alternately hailed as a realistic study of postwar urban corruption and vilified for its graphic depiction of mobster and cop violence, *The Big Heat* was a very potent film for its time. It seems much less strong today, although a number of scenes continue to pack a punch—notably Jocelyn Brando's death and the scene where Marvin scalds the face of girlfriend Grahame with boiling coffee in order to make a point.

Many recent films in the noir tradition have been drawn from the novels of Jim Thompson, a prolific though never very popular author of pulp thrillers in the late 1950s, 1960s, and 1970s. Thompson, who died in 1979, has lately become the focus of a one-man film noir revival. Adaptations of his books seem to be

Vengeful lawman Glenn Ford reluctantly turns killer Lee Marvin over to his no-help superiors in Fritz Lang's The Big Heat *(1953). (Copyright © 1953 Columbia Pictures)*

arriving on the screen every other week; he may ultimately become the most-filmed noir writer of them all.

Not all of Thompson's books deal with gangsterism, but gangsters usually feature importantly in their plots. A good example is Stephen Frears's *The Grifters* (1990); the most acclaimed adaptation of a Thompson novel to date,* it even captured several Oscar nominations. The gangster (Pat Hingle) for whom Lily (Anjelica Huston), one of the film's trio of con artists, works has only a few minutes of screen time. But his character is central to the plot. It's the pressure he puts on the devious Lily either to tow the line or risk execution that fates Lily's fellow grifters (John Cusack and Annette Bening) and propels the ugly tale of incest, double-dealing, and murder.

Frears successfully captures the mood of corruption and disillusionment of the classic films noir. But on the whole, his film has been wildly overpraised. Noirish mystery writer Max Allan Collins, a fervent promoter of Thompson's work, accurately summed up the film's major problems:

> John Cusack is wonderful as the young con artist, Roy Dillon. But the two women are dismally miscast. It is key [to the plot] that the two women look *alike* and be about the *same* age. Anjelica Huston is both too

---

*Drowned out by all the critical hoopla surrounding *The Grifters, After Dark, My Sweet,* another updated film noir based on a Jim Thompson novel released the same year, was much superior — largely because of a fascinating lead performance by Jason Patric. It's not a gangster film, though.

old and not conventionally attractive enough for [the role of Lily, Roy's mother]. Worse is Annette Bening, who is too young for her role of the "older" girlfriend (at least when contrasted with Huston). Attention to detail is not Frears' long suit—or he would have at least given Huston a blond wig that matched Bening's hair-color, so that their supposed resemblance (the women are mistaken for each other at several key moments) had some small credibility.

Seldom revived on television (and usually cut when it does turn up), writer-director Mike Hodges's *Get Carter* (1971) is one of a handful of British gangster films noir to rank right up there with the best American counterparts.

Michael Caine gives a powerful performance, perhaps one of the best of his career, as the title character, a tough, London-based contract killer who journeys home to Newcastle for the funeral of his upright younger brother. He discovers that his own mob cronies had the man murdered. Caine's niece had been drawn into a porno racket run by Caine's boss, a mob kingpin played by playwright John Osborne. When Caine's brother found out, he threatened to blow the whistle and Osborne had him killed. Caine employs all his skills to exact brutal revenge on the killers of his brother, particularly Osborne. Anticipating this, Osborne hires another contract killer to get Caine first, leading to the film's jolting and bitterly ironic conclusion.

Tough, violent, and beautifully photographed in a color adaptation of the moody film noir tradition, *Get Carter* is a small classic that deserves far more recognition than it has received.*

Michael Caine was also the star of Hodges's *Pulp* (1972), a bizarre follow-up to *Get Carter* that poked satiric fun at film noir and pulp fiction's influence on the gangster film. Caine plays a successful author of hard-boiled sex and death thrillers in the vein of Mickey Spillane. In fact, the character's name is Mickey King, although he writes under the pseudonym S. Odomy and O. R. Gann (one of his books is titled *My Gun Is Long*). Caine is hired to ghost the memoirs of a once-popular star of Hollywood gangster movies (played to the hilt by Mickey Rooney). Journeying to Rooney's villa, Caine discovers that an assassin is dogging his trail and realizes that someone obviously doesn't want Rooney's past revealed in print. Shortly after meeting with Caine, Rooney is assassinated at his own birthday party, a bizarre affair during which Rooney gets his jollies by rudely subjecting his guests to crass practical jokes. Caine's attempts to unravel why Rooney was murdered

---

*Rather than promoting the British-made *Get Carter* more aggressively and getting it widespread American distribution, MGM decided to make an American version of it instead. Capitalizing on the popularity of black-oriented action movies like *Shaft*, it remade *Get Carter* a year later as an all-black film under the title *Hit Man*.

lead him to a beach where he confronts the black-dressed assassin in a scene that parodies the finale to Hodges's earlier *Get Carter* and runs the assassin over in a truck, announcing to the corpse, "Thou art pulp and to pulp thou shalt return."

Wounded himself, Caine winds up in the dead Rooney's estate, imprisoned by the still-unknown conspirators behind the murder; he spends his convalescence plotting his revenge in the form of a new work of pulp fiction.

Pulp is both a gangster film and a parody of the genre—a parody of pulp fiction that is pulp fiction itself. We never do find out whether Caine is actually living out one of his pulp stories come to life or whether he's imagining the whole thing. Like *Get Carter*, it's a shadowy work full of acute paranoia. It also served as a stage-setter for Hodges's next film, the even *more* paranoid science fiction thriller *The Terminal Man* (1974).

THE BIG HEIST

Although armed holdups and robberies had been a fixture of the gangster film from the genre's earliest days, the heist movie itself did not come into its own as a distinct subgenre of the gangster and crime film until the 1950s. Before then, moviemakers usually left most of the details involved in the planning and execution of the crimes they showed largely unexplored. All we usually got to see was the gangsters' car pulling up to the bank and the exciting chase and gunplay that ensued as they made their breathless getaway from the law. The heist itself played a subordinate role in the overall context of such films. It was never the focus of the story, just one of a number of elements that moved the story along.

The reason for this was that the strict Motion Picture Production Code expressly forbid moviemakers from focusing on the heist as a film topic. "Methods of crime shall not be explicitly presented or detailed in a manner calculated to . . . inspire imitation," the code decreed. Since the Code Seal of Approval was mandatory, the studios complied.

All this began to change in the 1950s. Audiences' tastes and sensibilities had altered during the postwar years; the success of film noir reflected that. In addition, the Supreme Court had forced the major studios to release their monopolistic stranglehold on film exhibition by divesting themselves of their lucrative theater chains. With theaters now independently owned and operated, the studios no longer had ready outlets for their product. They had to compete with one another for theater space. Competition was fierce—and made even fiercer by the advent of television, which allowed moviegoers to stay at home and get their screen entertainment for free. Only the lure of something different would drag them away from the "box."

To give them something different, the studios came up with all sorts of technological gimmicks—from big screen Cinerama, CinemaScope, and Vista-Vision to 3-D. But they also began challenging the code's authority. If fans of gangster and crime movies required something new to get 'em off their duffs and into the theaters, then, by God, they'd give it to 'em, the code be damned.

Thus the heist film was born.

Among the earliest films to test the waters was the explicitly titled *Armored Car Robbery* (1950), an RKO B picture directed by Richard Fleischer. The son of animation pioneer Max Fleischer, Fleischer had cut his directorial teeth on a number of gangster and crime films for the studio in the late 1940s, such as the excellent suspense thriller *Follow Me Quietly* (1949). *Armored Car Robbery* was one of his last two B pictures for the studio before it moved into the Hollywood big leagues with such superproductions as Walt Disney's *20,000 Leagues Under the Sea* (1954). Earl Felton and Gerald Drayson Adams's screenplay continued to focus most of the attention on the aftermath of the robbery—the police manhunt for the criminals—but enough screen time was devoted to the setup and execution of the robbery to qualify the picture as a bona fide heist film.

William Talman, later to become famous as Hamilton Burger, the most losing prosecuting attorney in TV history on the long-running "Perry Mason" series, played the brains behind the action-filled heist. Charles McGraw played Talman's adversary, the dogged cop who hunts most of the gang down but repeatedly fails to nail Talman himself. With the loot and his moll (Adele Jergens) in tow, Talman flees to the airport to make his final escape. But McGraw and his men get a tip and swarm the place, and the gang leader is killed by an onrushing plane when he tries to make a break for it across a busy runway.

Though no masterpiece of the subgenre to be sure, *Armored Car Robbery* is a skillfully plotted, tautly made early heist film. Fleischer followed it two years later with a more exceptional gangster movie, *The Narrow Margin* (1952), though it's not

Below, left: William Talman and Adele Jergens gloat over their big score. They won't get to keep it, of course. From Armored Car Robbery *(1950). (Copyright © 1950 RKO)*

Right: The mob's hitmen get the wrong girl (Marie Windsor) in Richard Fleischer's claustrophic The Narrow Margin *(1952). (Copyright © 1952 RKO)*

a heist film. Earl Felton again wrote the screenplay and Charles McGraw played the lead, a Los Angeles cop assigned to transport a gangster's tough-talking widow (Marie Windsor) to the West Coast, where she is to testify before a grand jury about the mob's murderous activities. The bulk of the film's action is confined to the claustrophobic interior of the moving train itself as McGraw plays cat and mouse with several mob hit men to prevent the woman (whom the mobsters have never seen) from being found and killed. In one of several ingenious twists, Windsor *is* murdered. But she turns out to have been an undercover policewoman serving as a decoy for the real widow (Jacqueline White), an attractive blonde on the train, whom the in-the-dark McGraw has innocently befriended and whom he unwittingly puts in danger when the hit men realize their mistake.

An expertly made noir thriller, the film was remade in 1990 by director Peter Hyams as *Narrow Margin.* The remake featured Gene Hackman in the McGraw role and Anne Archer as the woman in jeopardy, the witness to a mob hit, whom Hackman bumblingly tries to protect while persuading her to testify. Again, the bulk of the action is set aboard a fast-moving train. In many ways, the remake is equally good, although Hyams takes a different approach by concentrating on stunt action and thrills rather than on claustrophobic suspense. By playing on the expectations of those familiar with the earlier version and by departing from the original's plot in several key ways, the remake successfully brings off a surprising twist or two itself. In the remake, for example, the identity of the targeted woman is never in doubt. It's one of the contract killers (the blond passenger Hackman befriends) who's playing the masquerade.

Fleischer returned to the heist film with the expensively mounted and more ambitious *Violent Saturday* (1954), the story of a trio of gangsters (Stephen McNally, Lee Marvin, J. Carrol Naish) out to rob a small Arizona mining town's bank. Sydney Boehm's script carefully laid out all the details of the heist while sluggishly weaving in the soap-operatic stories of various townspeople (mining engineer Victor Mature, librarian Sylvia Sidney, adulterer Richard Egan) whose lives are brutally affected by the robbers' weekend heist and its bloody aftermath. Looking forward to the much later (and much superior) crime thriller *Witness,* the conclusion takes place in peaceful Amish farm country, where hero Mature is almost done in by psychopathic gang member Marvin but is saved from death by Amish farmer Ernest Borgnine, who casts aside his pacifist beliefs for a moment in order to thrust a pitchfork into the murderous Marvin's back.

"Experience has taught me never to trust a policeman. Just when you think he's all right, he turns legit," caustically observes Doc Riedenschneider (Sam Jaffe), the mastermind behind the centerpiece robbery of John Huston's gritty *The Asphalt Jungle* (1950), the granddaddy of all "big heist" gangster films.

Doc's remarks refer to Lieutenant Ditrich (Barry Kelly), a cop on the take who is being forced to put the squeeze on his mobster friends due to pressure

from above, a situation that threatens Doc's scheme to get away with the biggest jewelry-store heist in midwestern history. In the end, though, it's not Ditrich who fouls up the scheme; it's Doc's partners in crime—and Doc himself, who dallies just long enough at a diner ogling a nubile teenage girl for the cops to catch up with him.

In *The Asphalt Jungle*, based on a novel by the ubiquitous W. R. Burnett, the "poet laureate" of American crime fiction, the law fairly disappears into the background. It's the criminals who do themselves in. To show how and why, Huston's script (cowritten with Ben Maddow) places the criminals' characters and crime under a microscope. Fully half the film is given over to scrutinizing such previously unexplored details as how such an elaborate heist is financed, determining what skills are needed for various aspects of the job, and what goes into recruiting the right people to pull the job off. Huston then uses up eleven minutes of screen time—an unheard-of amount in any crime film up to the time—to show us the mechanics of the robbery itself.

For suspense purposes, Huston doesn't fill in all the blanks; we're not aware upfront of *everything* that could go wrong during the course of the robbery. Nevertheless, *Jungle's* meticulous and spellbinding robbery sequence set the stage for every heist film to come in the gangster genre—many of them featuring even more elaborately planned and executed heists.*

Needless to say, the code was not amused by this, although Huston had

Above, left: *Sterling Hayden, Brad Dexter, Louis Calhern, and Sam Jaffe in John Huston's* The Asphalt Jungle *(1951), the granddaddy of all "big heist" films. (Copyright © 1951 Metro-Goldwyn-Mayer)*

Right: *Ocean's 11 (1961), starring Frank Sinatra and the "Rat Pack" played the "big heist" mostly for laughs. (Copyright © 1961 Warner Bros.)*

*Not all heist films that followed were gangster films. Nor were many in the same serious vein as Huston's classic study of crime as "a left-handed form of human endeavor." For example, Charles Crichton's *The Lavender Hill Mob* (1951) with Alec Guinness featured no gangsters at all—except, perhaps, for the two cockney lowlifes played by Sidney James and Alfie Bass, both of whom are professional crooks by delusion only. *Mob* was also played for laughs. A classic in its own right, it paved the way for a host of comedy heist films such as *The League of Gentlemen* (1960), *Big Deal on Madonna Street* (1958), *Ocean's Eleven* (1960) (which does involve gangsters, but only marginally), *How to Steal a Million* (1966), *$* (1971), and *The Hot Rock* (1972), to name but a few.

surprisingly little trouble getting his script passed. It was also not pleased by Huston's having one of his characters (the double-crossing Emmerich, played by Louis Calhern) commit suicide rather than face financial ruin and a jail term when he and his fellow coconspirators turn on one another and their successful enterprise begins to unravel. Even less content was studio head Louis B. Mayer, who criticized the film as "ugly" and not in the glossy MGM mold. "I wouldn't walk across the room to see a thing like that," Mayer said. Audiences disagreed, however: The film was a major box-office success for the studio, marking the beginning of the end for Mayer as head of MGM, though not for the heist film itself.

John Huston's *The Asphalt Jungle* established the basic ground rules for the big-heist gangster film, but Jules Dassin's French-made *Rififi* (1955) remains the definitive treatment of the subject. For sheer throat-clutching suspense, *Rififi*'s classic robbery sequence, which consumes a full half hour of the film's 117-minute running time, has never been topped—not even by Dassin himself, whose colorful caper comedy *Topkapi* (1964) boasts an even more intricate and elaborate heist.

The American-born Dassin was no stranger to Hollywood gangster films or films noir. He had directed Mark Hellinger's prison drama *Brute Force* (1947) and cop thriller *The Naked City* (1948), two preeminent films noir of the decade, as well as *The Night and the City* (1950), a moody mobster movie about a conniving American gangster (Richard Widmark) who gets in over his head in the seamy London underworld.* Dassin's career in Hollywood seemed assured until the blacklist intervened; he then went to France to find work. The first film he made there was *Rififi*, an American-style noir gangster film (a genre French audiences and critics loved) based on a popular French novel by Auguste le Breton. Breton wrote in the same hard-boiled style as such American counterparts as James M. Cain and W. R. Burnett and was obviously influenced by them—Burnett especially.

Rififi is by no means a clone of Huston's (and Burnett's) *The Asphalt Jungle*, but they certainly bear some plot similarities. In both films, a group of professional crooks with different specialties are led by a resourceful master criminal—Doc in *Asphalt*, Tony Stephanois (Carl Mohner) in *Rififi*—into successfully pulling off a big-time jewelry-store robbery that is shown in some detail. Then the caper goes sour. Both films end with the bad-guy hero—Dix Handley (Sterling Hayden) in *Asphalt*, Tony Stephanois in *Rififi*—setting things right by shooting it out with the worse guys and making off with the loot. But each dies from wounds received in the shoot-out before his ill-gotten gains can do him any good.

---

*The film was ineffectively remade in 1992 as *Night and the City*, with Robert De Niro in the Widmark role; the local shifted to contemporary New York.

There are significant differences between the two films as well, however. Huston's caper goes sour when one of the coconspirators (Emmerich) pulls a double cross. But in *Rififi*, the caper goes sour because of a rival gang led by gangster Pierre Grutter (Marcel Lupovici) that tries to horn in on the take. Grutter discovers who pulled off the job when one of the robbers (played by Dassin under the pseudonym Perlo Vita) starts flashing some of the jewels around in Grutter's nightclub. Grutter's gang then kidnaps Stephanois's nephew and demands the fortune in jewels as ransom for the boy's life, forcing the bloody confrontation that concludes the film.

The major difference between the two films is in their approach to the heist itself. Befitting his thematic interests, Huston's film is more concerned with what happens to its self-destructive cast of characters *after* they've grabbed "the stuff that dreams are made of." Dassin is no less concerned with this, but he turns the robbery into the focal point of the film. Every element of the plan is outlined for us beforehand so that we're aware of all the various obstacles the crooks face and see what they cook up to surmount them. This sets the stage for the thirty-minute robbery sequence itself, which contains no dialogue and unfolds in silence broken only by the clinking of the men's tools, the noise of which could trigger the store's supersensitive alarm system at any moment. Robbery scenes simply don't come any more heart-stopping than this.

Rififi was quite successful in the United States but even more so in Europe, where it was followed by three unofficial sequels (all drawn from novels or original screenplays by Auguste le Breton) and countless imitations and send-ups. The sequels were Alex Joffé's *Du Rififi chez les Femmes* (1959), in which molls joined with mobsters to pull off the big heist; Jacques Deray's Occidental *Rififi à Tokyo* (1961); and Denys de la Patelliere's south-of-the-border heist film *Du Rififi à Panamae* (1966), which featured one of the last screen performances by George Raft. Mario Monicelli satirized the mechanics of *Rififi*'s classic robbery sequence — and most other conventions of the big-heist subgenre, as well — in *Big Deal on Madonna Street* (1958), a hilarious caper comedy starring Marcello Mastroianni as the inept mirror image of *Rififi*'s scrupulous master planner, Tony Stephanois. Director Henri Verneuil aped the formula more seriously — and elaborately — in his big international hit *The Sicilian Clan* (1969), also based on a le Breton novel; it starred aging French superstar Jean Gabin as the Doc Reidenschneider/Tony Stephanois–like criminal mastermind. Even Little Caeser finally got into the act when Edward G. Robinson himself took on the role of criminal mastermind in a series of heist films made virtually back-to-back during the last years of his life: *Grand Slam* (1967), *The Biggest Bundle of Them All* (1968), *Mad Checkmate* a.k.a. *It's Your Move* (1968), and *Operation St. Peter's* (1968).

Stateside, a young director named Stanley Kubrick finally caught the eye of Hollywood with his experimental take on the heist-film formula, titled *The Killing* (1956), a film that combined elements of both *The Asphalt Jungle* and *Rififi* but that was mostly clearly influenced by the former. It's got the same star (Sterling Hayden), playing a roughly similar role (though he's the heist's ringleader this time around rather than just a strong-arm functionary). Hayden's assessment of his colleagues' motivations ("None of these guys are criminals in the usual sense . . . they've just got a little larceny in 'em") echoes the lawyer Emmerich's view of crime from the Huston film as "nothing more than a left-handed form of human endeavor." Many of Kubrick's character types are the same — especially Hayden's girlfriend (Coleen Gray), who is a virtual stand-in for the character played by Jean Hagen in *The Asphalt Jungle*. Both films share a subtext involving horse racing, as well. The film's title refers both to the gang's sought-after big score (the killing it hopes to make) and to the robbery's centerpiece, the killing of a racehorse. (It also hints at the bloodbath that climaxes the film, when most of the gang members are killed in a shoot-out with rivals who, like the Grutters in *Rififi*, attempt to horn in on the take.) In the film noir tradition, Kubrick also added a sexy, duplicitous dame (Marie Windsor). It is through Windsor, the scheming wife of one of the heist participants (Elisha Cook, Jr.), that outsiders Vince Edwards (her lover) and Joseph Turkel get wind of the plan and the rendezvous where the take is to be split up.

Like Dassin, Kubrick makes his robbery sequence the focal point and suspense showpiece of his film. But their approaches to creating suspense are very different. In *Rififi*, we hold our breath in anticipation that a slip of the men's tools will trigger the store's supersensitive alarm system at any second. In *The Killing*, Kubrick creates suspense by establishing a rigid timetable for each stage of the robbery and by using a narrator and repeated shots of the betting-room clock to keep us aware of that timetable every step of the way. The narrator is also used to keep the linear progression of the robbery straight in our mind while Kubrick's camera constantly shifts back and forth in time during the heist to show each gang member carrying out his concurrent task. Kubrick's experimental "time and motion study" may not be as consistently suspenseful as its counterpart robbery sequence in the Dassin film, but it's an equally effective piece of filmmaking.

After the robbery, Hayden takes the loot to the rendezvous to split it with his partners. As he arrives, he sees the bloodstained Elisha Cook, Jr., the sole survivor of the bloody shoot-out with the rival gang members, stagger into the street. Hayden and his partners had agreed beforehand that should he spot any trouble when he shows up, he is to drive away with the loot and not stop to investigate. So he does just that and heads straight to the airport with Colleen Gray to make his final getaway with the suitcase full of cash. In the film's ironic conclusion, Hayden's careful planning goes awry when he is unable to take the oversized suitcase onto the plane with him and is forced to check it through instead. As the baggage cart is being driven to the plane, a poodle belonging to one of the waiting passengers breaks loose and runs into the truck's path. The driver swerves to avoid hitting the dog and the suitcase falls onto the runway, where it breaks open and the $2 million in cash is blown away into the night by the wind from the plane's propellers.

Gray ushers the zombified Hayden away from the scene and tries to hail a taxi, but they're spotted by the authorities before they can get away. "Johnny, you've got to run," she tells him as two armed officers approach them from the terminal. But the failed master thief mutters a dispirited "Ah, what's the difference" and gives himself up instead.

Joseph Pevney's *Six Bridges to Cross* (1955) drew the inspiration for its centerpiece heist from a real-life event—the notorious Brink's payroll and securities-company robbery in Boston five years earlier.

Touted as "the crime of the century," the spectacular Brink's job was pulled off by a minor Boston criminal named Tony Pino and eleven of his closest crook pals, among them the colorful Adolphe "Jazz" Maffie and Specs O'Keefe. Pino and his associates planned the robbery over a two-year period, leaving nothing to chance. They broke into the place several times beforehand to have duplicate keys made for the various counting-room doors and security cages, studied the company's elaborate alarm system at the manufacturing firm where it was made, and even made Brink's uniforms for themselves so they could slip in and out unnoticed. They also conducted a brazen dress rehearsal for the robbery a month before the heist right inside Brink's itself. The actual robbery took place on January 17, 1950, and netted the thieves a cool $2.7 million, which they had agreed to keep on ice for six years until Massachusetts's statute of limitations ran out. The extraordinary discipline they had mustered for the planning and execution of the robbery fell apart at this stage of the game, however. Disputes arose over splitting the take; several gang members felt they'd been shortchanged, and they all began turning on one another. O'Keefe and fellow gang member Albert "Gus" Guscoria were subsequently arrested in Pennsylvania for robbing a series of hardware and clothing stores and sent up the river for three years. Fearing they might talk, Maffie and others started spending the loot. O'Keefe didn't talk (neither did Guscoria, who died in jail). When O'Keefe got out, he learned that Maffie had spent most of his share, too (he had placed it in Maffie's safekeeping while incarcerated), and demanded an extra share. Believing O'Keefe would squeal on them if not taken care of, the gang hired a hit man to kill him. Following two attempts on his life, the second one almost successful, O'Keefe got fed up and finally did spill his guts to the cops. Pino, Maffie, and most of the others were rounded up, tried, and sentenced to life in prison. Most of the $2.7 million, however, was never recovered.

Sydney Boehm's melodramatic script for *Six Bridges to Cross,* based on Joseph F. Dineen's best-selling account of the case, *They Stole Two and a Half Million Dollars* [sic] *and Got Away with It,* is at heart a tale of juvenile delinquency and ultimately more fiction than fact. Tony Curtis stars as the brains behind the heist, a fictional character named Jerry Florea who ran into trouble with the law when he was a kid and has since grown up to be a career criminal despite a sympathetic neighborhood cop's (George Nader) persistent efforts to rehabilitate him. As in Anthony Mann's *T-Men* and Kubrick's *The Killing,* a narrator is used to give the film a documentary flavor. The effect is enhanced by William Daniels's gritty black-and-white photography, much of it shot on location in Boston.

The film picks up Florea's saga during his early years as a youthful offender (played by Sal Mineo) with plans of making it big in the Boston underworld, and it climaxes several decades later with his pulling off "the crime of the century." The planning of the heist is outlined in fairly intricate detail, and the action-filled heist itself is realistic indeed, shot as it was in Brink's Prince Street garage, where the event actually occurred. In keeping with the big-heist subgenre, the robbery is a success, but the robbers fall out afterward and their dreams of living in wealth and luxury collapse. In this case, the authorities rightly pin the blame for the momentous caper on habitual criminal Curtis and threaten him with deportation. Nader, now a bigwig on the force, persuades him to give the money back to avoid

Habitual criminal Tony
Curtis ignores cop George
Nader's persistent efforts to
rehabilitate him and pulls
off the Brink's robbery in
Six Bridges to Cross
(1955). (Copyright ©
1955 Universal Pictures)

this fate. Curtis agrees, only to be shot by one of his cronies, after which the well-planned scheme goes to hell fast.

William Friedkin's *The Brink's Job* (1978) offers a much more factual look at the famous robbery and its aftermath. Like *Six Bridges to Cross,* the film benefits greatly from having been shot at the actual Boston locations, including the still-standing Brink's garage on Prince Street. Many of these sites had to undergo an expensive face-lift, however, to make them appear as they did back in the 1950s. Vinnie Costa (Tony Pino's brother-in-law), Adolphe "Jazz" Maffie, and Sandy Richardson, the sole surviving participants in the Brink's robbery, acted as consultants on the film.

Friedkin was no stranger to the gangster film. His genre debut, *The French Connection* (1971), had captured an Academy Award as Best Picture. Star Gene Hackman and director Friedkin also won Oscars for their work on the film, whose most enduring element is its classic car chase through the crowded streets of the Big Apple*—a scene designed to top Steve McQueen's equally memorable joyride in pursuit of the bad guys across the streets of San Francisco in *Bullitt* (1968), a much superior mob movie that shared the same producer, Philip D'Antoni.

The Brink's Job is based on Noel Behn's nonfiction account of the case, *Big*

---

*John Frankenheimer wittily parodied this scene — and the whole car-chase cliché — in his grim sequel to the Friedkin film, *The French Connection II* (1975). Gene Hackman recreated his role as drug-busting NYC cop Popeye Doyle, who, this time around, chases the bad guys on foot.

Stick-Up at Brink's. However, Walon Green's screenplay and Friedkin's direction seem to have been inspired in equal measure by Mario Monicelli's classic caper comedy *Big Deal on Madonna Street,* for much of the film is played for laughs. Pino (Peter Falk) and his coterie of small-time hoods are portrayed as the most unlikely prospects for pulling off such a grandiose scheme that one can imagine. This is not really stretching the truth. The authorities, in fact, were fully aware that Pino and his pals were casing the Brink's garage and vault all along, but they ignored them in the mistaken belief that they were too small-time and incompetent to pull off such a job. The authorities had reason to believe this, for Pino's biggest heist up to that time had been the knock-over of a gum-ball factory's safe, which had netted him a whopping thirteen dollars. And most of his colleagues hadn't even had *that* much success in their criminal endeavors.

The Brink's job would be different, though, for, as Pino spots early on, the joint's reputation for tight security is vastly overrated. He confirms this by stealing a couple of bags full of cash and securities from the back of an unwatched Brink's truck with no problem. Later, he sneaks into the garage at night to case the place and finds security measures there to be equally lax. "This joint is mine. I own this place!" he says in cockeyed consternation. "That building is asleep," he subsequently tells his wife (Gena Rowlands). "[That money] is screamin' at me through the walls. It's yelling, 'Hey, Tony, come in and grab me. Get me out o' here!'" And, of course, he decides to do just that.

Together with Costa (Allen Goorwitz), Albert "Gus" Guscoria (Kevin O'Connor), Sandy Richardson (Gerard Murphy), Joe McGinnis (Peter Boyle), Adolphe "Jazz" Maffie (Paul Sorvino), and safecracker Specs O'Keefe (Warren Oates), Pino successfully pulls off "the crime of the century," which Friedkin stages in suspenseful but humorous detail, climaxing with a fictional scene in which the boys whoop and holler and roll around on a mountain of cash inside the vault itself.

The remainder of the film authentically recreates the collapse of the scheme as the gang begins to fall out with one another, O'Keefe and Gus are arrested in Pennsylvania, and Pino and company are subsequently hauled in and sent up the river. Events occasionally turn grim, but the film manages to sustain its comic tone throughout. Overall, it's a most entertaining romp—a witty look back at a classic American caper that occasionally bordered on farce—and probably the overrated Friedkin's most underrated film. Not all the behind-the-scenes action was so lighthearted, however. At one point during the film's production, some real-life Boston hoodlums absconded with several cans of rushes at gunpoint and demanded a hefty ransom for their return. Since the rushes were just work prints and the original negatives were in safekeeping, Friedkin refused. The thieves were never caught and the stolen reels never recovered. Later, the production became the focus of a more serious investigation into charges of extortion involving payoffs to local mob figures connected with the Teamsters' union. The affair made the nightly news and several local racketeers were charged and sent up the river just like Tony Pino and his gang.

An earlier made-for-TV movie titled *Brink's: The Great Robbery* (1976), directed by Marvin J. Chomsky, offered a more straightforward—and much less entertaining—account of the case. Produced by Quinn Martin, the telefilm focused as much attention on the FBI's efforts to crack the case as it did on the heist itself. Darren McGavin, Cliff Gorman, and Michael V. Gazzo played the top members of the gang, whose names were changed in Robert W. Lenski's teleplay in order to protect the guilty.

Peter Yates's *Robbery* (1967), the film that paved the way for the young British director's American film debut with the popular Steve McQueen mob thriller *Bullitt*, dealt with an even more spectacular real-life heist—the 1964 theft of £2.5 million from a British Royal Mail train en route from Glasgow to London. Newspapers worldwide hailed the heist as "history's greatest robbery." The gang of twenty that pulled off the daring job was made up of bookies and other small-time British underworlders, plus others not at all connected with the world of crime—florists, mechanics, former military men, and several of their wives. Bruce Reynolds, a London antique dealer with a streak of larceny, was the ringleader who planned and led the military-style operation.

The key to the plan was ensuring that the train would stop at the precise time and place the robbers wanted it to—a spot on a secluded bridge not far from the rented farmhouse that served as the gang's headquarters. A truck on which the take was to be loaded was parked beneath the bridge. The gang accomplished the trick by rigging a track signal light to flash red rather than green as the train approached a crossroads near the bridge. The red light alerted the engineer to stop, as there was a delay ahead. When the engineer climbed down to use the telephone in a nearby signal box to find out the length of the delay, he found the wires cut, and he was quickly set upon by several men in heavy coats and ski masks. They and other members of the gang quickly boarded the train and smashed through all twelve cars to get at the mail bags full of money. In a matter of minutes, more than 120 bags of cash were loaded onto the truck and the robbery was over. The engineer and his crew were tied up and left behind on the stalled train, and the thieves sped to the farmhouse to quickly divide the take.

Although the robbers had executed the heist with great efficiency, they were more than a bit lax in covering their tracks afterward. The police discovered the deserted farmhouse several days later during a dragnet of the area, and a dusting of the place yielded tons of fingerprints and other significant clues that led to the arrest of all but Reynolds within a matter of weeks. The sentences were fairly stiff, depending upon each gang member's degree of participation in the heist. Reynolds was finally caught four years later and received a twenty-five-year stretch. A fellow gang member, Ronald Biggs, subsequently escaped from prison and was never recaptured. Less than £500,000 of the stolen loot was ever recovered.

Yates's film about the heist, written by Edward Boyd, George Markstein, and Yates himself, collapses Reynolds and Biggs into a single character, a former military man turned hoodlum played by Stanley Baker, who also coproduced the film. It is Baker who plans and leads the operation. He is also the only member of the gang to get away; he skips to the United States and then South America, leaving his wife (Joanna Pettet) behind in England. His character and all the others in the film are given fictional names.

The robbery is staged on the actual sites where it occurred and is tautly handled. It's by far the best scene in the film because it's also the most straight-forwardly presented. The rest of the film, like so many British pictures of the period, is staged and edited in the jumpy short-scene/quick-cut style of Richard Lester's influential Beatles films, a technique that worked for the Beatles and certainly keeps things hopping but that doesn't quite cut it in a suspense thriller. (Yates abandoned the technique in his more exciting *Bullitt* and has ever since.)

A little-seen German film titled *The Great British Train Robbery* chronicled the story of the landmark heist in a smoother and more straightforward manner and is consistently more absorbing and suspense-filled throughout.

Newcomer Quentin Tarantino injected some Scorsesian adrenaline—and an overdose of Scorsesian banter among his low-life gangster characters—into *Reservoir Dogs* (1992), a contemporary heist film that owes its plot to *White Heat* and its oddball structure to Stanley Kubrick's *The Killing*. Writer-director Tarantino even lifts one of his characters straight from *The Killing*—Michael Madsen's sadistic, sleepy-eyed psychopath, who is a virtual clone of the character played by Timothy Carey in the Kubrick film and of characters in many other crime films of the fifties, as well. In another nod to the genre's past, Tarantino also cast Lawrence Tierney in the pivotal role of the mob kingpin who plans and bankrolls the heist.

The film begins with the aftermath of the heist—a jewel robbery that has gone bloodily awry. Then it frequently doubles back to show us some details of the robbery, who the characters are, and what went wrong. The main focus of the story, however, is on how the mutually mistrustful cast of gangster characters comes undone when it becomes apparent that one of its members (Tim Roth) is an undercover cop who set the gang up.

Scorsese film veteran Harvey Keitel plays the ostensible hero, who is partnered with Roth for the heist and comes to like and trust him. Skeptical that there is a wolf in the fold at all, and doubly sure that it couldn't be Roth, who was mortally wounded during the getaway, Keitel forces a violent showdown with his finger-pointing colleagues when they attempt to execute Roth. The ironic—and bloody climax—leaves most of the gang dead and Keitel wounded. As the police storm the gang's hideout, the dying Roth assuages his guilt by confessing his identity to Keitel at last. Like Cagney's Cody Jarrett in *White Heat*, Keitel reacts with such anguish to this news that he moans like an animal injured to the depths of its soul—and is summarily gunned down by the cops.

Critically acclaimed—and controversial—because of its gritty gutter language, inventive (albeit derivative) narrative structure, and mixture of humor and extremely graphic violence, *Reservoir Dogs* put Tarantino on the filmmaking map. As a result, it is a heist film that is sure to be widely imitated in the years to come by other young filmmaking hopefuls, who will likely add yet more juice to the formula in an effort to win their own tickets to Hollywood.

MURDER FOR HIRE

The themes of crime and business converge most chillingly in the "murder for hire" film, another distinct subgenre of the gangster film that made its appearance in the 1950s. The character of the paid assassin or contract killer had appeared in gangster films before then, of course, but, like the big heist, he'd served mainly as a plot device, never a focal point. His motives and methods—like the details involved in planning and executing the big heist—had gone largely unexplored by moviemakers due to the restrictions of the Motion Picture Production Code. Even the two hit men played by William Conrad and Charles McGraw in Robert Siodmack's *The Killing*—the closest the movies had yet come to a murder-for-hire film—were essentially peripheral characters. The subject of the film was not them— or the amoral concept of murder for hire—but how the Swede (Burt Lancaster) got into the fix that set the killers on his trail.

As the power of the Motion Picture Production Code began to wane in the early 1950s, however, moviemakers began to delve more deeply into such heretofore-taboo subject matter as the mob's long-standing tradition of murder for hire, a subject much in the news at the time due to the Kefauver hearings on organized crime. It was during the hearings that Murder, Inc.—the corporate signature of the syndicate's professional hit squad, an organization that had first become known to the public in the early forties—hit the headlines once again.

The original Murder, Inc. (as the press dubbed it), headquartered in Brooklyn, was exposed and broken up in the 1940s, but the concept did not die with it. Mob contracts continue to be issued and gruesomely executed to this day.

Murder, Inc. was the enforcement arm of the burgeoning national crime syndicate created by Lucky Luciano and Meyer Lansky in the 1930s. Louis Lepke Buchalter, the mob's top union racketeer, ran the operation with the help of Albert Anastasia, his "lord high executioner." Notorious mobsters Joe Adonis, Bugsy

Siegel, Frank Costello, Vito Genovese, and Abner "Longy" Zwillman were the other "members of the board."

Murder, Inc. targeted only those gangsters who were thought to be double-crossing or in danger of squealing on the mob, or who failed to go along with the dictates of the national syndicate. Cops, politicians, and journalists were off-limits. A unanimous vote of approval was required of all board members before a contract could be issued. Murder, Inc. chieftains Buchalter or Anastasia would then give the contract to one of their lieutenants—Louis Capone, Mendy Weiss, or Abe "Kid Twist" Reles—who assigned the actual job to one of several hit men who free-lanced exclusively for them. In this way, the killers were unable to identify the top men who had ordered the hit and a legal system of plausible denial was established for those top men in the event they were ever questioned. It's been reported that between four and five hundred murders were carried out by the group before its activities finally came to light in the 1940s. The bodies of the victims were dumped in swamps and deserted farmlands all along the East Coast.

Exposure came as a result of a tip given to New York Assistant District Attorney Burton Turkus. The tip led to the arrest of Abe "Kid Twist" Reles and two of his free-lancers, Buggsy Goldstein and Dukey Maffetore. When Goldstein and Maffetore began spilling their guts to the authorities, Reles knew his days were numbered if he didn't make a deal and sing, too. Reles named other hit men on the Murder, Inc. payroll and implicated top man Buchalter, as well. At the time, Buchalter was serving a life sentence in Leavenworth on narcotics and other charges that had been successfully brought against him by Thomas E. Dewey. Murder was not among these charges, however, and an early parole for Buchalter seemed likely—until Reles fingered him as the head of Murder, Inc. Buchalter was charged with ordering the murder of a union leader named Joe Rosen, and Dewey's successful prosecution resulted in the death sentence. Buchalter and his other two lieutenants, Mendy Weiss and Louis Capone, went to the electric chair in 1944. Reles, the once-loyal lieutenant who had exposed their activities, never lived to testify against them or anyone else, though. He died in 1941 after a fall from the top floor of a Coney Island hotel where he was being held under police protection on Turkus's orders. The death was ruled accidental; bed sheets were found hanging from Reles's window, and it was assumed that the hoodlum, feeling trapped and fearing for his life from an inside job, had fallen while trying to escape. But most historians believe he was murdered on Luciano's orders to keep him from squealing on other members of the syndicate and that the killer, whoever he was, had simply paid one of Reles's guards to turn his back at the proper moment.

At the height of the televised Kefauver hearings, when the name Murder, Inc. was making news again, Warner Brothers capitalized on the notoriety and turned out a "today's headlines" picture entitled *The Enforcer* (1951), a semifictional account of the story. The film starred Humphrey Bogart (in his last role for the studio) as a crusading prosecutor modeled on Thomas E. Dewey and Burton Turkus. Everett Sloane played the Buchalter-like leader of the murder-for-hire organization whom Bogart finally brings to justice. The title refers to both the Bogart and Sloane characters (it was changed to *Murder, Inc.* for overseas release).

Director Bretaigne Windust began the film but was replaced by an uncredited Raoul Walsh. This may account for the film's overall unevenness of tone: Long stretches of the picture are talky and dull, while other sequences are quite powerful—even shocking. The likelihood is that these scenes belong to Walsh, a familiar hand at the brutal, hard-hitting style of gangster film pioneered by the studio, a style *The Enforcer* recaptures only in spots.

An example of this is the tense opening scene, which details the death of the Reles character, Joe Rico, played by Ted de Corsia. After months of frustrating work, Bogart has finally gotten the break he needs to send Sloane up the river for good. He's arrested a witness (de Corsia) to one of Sloane's many murders and the guy has agreed to sing at Sloane's trial if given airtight protection. Bogart stashes him in a hotel under armed guard, but the trapped and terrified de Corsia knows that Sloane has put out a contract on him and that it's only a matter of time before the organization's killers get to him, protection or not. He overcomes one of his guards by brutally slamming the man's head into the bathroom sink, knocking the man cold, then climbs out the window to escape. He's too high up to get away, however, and finds himself hanging precariously from the ledge. Bogart climbs out after him and extends his hand, but de Corsia loses his grip and falls to his death on the street below.

With de Corsia dead, Bogart's investigation grinds to a halt. But as a result of de Corsia's recorded testimony and the revelations of another informer (Zero Mostel), the persistent prosecutor uncovers a second eyewitness (Patricia Joiner) to Sloane's murderous activities, and she provides him with the evidence he needs to get Sloane sentenced to death.

The film's most gruesome scene (also based on fact) has Bogart and his men discovering one of the assassination squad's mass graves in a New Jersey swamp and unearthing bundles of pairs of shoes, the only traces remaining of the victims, whose bodies had been buried separately in lime. One of Murder, Inc.'s more subtle (compared to death by tommy gun) methods of execution—an ice pick thrust into the back of the victim's neck—is also faithfully delineated.

Published the same year *The Enforcer* was released, Assistant District Attorney Burton Turkus's own chronicle of the affair, *Murder, Inc.: The Story of the Syndicate*, became a movie itself in 1960 courtesy of Twentieth Century–Fox. Titled *Murder, Inc.*, the film unfolds in a gritty style similar to the TV series "The Untouchables,"

whose popularity at the time probably inspired the studio to make the film, and provides a much more accurate account of the killer organization's rise and exposure than the earlier Bogart film.

Henry Morgan plays Turkus, the narrator of the story; David J. Stewart turns in an utterly slimy performance as the villainous Louis Lepke Buchalter; and Peter Falk appeared in the role of the cagey but ultimately doomed Abe "Kid Twist" Reles, a performance that earned him an Academy Award nomination for Best Supporting Actor* and launched him on his career as one of the screen's most durable character actors.

Like *The Enforcer*, the film had two directors (producer Burt Balaban and Stuart Rosenberg share directorial credit), which again probably explains its similarly uneven qualities. The film's long expanses of languid and unexciting celluloid are offset by parts that are utterly compelling. The roles of the ill-fated young couple (Stuart Whitman and May Britt), who get caught up in a deadly syndicate power play when they agree to hide the fugitive Buchalter from the mob in their room, are considerably expanded to give the audience someone to root for. But the story belongs to Buchalter and Reles, and whenever Stewart and Falk are on screen, this minor but engaging docudrama about the infamous Murder, Inc. really cooks.

The writers of Menahem Golan's bloodthirsty biopic *Lepke* (1975) did a fair amount of research into their subject as well, although they managed to pull a few boners—like having Lucky Luciano (Vic Tayback) address syndicate colleague Ben Siegel as "Bugsy," the hated nickname used only by his enemies and the press. In another scene, narrator Lepke (Curtis) tells us how he ordered the death of Jack "Legs" Diamond and had his body dumped off a Coney Island pier, when

Below, left: Roy Roberts, Humphrey Bogart, and King Donovan uncover evidence of Murder Inc. in The Enforcer *(1951). (Copyright © 1951 Warner Bros.)*

Right: Peter Falk, May Britt, and Stuart Whitman in Murder Inc. *(1960). (Copyright © 1960 Twentieth Century-Fox)*

*Peter Ustinov won the Oscar instead for his performance as a similarly conniving weasel in the epic *Spartacus* (1960).

in fact Legs Diamond was murdered in a hotel room in Albany, New York. These are minor mistakes, yet they are curious lapses in a screenplay that, for most part, adheres quite closely to the facts.

The film plays like a dramatized rap sheet. It opens in 1923, when Lepke was an impoverished teenager (Barry Miller) on New York's Lower East Side. Several arrests for petty thievery land the kid in reform school. When he's released as an adult (Curtis, who gives a strong performance, though it lacks much depth), he joins up with childhood pal Gurrah Shapiro (Warren Berlinger), a member of a protection racket run by small-time hood Little Augie Orgen. Lepke kills Orgen, takes over the operation, and quickly expands activities to the city's labor unions. His success and deadly reputation win him a spot in Luciano's syndicate, where he heads up Murder, Inc., the syndicate's enforcement squad. Curiously, Murder, Inc. is never mentioned in the film. But its methods are graphically pictured—and also amusingly embellished, as in the scenes where hit man Mendy Weiss knocks off one victim with an exploding plate of spaghetti and another with a detonated stack of newspapers. However, most of Lepke's victims are dispatched by less colorful means—the familiar ice pick and tommy gun. These ongoing scenes of bloodshed are interspersed with tedious peeks into Lepke's more serene home life with vapid bride Bernice (Anjanette Comer), whose obliviousness to the source of her beloved husband's lavish living is positively astonishing. She makes the naïve and trusting Kay in *The Godfather* seem a hardened skeptic by comparison.

Eventually, the brutal Lepke pushes his ambitions too far and tries to horn in on Luciano's narcotics operation. A gang war erupts, and he becomes a targeted man forced to go into hiding. To cool things down, he agrees to give himself up to the feds on a lesser charge, but the feds pull a fast one and turn him over to New York prosecutor Thomas E. Dewey, who charges Lepke with murder and sends him to the electric chair—the only syndicate kingpin ever to die in this manner. Golan's staging of Lepke's execution in the "dance hall" (as the chair was referred to by death-row inmates) is the grisliest and most harrowing scene in the film and one of the most convincing in movie history. It's also the highpoint of what is otherwise just another mediocre mob movie spawned by the box-office success of Coppola's *Godfather* films. (Not to be outdone by Coppola, Golan announced his intentions to chronicle the lives of many more American gangsters in an ambitious series of ten feature films to be shot in Russia.) The first film in the proposed series, *Mad Dog Coll* (1991), received no theatrical release in the United States. Rather, it went straight to video here under the title *Killer Instinct* (1993). It was followed by *Hit the Dutchman* (1933), another version of the life of Dutch Schultz, with which the series seems to have ended.

A less bloody but more powerful look at the mechanics of murder for hire is provided by Irving Lerner's taut and suspenseful *Murder by Contract* (1958). Vince

Hitman Vince Edwards prepares to rub out wealthy socialite Caprice Toriel in Irving Lerner's arty low-budget sleeper Murder by Contract *(1958). (Copyright © 1958 Columbia Pictures).*

Edwards plays one of three contract killers hired to rub out a wealthy socialite (Caprice Toriel) scheduled to testify against their gangland boss. Herschel Bernardi (in a marvelously chilling performance) and Phillip Pine are his associates in the relentless stalk. Most of the action in this self-consciously arty but quite compelling low-budget sleeper is confined to the area in and around Toriel's heavily guarded apartment, a veritable fortress that the persistent Edwards manages to penetrate in a most unusual manner during the film's tense closing minutes — only to fall victim to Murphy's Law as everything suddenly goes wrong for him, at the worst possible time.

On the opposite end of the excitement scale is writer-director S. Lee Pogostin's *Hard Contract* (1969), the turgid tale of a professional hit man (James Coburn) who suffers a crisis of conscience when he's assigned to rub out one of his own (Sterling Hayden), an aging killer now living in comfortable retirement in Spain. Murder-for-hire films don't have to be filled with relentless action to engage our interest, but this one replaces action with so much talk and endless angst-ridden self-reflection on the part of the conscience-stricken hit man (indeed, *all* the characters) that even the most pacifist members of the audience are likely to grow a little bloodthirsty by the final reels. One feels like shouting at Coburn to button his lip and get on with it. That he finally chooses to let Hayden live is a real letdown — which is not quite the point Pogostin's interminable morality tale set out to make.

In between the polar extremes of *Murder by Contract* and *Hard Contract* are such typical murder-for-hire films as the Charles Bronson vehicle *The Mechanic* (1972), a film in which two syndicate killers (Bronson and Jan-Michael Vincent) also find themselves pitted against one another. Lewis John Carlino's script has the two killers engage in a bit of soul-searching as well. But at least they finally get on with the job.

The meticulous recreation of New York's Lower East Side at the turn of the century in Sergio Leone's epic Once Upon a Time in America *(1984). (Copyright © 1984 Warner Bros.)*

CHAPTER 7

THE

GODFATHER SAGAS

Theories abound as to why America's most influential lawman, J. Edgar Hoover, was so reluctant to pit the power of the FBI against America's most insidious criminal network, the Mafia—and why, for most of Hoover's tenure as Bureau chief, he even denied its existence. One theory is that mobster Meyer Lansky had insurance in the form of scandalous photos of Hoover, rumored to have been homosexual, in compromising situations with his longtime aide and companion, Clyde Tolson. Another theory is that Hoover himself was on the mob's payroll. And a third, and perhaps more convincing, explanation is that Hoover simply didn't want to risk tarnishing the Bureau's image by going after a bunch of shadowy, sleazy drug and prostitution merchants whose vast sums of money might tempt Hoover's FBI agents just as they had corrupted so many other police organizations. The mob was dirty, and some of that dirt might rub off. Much better for the Bureau's image and reputation to go after headline-grabbing desperadoes like Dillinger and seditious elements posing a threat to the fabric of American society like the dreaded Commies. At least gangsters were capitalists.

Not until the Kennedy administration, when Robert F. Kennedy became U.S. Attorney General, was the full force of the FBI finally committed to an all-out war against the mob. And not until 1963, when a low-level hit man named Joe

On the Waterfront
(1954) harrowingly
depicted mob control of the
Longshoreman's Union.
With Lee. J. Cobb and
Marlon Brando.
(Copyright © 1962
Columbia Pictures)

Valachi testified before the McClellan committee about the activities of the mob—which he had joined in 1929—did Hoover finally own up to the fact that, yes, Virginia, there really was such a thing as organized crime. Valachi offered Hoover a neat way out, though, giving the organization a different name, La Cosa Nostra ("Our Thing"); Hoover allegedly responded that of course he'd known of *that* organization and that his beloved FBI had been successfully infiltrating it for years.

Unlike Hoover, the gangster film was no late bloomer in coming to grips with the existence of the Mafia. The shadowy workings of an evolving (but unnamed) national crime syndicate had been exposed to moviegoers as far back as Lewis Milestone's ground-breaking *The Racket*, and in several other silent films, as well. And though still not referred to by name, the specter of organized crime reared its ugly head throughout *Little Caesar*, *Scarface*, *The Gangster*, and many other gangster and crime films of the 1930s and 1940s. *On the Waterfront* (1954), *The Garment Jungle* (1957), and the 1959 *The Big Operator* (a.k.a. *Anatomy of a Syndicate*) dramatized details of the mob's tentacled reach into America's various labor unions in realistic, hard-hitting, and sometimes harrowing terms. And Edward L. Cahn's exciting little B movie about a vicious mob power play, *Inside the Mafia* (1959), not only provided moviegoers with a realistic look at the inner workings of the mob, it exploited the name of the organization in the title.

Perhaps J. Edgar Hoover should have spent more time at the movies.

LA MANO NERA

Director Richard Wilson followed up his mediocre (and highly fictionalized) *Al Capone* (1959) with the much superior *Pay or Die* (1960), a realistic look back at the roots of organized crime in the Black Handers of turn-of-the-century New York. Often referred to as a criminal organization, the Black Hand (*La Mano Nera*) was actually a terrorist method used by the seedier elements of New York's Little Italy to extort protection money from the immigrant population. Those who refused to cooperate with the Black Handers were mutilated or murdered and a slip of paper bearing a black palm print and the words *pay or die* was left behind to warn others. The practice was so successful in intimidating the Italian immigrants from going to the police and persuading them to pay off that many mafiosi adopted it, as well.

Pay or Die tells the true story of Lt. Joseph Petrosino (Ernest Borgnine), an immigrant policeman in Little Italy who crusaded against the Black Hand extortionists during the years 1906 to 1909 and exposed the existence of the Sicilian-controlled New York Mafia at the expense of his own life. Petrosino is initially skeptical that a conspiratorial organization is behind the activities of the Black Handers. While studying to make captain, a goal he's repeatedly failed to achieve due to interdepartmental prejudice and his lack of proficiency in reading the English language, Petrosino comes up with the idea of putting together a team of fellow immigrants on the force to improve relations within the Italian community and to go after the Black Handers. The commissioner (Robert F. Simon) agrees and Petrosino's Italian Squad—a forerunner of Eliot Ness's Untouchables—gets its first big job when it's assigned to protect singer Enrico Caruso (Howard Caine), who's been targeted by the Black Handers for refusing to pay protection money. The Black Handers plant a bomb in Caruso's car, but Petrosino and his squad foil the assassination attempt and the bomber is killed.

Following this initial success of the Italian Squad, the Black Handers proceed to get bolder, and influential members of the Italian community, believing the squad needs a leader of more stature than Petrosino, urge the commissioner and the mayor (Paul Birch) to replace him. But Petrosino is kept on, and through his courage and persistence he and his squad get the frightened citizens to trust them and score an impressive record of arrests and convictions.

When an important criminal witness (Robert Ellenstein) adheres to the Mafia's code of silence by killing himself, Petrosino comes to realize that the Black Handers are not just a loose-knit bunch of extortionists but part of a larger criminal conspiracy whose unknown New York ringleaders are having their strings pulled by Mafia elders in Sicily. Petrosino finally passes the exam and makes captain, then sails to Italy to discover as much as he can about the Mafia's tentacled reach into the United States and to smoke out the name of the Mafia capo running things in New York.

Petrosino finds out that Zarillo (Franco Corsaro), one of Little Italy's most respected citizens, is the capo, and he acquires the names and identifying photos of numerous other capos the Mafia string-pullers have sent to the United States to develop their organization. In the surprising conclusion, he's stalked by Mafia goons and murdered on the streets of Palermo before he can deliver the critical information. Back home, the murdered policeman's protégé (Alan Austin) finally nails Zarillo, but the Mafia's infiltration of the United States goes on.

A decade earlier, Richard Thorpe's *Black Hand* (1950) recounted essentially the same story, but in more fictionalized terms. The plot centers on Johnny

Columbo, the son of an immigrant lawyer (Peter Brocco) who was murdered by the Black Handers for trying to expose them. Columbo and his mother flee to Italy, but Johnny (Gene Kelly) returns as an adult to exact *la vendetta* against the men responsible for his father's death. Johnny renews his relationship with his childhood sweetheart (Teresa Celli) and is taken under the wing of a tough Italian cop and old family friend named Lorelli (J. Carrol Naish), a character modeled on the real-life Petrosino. They turn Johnny away from revenge and get him to join in organizing the Italian community to fight back against the Black Handers and their mafiosi ringleaders.

On a secret mission to Italy, Lorelli discovers the name of the New York head man, Serpi (Marc Lawrence), and comes up with a list of names of other mafiosi sent to the United States, as well. Like Petrosino, he's killed for knowing too much. But he manages to mail off the list of names before expiring from his wounds. Johnny, who has become a member of the police force, receives the list and eventually revenges himself against Serpi and runs the other Black Handers to ground.

Tough and violent, *Black Hand* and *Pay or Die* are beautifully photographed by Paul C. Vogel and Lucien Ballard, respectively, and evoke the ethnic atmosphere of turn-of-the-century New York's teeming Little Italy quite vividly. Both films openly make use of the terms *mafioso, mafiosi,* and *Mafia;* in *Black Hand,* Naish even alludes to the purported derivation of the word *Mafia,* an acronym of *Morte alla*

Inspector Lorelli (J. Carrol Naish) prepares to mail the list of Mafioso names and photos to America. Lorelli was also based on Joseph Petrosino. From Black Hand *(1950). (Copyright © 1950 Metro-Goldwyn-Mayer)*

Francia Italia anela ("Death to the French cries Italy"), when he talks about the Bourbon kings' domination of Italy in the late eighteenth and early nineteenth centuries.

Of the two films, *Black Hand* is the less dramatically satisfying, however. For one thing, it is very oddly structured. Kelly (an unusual choice for the dramatic role of a revenge-seeking young Italian, though he acquits himself fairly well) is supposed to be the hero. But his character disappears for large chunks of the film as the story focuses on Naish, ostensibly a supporting character but the most interesting figure in the film. And the film's revelation of the capo comes as no surprise, since we see Serpi—though we don't know his name—engineer the murder of Johnny's father at the beginning of the film, as well as various other misdeeds throughout.

His Little Italy roots and the popularity of the gangster film provided Martin Scorsese with his successful entrée into the Hollywood big leagues via *Mean Streets* (1973), a gritty portrait of the legacy and influence of the Black Handers and organized crime on three modern-day second-generation Italian Americans. In many ways, the film is a warm-up for Scorsese's more polished and even more highly acclaimed *GoodFellas* (1990), set in the same Lower East Side/Little Italy milieu during roughly the same time period and that makes similar use of period rock and roll tunes to punctuate the visceral action.

Like a character out of an old Jimmy Cagney/Pat O'Brien gangster movie,

Gang war erupts in New York's Little Italy. From Martin Scorsese's Mean Streets *(1973) with Harvey Keitel. (Copyright © 1973 Warner Bros.)*

Mean Streets hero Harvey Keitel is torn between his religious convictions and desire to become a priest and his attraction to the money-making world of crime. That world is represented by his uncle (Cesare Danova), a successful restauranteur and mafioso. As Keitel searches his soul, he and pal David Proval get progressively more involved in low-level loan-sharking and numbers racketeering while the violent third member of their group, Robert De Niro, gets in over his head with a vicious small-time hood (Richard Romanus) bent on moving up the syndicate ladder and becoming a capo. Part coming-of-age tale on the order of Fellini's *I Vitelloni* (1953) and all gangster film, *Mean Streets* effectively shows how little the cultural landscape of Scorsese's Little Italy had changed since the early days of the Black Handers—when the power of gangland's allure and muscle posed just as much a threat and forced similarly hard moral choices.

Neither Scorsese nor De Niro were strangers to the gangster film when they collaborated on *Mean Streets*, their first film together. De Niro had appeared as one of Ma Barker's killer brood in Roger Corman's *Bloody Mama* (1970), one of a number of Depression-era gangster films made by Corman and others in the wake of the success of *Bonnie and Clyde*. De Niro also had a small part as a mafioso belonging to the all-thumbs Kid Sally Palumbo (Jerry Orbach) mob in James Goldstone's *The Gang That Couldn't Shoot Straight* (1971), an unfunny gangland farce in the tradition of Edward G. Robinson's mob comedies, based on Jimmy Breslin's amusing roman à clef about the notorious Brooklyn mobster Crazy Joe Gallo. And Scorsese had gotten his feet wet in Hollywood making *Boxcar Bertha* (1972), another Depression-era saga of young guns on the run inspired by the success of *Bonnie and Clyde*. Produced by Roger Corman, the film was loosely based on the autobiography *Sister of the Road* by Boxcar Bertha Thompson, a minor thirties hobo and bank robber. Barbara Hershey played the title role and David Carradine played her doomed lover, a character named Big Bill Shelley.

Jacques Deray's *Borsalino* (1970) examined the growth of organized crime from

Below, left: Borsalino (1970) examined the growth of organized crime from the European perspective. With Jean-Paul Belmondo, Alain Delon, and Catherine Rouvel. (Copyright © 1970 Adel Productions)

Right: Angelo Infanti (in light coat) as Lucky Luciano, Lino Ventura (to his left) as Vito Genovese, and Charles Bronson as Joe Valachi in The Valachi Papers *(1972). (Copyright © 1973 Columbia Pictures)*

the European perspective. The film is set in the Mafia-dominated port city of Marseilles during the early 1930s and atmospherically recaptures the flavor of some of the French gangster films starring Jean Gabin made during that period. Its style, however, is pure seventies mod (blood and laughs) mixed with Warner Brothers rat-a-tat-tat from the halcyon days of Robinson, Cagney, and Bogart.

Alain Delon and Jean-Paul Belmondo (doing his Bogie bit once again) play a pair of competitive gangster pals, two small-time hoodlums who laugh, love, and shoot their way to the top of the Corsican underworld until Belmondo is killed. The settings, photography, and costumes are lush, and the Claude Bolling score is wonderfully evocative of the era. But the film is a bit static and, at 126 minutes, much too long, which is probably why it was not a hit in the United States, where the type of lengthy, lavish, and epic period gangster film *Borsalino* inaugurated would have to wait two years until *The Godfather* finally to catch on. It was a big-enough hit in Europe, though, to spawn a slew of smaller European-style period gangster films, including one sequel, *Borsalino & Co.* (1974), which recounted the further gangland adventures of Delon following the death of the Belmondo character.

The Valachi Papers (1972) was a European production as well, but its setting is the United States. Based on the best-selling book by reporter Peter Maas, it looks at the growth of organized crime in the United States from the days of the Black Handers and "Mustache Petes" to the 1970s as seen through the eyes of Joe Valachi, real-life mob hit man turned informer. A few location scenes were filmed in New York, but most of the picture was shot on the gigantic sound-stages of Cinecittà studios in Italy. The cast is predominantly Italian as well, with a few American and British actors tossed in for good measure to enhance the international flavor. The film catapulted Charles Bronson to international stardom as Valachi.

Perhaps to offset the ethnic controversy that had plagued *The Godfather* (*The Valachi Papers* was released later the same year), the film was introduced by a quote from former U.S. Attorney General Robert F. Kennedy: "Crime is a question of criminal. It is not a matter of race, color or religion." We first meet Valachi in the Atlanta Penitentiary, where he's been incarcerated for murder. Big-time mob boss Vito Genovese (Lino Ventura) has been sent to the same pen on a narcotics rap and suspects Valachi of having ratted on him, a charge Valachi, a loyal Mafia soldier all his life, violently denies. When Genovese gives him the Sicilian kiss of death nonetheless, Valachi realizes his loyalty is for nothing and makes a deal with the feds to protect him and his family in exchange for the complete lowdown on the history and workings of the mob (which Valachi calls La Cosa Nostra), testimony the criminal will later repeat on live television before the McClellan committee.

As Valachi spills his guts to Special Agent Ryan (Gerald S. O'Loughlin), the film flashes back to the late 1920s. Valachi, a small-time hood just released from prison, lands the job of bodyguard to big-time "Mustache Pete" boss Salvatore Maranzano (Joseph Wiseman in an entertainingly ripe performance). Maranzano and rival Joey "the Boss" Masseria (Alessandro Sperli) are done away with by Lucky Luciano (Angelo Infanti, a virtual double for the real Lucky) and other ambitious mobsters, leading to the creation of New York's notorious Five Families. Valachi gets carried along and eventually becomes a hit man for the brutal Genovese and his psychotic sidekick Albert Anastasia—and an eyewitness to the mob's vicious intrigues and corruptive influence on America over the next several decades, culminating with the historic 1957 underworld conference in Apalachin, New York, which is raided by the feds and ultimately leads to Genovese's undoing as the "boss of bosses." For giving them the goods on the mob (even though much of his testimony is not believed at the time), Valachi is placed in tight security at a federal correctional facility in Texas. He dies there in 1971, having outlived the vengeful Genovese by six months.

Coming on the heels of Coppola's fastidiously made *The Godfather*, *The Valachi Papers* is an unusually shoddy affair. Perhaps to capitalize on the notoriety and big box office the Coppola film was mustering, it seems to have been slapped together and rushed into release: The English lip-synching of the mostly Italian cast is always just a bit off; action sequences are clumsily staged and rather unconvincing as well, the explosions of "blood squibs" as mobster bodies are racked by gunfire occasionally as badly synchronized as the actors' lips. The scene in which one of Valachi's close pals, Dominick "the Gap" Petrillo (Walter Chari), is castrated for dallying with Genovese's slutty show-girl mistress is, nevertheless, harrowingly effective. And Stephen Geller's script, which veers wildly from broad comedy to stark drama, does a good job of laying out the complex cast of real-life characters and explaining their sometimes Byzantine relationships. Bronson is typically impassive as Valachi, an essentially dumb guy who goes along until he can no longer afford to, but his performance, like the film itself, manages to be fairly engaging. Unlike *Borsalino*, which also clocks in at over two hours and mixes comedy with drama, *The Valachi Papers* at least manages to sustain viewer interest. And by adhering mostly to fact, it provides some solid inside dope on the history of the mob, as well.

The Sicilian kiss of death also figures prominently in the plot of *The Brotherhood* (1968), a small-scale mob melodrama starring Kirk Douglas as an old-style Mafia don whose reluctance to go along with the organization's more progressive schemes lands him on the hit list. Douglas's younger brother (Alex Cord), a college grad being groomed for big things within the organization, is given the death-dealing contract as a way to prove himself.

Douglas learns from some of the old-time mobsters he still pals around with that a fellow member of the syndicate's board of directors (Luther Adler) was responsible for the murder of his and Cord's mafioso father thirty-five years earlier. When Douglas kills Adler in revenge, he finds himself even more on the outs with the mob and is forced to go into hiding in Sicily. Cord hunts him down and tries to persuade him to patch things up, but Douglas knows the Mafia code renders that impossible and that he's a doomed man—and that Cord will be, too, if he doesn't fulfill the contract. In the film's powerful final scene, he forces the reluctant Cord into accepting the rules of the brotherhood and the fate those rules have dealt them. After embracing and exchanging the Sicilian kiss of death, Douglas backs away and Cord lets him have it with a shotgun. The film ends here, but the look of devastation and grim determination on Cord's face as he pulls the trigger suggests that the drama is not yet over and that, as the vicious circle of the brotherhood comes around, Cord will eventually turn into Douglas and exact his own vendetta against the mob someday. Douglas hints as much moments before his death, when he tells Cord, "Me like papa, you like me. It's like we're all the same guy."

The Brotherhood is a strongly acted film, particularly by Douglas, who also produced and therefore gave himself the best and showiest part. The scene where he literally takes Adler "for a ride" is especially well written and performed, the film's brutal highpoint. Cord's performance is bland and insufficiently realized, but

Kirk Douglas and Alex Cord exchange the Sicilian "kiss of death" in The Brotherhood *(1968). (Copyright © 1968 Paramount Pictures)*

his character remarkably foreshadows the part played by Al Pacino in *The Godfather*. *The Brotherhood*'s strong ethnic flavor is strikingly similar to that of the Coppola film as well, and there is even a reference to a Mafia family named Corleone in the film.

For the most part, *The Brotherhood* unfolds like a talky, slice-of-life drama from the golden age of television; for that reason, perhaps, it was not a box-office success. Having flopped with *The Brotherhood* and the domestic release of *Borsalino*, Paramount was understandably reluctant to pour money into yet another film about the Mafia. But *The Godfather* went ahead anyway, and the third time proved the charm.

AN OFFER HOLLYWOOD COULDN'T REFUSE

Mario Puzo says that one of the reasons he wrote *The Godfather* was to get out of debt. His first two novels, *The Dark Arena* (1955) and *The Fortunate Pilgrim* (1965), earned him some excellent reviews but not a lot of royalties. With *The Godfather*, he was aiming for a best-seller. And he achieved his goal. Published in 1969, the novel sold 500,000 copies in hardcover and more than 10 million copies in paperback by the time the film version was released. To put the frosting on the cake (or the sauce on the pasta, as it were), *The Godfather* also earned a great deal of critical acclaim for a commercial best-seller. *The Saturday Review* called it "A staggering triumph . . . the most revealing novel ever written about the criminal underworld of the Mafia." Like W. R. Burnett's *Little Caesar* forty years earlier, it set the standard for a whole new generation of novels about gangsters and gangland. And like Mervyn LeRoy's film version of *Little Caesar*, Francis Coppola's movie of *The Godfather* would become the yardstick by which all future gangster films would be measured.

The novel is a richly detailed roman à clef about the history and structure of organized crime in the United States, from the turn of the century to the bloody Mafia wars among New York's powerful Five Families in the late 1940s. The story and characters are modeled on a wide spectrum of events and underworld figures, politicians, entertainers, and other historical personages of that era. The novel's aging Don Vito Corleone, for example, is a composite of many real Mafia crime bosses, but primarily a portrait of Frank Costello, one of the original pioneers of the syndicate along with Meyer Lansky, Lucky Luciano, and Bugsy Siegel. Like Vito Corleone's, Costello's power in the organization derived from the number of politicians, judges, and police officials he had in his pocket and was able to strong-arm for the benefit of the organization. Michael Corleone, the youngest son, who ultimately claims his father's Mafia throne, is also a composite, but his most striking resemblance is to Vito Genovese. In the novel, Michael murders a crooked cop and an ambitious drug dealer for their participation in an assassination

Mafia justice. From
Lucky Luciano *(1974).*
(Copyright © 1974
Avco-Embassy Pictures)

attempt on his father's life and is then forced to hide out in Italy until things blow over. When he returns to the United States, his superior cunning makes him the natural candidate to take over the family's beleaguered operations after his father's death. The equally cunning Genovese had escaped to Italy to avoid a mob-related murder charge and returned to assume leadership of the powerful Luciano crime family. Like Costello, Vito Corleone is opposed to the syndicate's getting involved in narcotics, deeming them "bad business" and "bad for business," and his reluctance to use his political strings to assist fellow mobsters involved in the drug trade is what, in part, triggers the gang war for power among the Five Families that constitutes the book's plot.

In addition to exposing the secret lore and laws of the Mafia in skillful dramatic terms, the book also provides a richly authentic look at Italian-American life—something the film version would do even more fully, creating a furor, since the particular Italian-Americans being portrayed happened to be gangsters. Neither the book nor the movie suggests that all Italian-Americans are mafiosi. Nevertheless, Italian-American pressure groups forced the filmmakers to excise all reference to the words *Mafia* and *La Cosa Nostra* from the film's script. Less familiar Italian words like *capo*, *caporegime*, and *consigliere* would remain, however, and soon become part of the American vocabulary.

Paramount bought the rights to Puzo's sprawling period saga in manuscript form for the bargain price of eighty thousand dollars. Still smarting over the box-office failure of *The Brotherhood* and the poor U.S. performance of *Borsalino*, the

studio proposed to make the film on a modest budget of $2.5 million, a price that would virtually guarantee the studio a profit. To keep within the $2.5 million, the studio decided to update Puzo's story to the present to eliminate the costs of creating expensive period sets, with vintage cars and costuming, that would result. When the book became a runaway best-seller, however, Paramount decided to pour a few more million into the film's production and turn *The Godfather* into an "event movie," with widespread release and higher-than-usual ticket prices. At the insistence of producer Al Ruddy and director Francis Ford Coppola, the studio was also persuaded to return the story to its period milieu.

Many directors turned the project down before Coppola finally came on board. According to Robert Evans, Paramount's production chief at the time, Coppola was chosen for the assignment because he was Italian and would be able to invest the film with the required ethnic atmosphere. Coppola was also a young director in need of a major hit, and would, therefore, be easier for the studio to control. The likes of Laurence Olivier, Edward G. Robinson, and Richard Conte (who would ultimately be given the role of the godfather's chief rival, the insidious Don Barzini) were considered for the title role. Orson Welles actively campaigned for the part, as well. Demonstrating his independence early on, however, Coppola insisted on Marlon Brando, who had not had a box-office hit in years and whose name was anathema to the studio that had lost a fortune on Brando's profligate directorial debut *One-Eyed Jacks* (1961). To convince studio execs that Brando was

Right: The Family. James Caan, Marlon Brando, Al Pacino, and John Cazale in The Godfather *(1972). (Copyright © 1972 Paramount Pictures)*

Below, left: "Look how they massacred my boy!" Marlon Brando as The Godfather *(1972). (Copyright © 1972 Paramount Pictures)*

the right man for the job, Coppola persuaded the legendary actor to do a screen test in full makeup. That did the trick and Brando got the part—for which he was paid a percentage of the film's profits rather than a salary. For the pivotal role of Michael Corleone, the reluctant war-hero son who ultimately becomes an even more brutal don than his old man, the studio sought someone with the right mix of star power and bankability. Coppola insisted on the relatively unknown Al Pacino, and won that battle, as well. Coppola handpicked the rest of the cast and even wrote the script with Puzo.

One of the few things Coppola didn't get his way on was the film's conclusion. Coppola wanted to retain the book's original ending, in which Michael's long-suffering wife, Kay (Diane Keaton), who is much more aware of Michael's criminal involvements and darker side in the book than she is in the film, takes communion and prays for her husband's lost soul. It was Robert Evans who insisted that the film conclude with Michael's lie to Kay about his complicity in the murder of Carlo Rizzi (Gianni Russo), his sister's (Talia Shire) husband, and the closing of the door on Kay (and us, the audience) as he takes his place as dynastic head of the secrecy-bound family. With all deference to Coppola, Evans's revised ending is tremendously effective.

With *The Godfather*, Coppola took a tired cinematic genre in which all had seemingly been done and, just as Akira Kurosawa had with *Seven Samurai* (1954) and Sam Peckinpah with *The Wild Bunch* (1969), pushed it in an epic new direction.

Michael Corleone (Al Pacino) takes his place as dynastic head of the Family at the conclusion of The Godfather *(1972). (Copyright © 1972 Paramount Pictures)*

Brutal, bloody, shocking, scary, funny, socially and politically observant, and meticulously performed by everyone from the leads to the bit players, the film offered a panoramic glimpse into the closed society of organized crime in the United States—a society ruled by la vendetta, where the most sought-after currency, respect, is acquired through fear and intimidation. It's a society where murder is "nothing personal—just business" and casts a shadow over many other levels of American life, as well. As Kurosawa said of *Seven Samurai*, Coppola had made a film that was rich and "entertaining enough to eat." Not for nothing was it quickly dubbed the "*Gone With the Wind* of Gangster Movies."

Coppola had also made a financial blockbuster, a film whose huge box-office success prompted Paramount to demand a sequel as quickly as possible. For the sequel, however, Coppola demanded and got complete creative autonomy: He would not only write the script with Puzo and direct the film as he chose but would produce *The Godfather, Part II* (1974), as well.

The main criticism leveled at *The Godfather* was that Coppola had made his Mafia characters sympathetic by giving them too human a face. They *are* killers, after all, the film's critics wrote, even if they do have wives and families. Coppola's point about the banality of evil, that members of the underworld are not all eye-rolling, saliva-dripping goons, was apparently lost on them. (Interestingly, Puzo was acclaimed by many literary critics for having made "his frightening cast of characters seem human and possible.") Coppola took this criticism to heart, however, and in the sequel he determined to make the point that Michael Corleone, an antihero who kills to hold his family together through the turmoil of the Mafia wars in the first film, is a Machiavellian figure whose soul is clearly lost by the final reel of the second film. The first film ends with the christening of Michael and Kay's son, Tony, and Michael's concurrent baptism of fire as his father's rightful heir. The sequel begins with Tony's first communion and Michael's own symbolic first communion as head of the family, dispensing favors, orders, and "justice" as his father had done at the beginning of the first film. The point that what drives Michael is not what drove his father, that Michael is a more bitter and ruthless character who is finally capable of murdering his own brother (John Cazale), is potently made by flashing back in time throughout the sequel in order to contrast the two godfathers' characters at similar points in their lives.* Vito is

---

*The flashback scenes in which the young Vito (Robert De Niro) flees Italy following the Mafia murders of his family and builds his power base in the United States by taking a leaf from the book of the Black Handers are taken from Puzo's novel. When *The Godfather* and *The Godfather, Part II* films were sold to NBC, Coppola eliminated the flashback structure of the second film and reedited both films so that they unfolded chronologically. He also added several sequences that had been cut from the theatrical versions. The result was an epic generational saga that enabled viewers to marvel at how convincingly De Niro turns into Brando in terms of gesture, voice, and makeup. But the loss of the flashback structure muted our understanding of the differences between Michael and Vito.

clearly a product of his old country ways. He views the world as a place where only the strong can survive. He functions on the instinctive level of pure animal cunning. Even *la vendetta* is no more than the natural order of things in his world. By contrast, Michael is a bitter man because he'd wanted no part of his father's world, yet has been drawn into it, anyway. His dreams of not being a criminal like his father having been crushed by circumstances, he views the world as a sewer and acts accordingly. By the end of the film, his outlook has turned him into a conscienceless, dead-eyed monster.

Coppola saw the sequel not as a way of simply cashing in on the success of the first film but of expanding its elements into a much broader and richer tapestry. The film chronicles the business of organized crime in the United States from 1900 to the 1960s, weaving fact with fiction in the manner of its predecessor. The opening sequence in Sicily depicts the funeral of Vito's slain father, the murder of his mother, and his escape to New York's Little Italy, which production designer Dean Tavoularis reconstructed in spectacular fashion. Coppola's use of the Neopolitan opera *Senza Mamma,* a popular musical of the period written by the director's paternal grandfather, serves as a coda to the Little Italy sequences where the adult Vito murders the Black Hander Don Fanucci (Gaston Moschin) and begins his rise to power in the underworld. When he becomes a successful figure in organized crime, Vito returns to his native hill village in Sicily to revenge himself on the mafiosi who murdered his family. In the modern sequences, Coppola introduces a Meyer Lansky character named Hyman Roth (Lee Strasberg), the syndicate boss

Robert De Niro as the young Vito Corleone in The Godfather Part II *(1974). (Copyright © 1974 Paramount Pictures)*

Vito (Robert De Niro) gets even with the mob boss who killed his family. From The Godfather Part II *(1974). (Copyright © 1974 Paramount Pictures)*

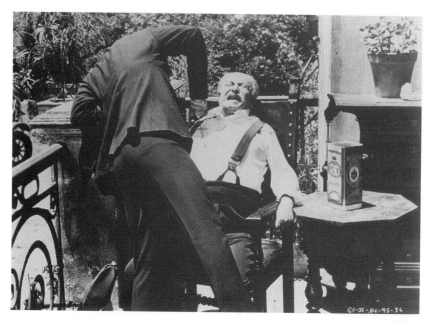

and financial wizard who plays up to Michael but secretly plots to overthrow him. These scenes take the film to Cuba (the scenes were shot in the Dominican Republic), where organized crime's vast holdings in nightclubs and gambling are lost in the wake of Castro's overthrow of the mob-controlled Batista government.* The film also includes a reenactment of the McClellan committee hearings, where a Joe Valachi–like character (Joe Spinell) amuses the senators with his description of the mob's killers as "button men," just as Valachi had done. As an in-joke, Coppola assigned the roles of the senators on the committee to various nonactors who had been instrumental in shaping his career. They include the late Phil Feldman, the producer of Coppola's first big Hollywood film, *You're a Big Boy Now* (1966); writer-producer William Bowers; producer-director Roger Corman; and Buck Houghton, the producer of the legendary TV series "The Twilight Zone." Peter Donat plays the McClellan character, here named Senator Questadt. At the conclusion, Michael's Mafia "soldiers" brutally take care of "all family business," including the murder of Hyman Roth and Michael's brother, as the ruthless criminal chieftain gazes upon the chilly waters of Lake Tahoe from the windows of his heavily fortified estate.

Of *The Godfather, Part II,* Coppola said: "The only way [it] can be an excellent film is, if when it's done and seen, the audience, including myself, looks at it and

*Richard Lester's *Cuba* (1979) and Sydney Pollack's overblown and *Casablanca*-like *Havana* (1990) explore this critical event in the mob's history in more detail but much less vividly.

says that it was essential that it was made." He succeeded. *The Godfather, Part II* is a rarity indeed, a sequel that not only deepens our understanding of the original film but betters it artistically. It remains, as well, the only sequel to date to repeat the success of its predecessor in capturing a Best Picture Oscar. As of this writing, it also remains Coppola's masterpiece, his perhaps more ambitious and controversial *Apocalypse Now* (1979) notwithstanding.

The Godfather, Part II was a huge financial success but, at twice the budget of its predecessor, not quite the blockbuster the original had been. Paramount was savvy enough to realize that since the film ended in the 1960s with Michael Corleone still very much alive (physically, if not spiritually), the mine had yet to be played out. It wanted another sequel. Coppola wasn't interested, however, and shelved the offer to make *The Godfather, Part III* for almost twenty years.

In the interim, Puzo turned out another Mafia-themed novel called *The Sicilian*, a fictionalized account of the life and death of the legendary Sicilian bandit and revolutionary Salvatore Guiliano, who was assassinated in 1950 for warring against the Italian government, the country's rich landowners, and powerful mafiosi. The character of Michael Corleone appears briefly in the novel.

A big-budget film version of the book was made in 1987 with the uncharismatic Christopher Lambert in the title role. The Michael Corleone scenes were dropped from the film version, which was directed by Michael Cimino, the profligate filmmaker who had sunk United Artists and almost ruined his career with the megabuck spectacular (and spectacularly awful) *Heaven's Gate* (1980). A large-scale but plodding film completely lacking the operatic drama of Coppola's two *Godfather* films, *The Sicilian* proved once again that Cimino's powerful, Oscar-winning *The Deer Hunter* (1978) had been a fluke. Shorn of more than thirty excruciatingly tedious minutes (the complete version is available on videocassette) to improve its chances at U.S. box offices, *The Sicilian* deservedly belly flopped nonetheless. Though less epic in scope and made for a fraction of *The Sicilian*'s cost, Francesco Rosi's documentarylike *Salvatore Guiliano* (1962) was an infinitely more illuminating and gripping treatment of the same story.

Ironically, Coppola finally resumed the *Godfather* saga for the same reason he'd launched it in the first place: He needed a box-office hit and an infusion of capital to boost his sagging filmmaking and personal fortunes. Paramount had been talking about doing *The Godfather, Part III* for years, without Coppola; stars such as John Travolta and Sylvester Stallone had been courted for the project, which was to have focused on Michael's son, Tony, now grown and heading up the family business. Following the box-office failure of Coppola's long-cherished project *Tucker: The Man and His Dream* (1988), Paramount chairman Frank Mancuso approached Coppola about taking the reins on *The Godfather, Part III*, and this time the director was interested. To sweeten the offer, Mancuso agreed to give the director the total artistic control Coppola had had on *The Godfather, Part II,* plus a $5 million salary and 15 percent of the film's gross. This proved the proverbial offer Coppola couldn't refuse, and he and Mario Puzo agreed to come up in six months with an original script focusing on the further adventures of Michael Corleone. Paramount wanted the film for a Christmas 1990 release, however, and so the collaborators were forced to pare down their schedule and turn out their script in a brisk six weeks. Coppola was revising the script even as shooting began in November 1989, and he would continue to do so throughout the film's production, tallying approximately thirty drafts before the film was finally completed. Pressure mounted on Coppola during the editing stage of the nearly three-hour film, and rumors spread throughout the industry that the movie was in trouble and would not be ready in time for the lucrative Christmas season—a deadline that had to be met to qualify the film for Academy Award consideration that year, as well. The film opened on time, however, and proved to be the hit everyone expected it to be. But it was not the blockbuster *The Godfather* had been, nor did it receive the unanimous critical accolades heaped upon *The Godfather, Part II;* like its predecessors, *The Godfather, Part III* did receive an Academy Award nomination as Best Picture, but, unlike them, it failed to take home the prize.

The film takes up the saga of Michael Corleone in 1979, as the now sixty-year-old don (Pacino again) is receiving the Order of San Sebastian, the highest honor the Catholic Church can bestow upon a layman. Haunted by the murder of his brother Fredo and his long unkept promise to his ex-wife, Kay (Keaton), to make the family business legitimate, Michael takes advantage of the Vatican Bank scandals to buy his way into respectability, and to redeem himself at the same time. Through the Vito Corleone Foundation, a charitable organization innocently fronted by his daughter, Mary (Sofia Coppola), Michael makes a $600 million donation to assist the Vatican with its real estate and loan troubles in exchange for controlling interest in International Immobiliare, an outwardly respectable but secretly shady European multiconglomerate whose largest share-holder is the Vatican Bank. Pope Paul VI himself must ratify the deal, but the pontiff's untimely death and the delay in electing a new Pope stalls Michael's takeover plans long enough for his former syndicate associates to thwart his dream of washing away his sins and becoming respectable. Unhappy that Michael has severed himself from them and is going it alone on the lucrative Immobiliare deal, the heads of the other crime families conspire to draw Michael back into the Mafia world of violence and double-dealing—a conspiracy that, among other things, involves assassinating the honest new Pope (Raf Vallone) and, ultimately, Michael himself.

In between coping with Mafia plotters, crooked Vatican officials, and cutthroat European businessmen, Michael faces trouble on the home front, as well. His

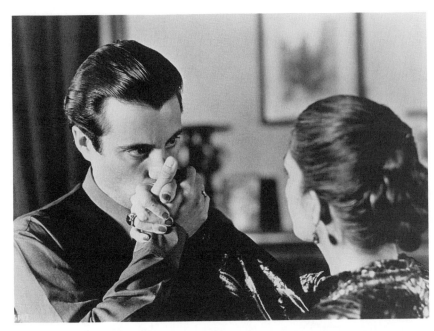

Sonny's illegitimate son, Vincent Mancini (Andy Garcia), takes over as head of the Family in The Godfather Part III *(1990). With Talia Shire. (Copyright © 1990 Paramount Pictures)*

grown son, Tony (Franc D'Ambrosio), has rejected the family business (just as Michael himself had wanted to at Tony's age) to become an opera singer. Meanwhile, his daughter, Mary, is carrying on a tempestuous affair with her first cousin Vincent (Andy Garcia), the hotheaded illegitimate son of Michael's late brother Sonny. Michael has taken Vincent under his wing and ultimately enthrones him as the family's next godfather (thereby paving the way for a *Godfather, Part IV*). Michael is also attempting to reunite himself with his ex-wife, Kay. All these intrigues come to a climax in the film's vigorous last half hour, during Tony's operatic debut, when, with Vincent's help, Michael bloodily settles "all family business" once more—this time, he hopes, for good. In the process, Mary takes an assassin's bullet that was meant for him and the veteran gangster collapses with grief, realizing he has not only lost his beloved daughter but his dreams of redemption, as well. The final scene shows the white-haired Lear-like don sitting alone in the yard of his Sicilian palazzo many years later; he slumps over dead from a heart attack and falls to the ground, bringing the curtain down at last on his awful life.

The Godfather, Part III is not without its virtues. Its rich, warm photography by Gordon Willis, sumptuous production design by Dean Tavoularis (and others), and operatic style are all remarkably consistent with the first two films in the series. But its flaws are not insignificant. Considering its whopping $55 million budget (more than four times that of *The Godfather, Part II*), its failure to provide a

Sitting ducks. Sofia Coppola, Diane Keaton, Al Pacino, George Hamilton, John Savage, Don Novello, Andy Garcia, and Talia Shire in the operatic finale of The Godfather Part III *(1990). (Copyright © 1990 Paramount Pictures)*

conclusion to the Corleone saga in keeping with the epic vision of the first two films is a big disappointment. Coppola intended the film to be contemplative, but the effect it produces is ennui. Compared to the first two films, it is dull. Its mostly new cast of mafioso characters and scheming outsiders is simply no match for the colorful Don Barzinis, Clemenzas, Tessios, Sollozzos, Sonny Corleones, Tom Hagens, Hyman Roths, Frankie Pentangelis, and other underworld killers and victims who populated the earlier films, riveting our interest even as they repelled us. Nor is the similarly intricate plot as gripping as those of the earlier films. In fact, it's downright hard to follow at times.

Coppola's casting of his nonactress daughter, Sofia, in the pivotal role of Mary also fails to serve the film very well. Awkward and inexperienced, she fails to make the character come alive. That we feel any emotion at all when Mary is killed in the film's climax is solely due to the wrenching performances of Al Pacino and Diane Keaton in this admittedly powerful scene.

To the role of Vincent, Michael's surrogate son and heir to his position as godfather, Andy Garcia brings a considerable amount of fire and grit, but the character is fairly one-dimensional and hardly the stuff of which gangland sagas are made.

The film's most serious flaw, however, is the change Coppola and Puzo have wrought in their main characters. They are simply not the people they were at the close of *The Godfather, Part II*—a fact that becomes strikingly apparent when the two films are watched back-to-back.

Connie (Talia Shire), Michael's long-victimized sister and an embittered, vulnerable woman in *The Godfather, Part II*, is turned into a scheming Lady Macbeth in *The Godfather, Part III*. In *The Godfather, Part II*, Kay revenges herself on Michael by aborting a child to keep it from being born into the violent world of "this Sicilian thing" her dreaded husband has subjected her to—an act that loses her custody of their children when they divorce and that cements their mutual hatred. Yet in *The Godfather, Part III*, the two attempt a reconciliation and Kay admits she still loves him, a revelation that is impossible to swallow given the past they've shared. But the most extreme, and damaging, alteration is in Michael's character.

Monsters may get old and tired, but the outlook that made them monsters does not vanish. Guilt and the need for redemption are simply not a part of the emotionally dead, cold-eyed character Michael had become when *The Godfather, Part II* faded to black. Nor would the Michael of the second film, who cynically observed to the naïve Kay that even governments are corrupt and order people killed, have commented with such surprise and chagrin (as he does in *The Godfather, Part III*) that "the higher I go, the crookeder it gets." We do feel a sense of loss when Michael slumps over dead in his chair, but this has less to do with Coppola and Puzo's forced attempt to make him into a tragic King Lear than it does with our feelings of nostalgia for the overall series now that it has ended. Coppola and Puzo would have been wiser to make *The Godfather, Part III*'s Michael Corleone a Captain Ahab instead; that at least would have made it more consistent with—and as interesting as—its predecessors.

The film offered a nice touch, though, by having the character of Joey Zasa (Joe Mantegna), a character modeled on Joe Colombo, the flashy gangland boss whose Italian-American and antidefamation organization forced the removal of all reference to the words *Mafia* and *Cosa Nostra* from the first film, mowed down by gangland bullets after proclaiming that there was no such thing as the Mafia or La Cosa Nostra.

Akira Kurosawa alluded to another of Shakespeare's tragic heroes in *The Bad Sleep Well* (1960), a tale of vendetta and corporate gangsterism that foreshadowed Coppola's *Godfather* films in many ways.

Iwabuchi (Masayuki Mori), the Vito Corleone–like head of a government housing corporation that is being investigated for corruption, rules his empire in the same brutal style as Coppola's Mafia gangsters. His corporate officers and their underlings function like capos and Mafia soldiers; disloyal employees or potential whistle-blowers are murdered, their deaths made to appear like suicides or accidents. Iwabuchi's hold over his corporate family is so strong and his code of silence so ingrained that when one official finds himself boxed in by the police and is told by the corporation's lawyer that the only way out is suicide, the man instantly complies by jumping in front of a truck moments before the police are to take him into custody. (*The Godfather, Part II* has a similar scene, in which reluctant government witness Frankie Pentangeli [Michael V. Gazzo] finds himself in a kindred bind and the family's consigliere [Robert Duvall] also suggests suicide as the only honorable way out. Frankie complies shortly after by slashing his wrists in a warm bath while his government guards obliviously play cards in an adjoining room.) As in the *Godfather* films, such deaths are "nothing personal—just business." The victims' funerals are lavish and well attended by friend and foe alike. And the victims' families are taken care of financially by the corporation from then on.

Like Coppola's Mafia types, the contrast between Iwabuchi's professional and private life is stark. On the home front, the gray-haired old man seems the ideal father figure as he dotes on his crippled daughter (Kyoko Kagawa) and patiently puts up with his ne'er-do-well son (Tatsuya Mihashi). Even his son says of him, "It's hard to believe he's a bad man."

The situation comes to a head when Iwabuchi's masquerade as honest businessman and loving father is threatened with exposure from within by Nishi (Toshiro Mifune), Iwabuchi's son-in-law and seemingly loyal personal secretary. In fact, Nishi is the illegitimate son of a corporate official Iwabuchi had ordered killed. Like Shakespeare's Hamlet, however, Nishi is a man torn between the desire for revenge and the power of his conscience. He has married Iwabuchi's Ophelia-like daughter in order to get close to the old man and bring him down. But he unexpectedly finds that he has fallen in love with the vulnerable girl. Guilt-ridden over what he plans to do and the devastating effect it will have on her, he refuses to consummate their marriage, in effect sending her to a symbolic nunnery. As Nishi weaves his web of retribution, using "ghosts" and other theatrics (if not precisely a play within a play), he finds himself unable to carry his vendetta through to its extreme conclusion. "I'm not tough enough, I don't hate enough," he reveals to his friend and confidant Itakura (Takeshi Kato), the film's combination of Horatio and Laertes. And the dilemma ends in tragedy. Nishi is killed when his wife (who finds out too late that he does love her and sought to shield her) inadvertently leads her father's goons to him. The evidence of the corporation's misdeeds is destroyed. An important witness is killed along with Nishi. The lives of Iwabuchi's daughter and son are shattered by the loss of Nishi and the knowledge of what their father really is. But Iwabuchi remains atop his throne as the crime and corruption persist, although there is a strong hint that his tenure may not be long—that he, too, may be marked for death for having let the corporation's dirty dealings come so close to exposure.

Kurosawa's allusions to *Hamlet* add resonance to the story and characters, for they are subtle and never pushed too far. In *Men of Respect* (1991), writer-director William Reilly's distinctly unsubtle and overwrought retelling of Shakespeare's *Macbeth* as a bloody modern-day gangland melodrama, gun-toting hoods take the place of the Bard's warring Scottish clans—and bludgeoning allusion the place of effective drama. John Turturro plays Mike Battaglia, an ambitious mob hit man who slaughters his way to the top of the underworld (an oxymoron if ever there was one), with scheming wife Katherine Borowitz urging him on all the way because Turturro had forced her to have an abortion that left her unable to bear children, so she now feels he owes her. Reilly doesn't just draw parallels with Shakespeare's play; he attempts to recreate *Macbeth*'s classic scenes, often with unintentionally amusing results. Turturro's basement apartment encounter with a tarot-card reader who foretells of his ascension to power and Borowitz's ripely performed "out damn spot" scene in a rainstorm are but two notable examples. The film was an unacknowledged remake of director Ken Hughes's British-made *Joe Macbeth* (1955) starring Paul Douglas and Ruth Roman as another pair of contemporary underworlders inspired by the Bard's conniving couple. Hughes's film was a bit less pretentious but just as funny. One can only wonder, what with at least two gangster movies based on *Macbeth* now under Hollywood's belt, when a gangland retelling of *Julius Caesar* will come our way. It's certainly got all the right ingredients.

One wonders why Francis Ford Coppola never wove the sensational subject of the underworld's alleged involvement in the American crime of the century—the assassination of President John F. Kennedy—into his epic Mafia saga. Perhaps he felt the subject was just too controversial and inflammatory—or maybe just so ugly that it would have tarnished the romantic veneer of his epic tale. Then again, maybe he's one of the diehards who still believes the Warren Report. In any case, Coppola left it to other filmmakers to speculate about this disquieting possibility.

Ironically, the two most provocative films to raise the issue of mob involvement in the murder of President Kennedy were both made by Britishers. The first was the excellent television docudrama *Blood Feud* (1983), directed by Mike Newell. A two-part miniseries that aired in syndication as part of an independent-network experiment called Operation Prime Time, the telefilm chronicles the decade-long effort of Robert F. Kennedy to nail Teamsters union boss Jimmy Hoffa on racketeering and criminal conspiracy charges.* The film picks up the still-controversial story in the 1950s when RFK was serving as chief counsel of the organized crime investigation committee headed by Senator John McClellan (Philip Bruns). Brother John (Sam Groom), then a senator, also sits on the committee, whose

*Other films dealing with Hoffa and/or the Hoffa/RFK feud include: Norman Jewison's roman à clef *F.I.S.T.* (1978), starring Sylvester Stallone, and Danny DeVito's big budget biopic *Hoffa* (1992), starring Jack Nicholson. Larry Cohen's *The Private Files of J. Edgar Hoover* (1977) also covers some of the same ground but in high-camp fashion. Michael Parks's interpretation of RFK has to be seen to be believed.

Corrupt union leader Sylvester Stallone toughs it out at the Senate hearings in F.I.S.T. (1978), director Norman Jewison's roman à clef of the life of Jimmy Hoffa. (Copyright © 1978 United Artists)

work culminated with the televised hearings discussed elsewhere in this chapter. When JFK becomes President, he makes brother Bobby Attorney General, and the crusade against the mob in general and Hoffa in particular reaches critical mass.

Squeezed by his mob bosses, who are not at all pleased by the attention Hoffa's travails have focused on them, and by RFK's relentless (some said ruthless) assault, Hoffa determines to get Bobby before Bobby gets him. But Hoffa's assassination plans go awry, and despite the best efforts of hotshot lawyer Edward Bennett Williams (Jose Ferrer) to keep the corrupt union leader out of jail, Hoffa is convicted in 1967 on charges of misappropriation of Teamster pension funds and jury tampering and sent to the slammer. By this time, of course, President Kennedy has been assassinated and Bobby is merely another senator from New York with presidential aspirations.

Robert Boris's well-researched and incisive script focuses entirely on the titular "blood feud" between Bobby (Cotter Smith), a child of privilege, and Hoffa (Robert Blake), a child of poverty, both of whom, the script suggests, got in over their heads with the mob. The beleaguered tough guy Hoffa says as much in one fictionalized scene, when he rings up Bobby to warn him of the dangerous game both are playing. When President Kennedy is killed, Bobby understands the disquieting import of Hoffa's words. The script boldly suggests that it was not a lone gunman who was behind the murder of President Kennedy but, rather, the mob, and that the motive was to defang his threatening Attorney General brother.

Or, as New Orleans crime boss Carlos Marcello was reported to have said just months before the assassination: "[A] dog will keep biting you if you only cut off its tail, but cut off the head and the dog will die, tail and all."

This and another standard Mafia message of Marcello's ("Take the stone out of my shoes") are featured prominently in British director John Mackenzie's haunting speculation into the motives of "the man who killed the man who killed Kennedy" in *Ruby* (1992) — although the quotes are attributed to a fictional character, Santos Alicante (Marc Lawrence), based on Marcello and another real-life Mafia boss, Santos Trafficante.

Ruby was released a few months after Oliver Stone's monumental *JFK* (1991). The story has circulated that Stone attempted to keep the film from being made at all so that it wouldn't compete with his own. But they are hardly competitive in substance. Drawing on Jim Marr's book *Crossfire: The Plot That Killed Kennedy* and Jim Garrison's autobiographical account *On the Trail of the Assassins*, Stone's controversial epic marshaled the mountains of information uncovered by Warren Report critics over the years into a provocative docudrama that concluded the mob served as functionaries in a much broader and more insidious government-managed conspiracy. *Ruby*, on the other hand, isn't really about the assassination at all. It mixes assassination facts and lore to tell the story of an ambitious gangster who is destroyed by his ignorance of a larger scheme to grab power and revenge in which he has unwittingly become ensnared. In this respect, the film resembles Mackenzie's earlier *The Long Good Friday* (1980), whose main character, Harold Shand, is kin to Danny Aiello's Jack Ruby in many ways.

The facts surrounding the real Jack Ruby and his involvement with mob, CIA, and various other figures who may have been part of a conspiracy to kill the President are presented in the film. But they are telescoped, treated offhandedly, and often made to serve a symbolic rather than straightforward purpose. Witness the big Las Vegas nightclub scene, where Ruby, the mob, the CIA, and the President all converge and interact in the same room. The incident never took place, but the image recalls their tragic convergence over the assassination later. Likewise, the character of Candy Cane (Sherilyn Fenn), the stripper from Ruby's Carousel Club who is enlisted by the mob as its conduit to Kennedy: She is not fact. She's a fictional composite* through whom fact and rumor are mixed and revealed. Many critics of the film (which received mostly negative reviews) had problems with this sometimes-confusing and occasionally satiric approach, which

---

*Among them: Judith Exner, the girlfriend of mobster Sam Giancana and alleged bedmate of the President's; Beverly Oliver, another acquaintance of Ruby's and an eyewitness to the assassination, nicknamed the "Babushka Lady"; and, of course, Marilyn Monroe, with whom Kennedy reportedly had an affair and who some conspiracy theorists maintain may have been killed by the mob, as well. Fenn is made up to resemble Monroe, and the innocence combined with sexiness she brings to her performance captures the Monroe image to a T.

probably derived from the film's origins in the stage play *Love Field* by Stephen Davis (who also wrote the screenplay).

The film portrays Jack Ruby as the assassination plot's real Lee Harvey Oswald—the outsider nobody who commits a momentous act to demonstrate that he's really a somebody. Ruby works as a mob liaison with the Dallas police and the CIA. Each treats him with disdain. But it's the mob's lack of respect for this Jewish outsider amidst a sea of Italians that's the worst insult, for respect is the mob's most valued currency. And Ruby has given his life to the mob. Even his refusal to assassinate crime boss Alicante is treated with scorn by the very man whose life he saves; Alicante sees him as a low-level slob whose loyalty stems from a lack of guts. Ruby is swept up into the conspiracy, though not part of it, his silence taken for granted by his mob bosses. Ruby's "How dare they try to get away with this!" when the President is killed is not just a cry of patriotic outrage over what the mob has done to Kennedy and the country but of personal outrage over what it has long done to him. His murder of Oswald is an act of defiance against the mob wrongdoers, for he believes that doing so will expose the conspiracy and reveal him as a hero in the bargain. But like *The Long Good Friday*'s Harold Shand, he fails to comprehend the nature of the forces he's up against, and he's fatally trapped by his own desperate act of reprisal. The Warren Commission denies his request to be taken to Washington, the only place he feels safe to testify freely. And he takes his secrets with him to the grave when he dies in prison of cancer—the deadly cells vengefully injected into his veins on purpose by murderous "guards" (a frightening scenario many Kennedy conspiracy researchers have expounded upon).

The success of *The Godfather* resulted in a flood of underworld dramas not seen since the 1930s as producers everywhere scrambled to get on the Coppola bandwagon and rush their own tales of deadly dons, Mafia princesses, and gangland warfare to theater and television screens. The quality of these productions varied widely. Most films in the post-*Godfather* wave—among them *Across 110th Street* (1972), *The Don Is Dead* (1973), *Hell Up in Harlem* (1973), et al.—tended to pick up only on the graphic violence of Coppola's film in an attempt to outbloody it. The majority of gangland dramas made for television, constrained by networks from showing much graphic violence, repackaged the family rivalries and generational conflicts of Coppola's film into high-class soap operas suitable for prime time. But there were, too, some exceptional films.

Paul Wendkos's telefilm *Honor Thy Father* (1971), adapted by Lewis John Carlino from the best-seller by Gay Talese, offered a compelling inside look at the rise and fall of the notorious Bonnano Mafia family, a film as rich with detail and breathing with authenticity as Coppola's, save only the graphic rough stuff.

More substantial was Sergio Leone's big-screen *Once Upon a Time in America*

James Woods and pals blaze away in Once Upon a Time in America *(1984). (Copyright © 1984 Warner Bros.)*

(1984), which achieved the near impossible by being as epic in scope as Coppola's first two *Godfather* films, and almost as good. It also provided audiences a refreshing change, offering a look at the world of Jewish gangsters in place of the increasingly familiar Italian bunch.

Based on Harry Grey's slim novel *The Hoods*, Leone's more complex and expansive film chronicles the lives of its gangster characters from the Roaring Twenties to the late 1960s, shifting back and forth in time in the manner of *The Godfather, Part II*. Like Leone's spaghetti Westerns, it is primarily a tale of deceit and revenge. The protagonist is David Aaronson (Robert De Niro), nicknamed "Noodles," the only surviving member of a quartet of Jewish gangsters whose power in the New York underworld and labor rackets once equaled that of their Mafia counterparts. Noodles returns to his Lower East Side roots after many years of exile, haunted by the memory that it was he who'd been responsible for the deaths of his boyhood pals and former cronies in crime. At the peak of the gang's success, Noodles's ambitious and unbalanced partner, Max (James Woods), the brains of their organization, had set in motion a daring plan to knock over a federal bank, a crime that would likely have resulted in the fullest wrath of the law — and death for them all. To save Max from himself and salvage the gang's future (a prison sentence being preferable to being killed), Noodles had exposed the robbery plan to the cops, hoping it could be nipped in the bud with no casualties, but the betrayal went wrong and Noodles's cronies were killed, after all. Years later, when he returns to New York, the guilt-ridden Noodles discovers that it was the ambitious, double-dealing Max who'd orchestrated the betrayal in a move to get the gang out of the way and grab everything for himself. Still alive and now a wealthy prominent citizen married to Noodles's childhood sweetheart (Elizabeth McGovern), who'd also played a part in the deception, Max awaits — indeed invites — Noodles's revenge. But unlike in Leone's spaghetti Westerns, there is no purging of grievances or ritualistic shoot-out at the end of *Once Upon a Time in America*. The film concludes with a curious yet haunting ambiguity as Noodles simply walks away, disappearing into the predawn mist.

Unlike *The Godfather, Part II, Once Upon a Time in America* is not quite the sum of its parts. But its parts — from the breathtaking recreation of New York City during the twenties, spectacular photography, and stylized reverence for the ingredients of the genre, to the performances of De Niro, Woods, and all others — are magnificent indeed. Although it was not a box-office success (Warner Brothers released it in a severely truncated and confusing 139-minute version, though Leone's 227-minute version, now available on videocassette and disc, is the full masterpiece), it remains Leone's best film. Unfortunately, it was also his last. He died in 1989.

Coppola's *Godfather* films had turned the subject of organized crime in America into grand opera; Leone's into an epic myth. In John Huston's *Prizzi's Honor* (1985), based on a novel by Richard Condon, the same material was treated as grand farce. A satiric look at the Mafia's skewed morality and obsession with honor, the film has as its protagonist Charley Partanna (Jack Nicholson), a dim-witted hit man for Brooklyn's powerful Prizzi crime family (a comic version of the Corleones). Charley is being groomed by the mob for big things, but his future hinges on marrying one of the Prizzi daughters, Maerose (Anjelica Huston). But she unexpectedly stands him up. Out of honor to Charley, the Prizzis disown her until Charley agrees to take her back or marries someone else. As Maerose schemes to win Charley back and regain her position, Charley falls for the mysterious Irene (Kathleen Turner), a professional killer like him, and marries her — not realizing that she's the brains behind a recent scam of the Prizzis' Las Vegas operation. The heated situation comes to a head when the cops crack down on the Prizzis after Irene shoots a police officer's wife during an entrepreneurial kidnapping she and Charley had hoped would put her back in the mob's good graces. The Prizzis order Charley to murder Irene, while, at the same time, one of the devious Prizzi brothers contracts Irene to kill Charley, who stands in the brother's way of becoming the mob's top man. Irene loses the climactic duel. And Charley gets back together with the wily Maerose, her honor now fully restored, having learned an important lesson about the perils of trying to marry and work outside the family.

Though not as clever and biting a *Godfather* satire as *Prizzi's Honor,* the 1990 *The Freshman* offered a few solid chuckles of its own, most of them provided by costar Marlon Brando's hilarious send-up of his classic performance as Don Corleone in the Coppola film. And David Mamet's earlier *Things Change* (1988), a gangland comedy starring Don Ameche as an Italian shoemaker who changes places with a big-time don to keep the gang leader out of jail, played the machinations of the mob for, of all things, *whimsy.*

Brutal realism and caustic satire were combined in Martin Scorsese's *GoodFellas* (1990), one of the most critically acclaimed gangster films of the post-*Godfather* years. A follow-up to *Mean Streets,* which it resembles in many ways, *GoodFellas* was based on reporter Nicholas Pileggi's gritty biography—titled *Wiseguy* (Mafia slang for *gangster*)—of ex-Mafia goon Henry Hill. The film was titled *GoodFellas,* another Mafia slang term, probably to avoid confusion with the popular TV series of the period called "Wiseguy," which also dealt with the mob.

Ray Liotta stars as Hill, an Irish-Italian kid from Brooklyn, who, like Harvey Keitel's character in *Mean Streets,* is impressed early on by the flashy cars the wise guys in the neighborhood drive, by the expensive clothes they wear, and by the power they wield. Deciding to become a gangster himself, he gets his start doing odd jobs and running numbers for syndicate boss Paul Cicero (Paul Sorvino), who makes his real money, in Hill's words, "offering protection for people who can't go to the cops." Hill later falls in with two other local hoods, Jimmy Conway (Robert De Niro)* and Tommy DeVito (Joe Pesci), a psychotic punk reminiscent of the De Niro character in *Mean Streets,* who kills people for not treating him with respect (or, as he says, for "busting my balls").

De Niro's warning code is "Never rat on your friends and always keep your mouth shut." Ironically, Liotta eventually breaks that code and turns on De Niro largely because of De Niro himself.

When De Niro and Pesci kill a guy, Liotta gets himself in deep by helping them dispose of the body. The three goodfellas rise in the mob, but then everything falls apart. Liotta gets involved in a drug-trafficking sideline, a venture prohibited by mob boss Sorvino, and finds himself on the outs with his former patron. A contract is put out on Pesci for having murdered a fellow wise guy without the syndicate's approval, and he's killed at the very moment he thinks he's being initiated into the upper echelons of the family. And De Niro engineers the notorious 1978 Lufthansa robbery at Kennedy Airport, netting the gang a fortune in cash and jewels, most of which De Niro decides to keep for himself.

---

*The hood De Niro's character is based on was named James "Jimmy the Gent" Burke, a moniker inspired, perhaps, by the Irish-American tough guy played by James Cagney in the 1934 gangster film of the same name.

When the feds start closing in on his narcotics operation, and De Niro begins knocking off his coconspirators in the Lufthansa heist (from which Liotta collected a share), Liotta realizes the jig is up and makes a deal with the feds to rat on the mob in exchange for his freedom. As a result of Liotta's evidence, De Niro, Sorvino, and many other mobsters are sent to jail in one of the biggest gangland sweeps in history.

The film ends with Liotta entering the Federal Witness Protection Program and mourning his lost glory days as a high-rolling goodfella with the observation, "I miss the action. Now, I'm just a shnook like everybody else." (Not quite. As a result of the U.S. Supreme Court's overturning of New York State's "Son of Sam law," which had prohibited criminals from sharing in the profits of books or movies about their crimes, the actual Hill collected almost $200,000. Hill has since made even more money appearing [in disguise] on numerous TV talk shows, and, as of this writing, was negotiating with several independent producers to act as paid consultant on a proposed TV series about the mob. Who *says*, "Crime doesn't pay?" Not Henry Hill.)

Scorsese's vivid slice-of-life glimpse at contemporary gangland reveals a society that is totally amoral—a society ruled by blood and ritual, where greedy guys and killers are named after saints and their wives and daughters after the Virgin Mary; a society where notions of right and wrong have become so skewed that ratting on your friends is wrong and everything from petty larceny to murder is okay, just part of the daily routine—like a regular nine-to-five job. "It got to be normal," observes Liotta's Jewish outsider wife (Lorraine Bracco). "It didn't seem like crime at all."

There is another pervasive characteristic within Scorsese's society of goodfellas, as well, and that characteristic is stupidity. As the film drives home, real-life goons are a far cry from Coppola's Machiavellian schemers. They're "dumbfellas" one and all.

"Clothes are important. They make you what you are." "Glamour is fear. If people are afraid of you, you can do anything." These are the credos of Gary Kemp's Ronald Kray in *The Krays* (1990), director Peter Medak's account of the notorious gangster twins who plagued London's East End during the 1960s. Kemp's brother, Martin, plays Reginald Kray, the other half of the deadly duo who modeled their brutal ways after their Mafia counterparts in the United States and dressed to the Robinson-Raft nines in emulation of their heroes. In fact, the Krays' enemies often referred to them as "just a pair of movie gangsters," if always behind their backs.

British gangsters were never quite as genteel as many crime writers would have us believe. But as Medak's film accurately shows, the Krays heralded a new British gangster, one who killed not just for money but because, as Reginald Kray once confessed, he got such a "nice feeling" from it. Like their mob brothers in *GoodFellas*, the Krays build their criminal empire offering protection to people who can't go to the cops. Anyone who crosses them or offers the slightest offense (real or imagined) is dealt with viciously and publicly in order to impress London's underworld that the twins are not to be trifled with. At one point, Ronald Kray, the more unstable and sadistic of the pair, glimpses a fellow mobster grinning innocently at him, and he vengefully carves a permanent smile into the poor man's face with a sword. The twins are so brazen and unconcerned about people ratting on them that they walk into public places and machine-gun rival gang members right in front of witnesses. Their bold behavior proves their undoing, however, when Ron pursues a thug named Cornell (Steven Berkoff), who's made derisive comments about Ron's homosexuality, into the Blind Beggar pub and shoots him in the forehead as the customers watch in horror. The film doesn't reveal how or why the twins are eventually imprisoned; it simply concludes with a shot of the aging badfellas attending the funeral of their beloved mother (superbly played by Billie Whitelaw) and a title card that informs us they're still in jail. (Both will be eligible for parole in 1999.)

Unlike *GoodFellas*, *The Krays* doesn't provide much inside dope on the underworld milieu in which the Krays operated and, for a time, flourished. It's also a bit confusing at times. Characters are introduced, disappear, then reemerge, only to be beaten or killed without much rhyme or reason. Often we don't know who they are, what role they play in London's underworld, or how they connect to the

"Glamour is fear. If people are afraid of you, you can do anything." Gary Kemp (left) and Martin Kemp (right) as The Krays (1990). (Copyright © 1990 Miramax Films)

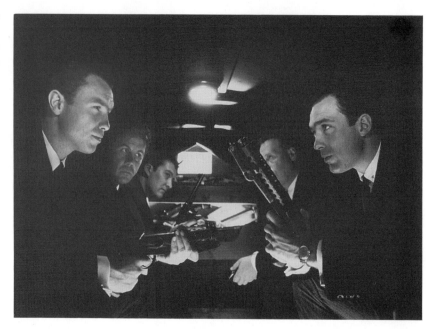

Krays. We see the Krays' crimes in vivid and sometimes harrowing detail but are denied the strong feeling for time and place and potent sense of atmosphere that characterize such superior British gangster films as *Get Carter, The Long Good Friday,* Val Guest's gritty and neglected *Hell Is a City* (1960), and director Medak's later *Let Him Have It* (1991).

Given the sleazy elements of the story, *The Krays* also fails to outsensationalize St. John Clowes's *No Orchids for Miss Blandish* (1948),* the most notorious British gangster film ever made, which was deemed a "disgrace to British films" by London's *Evening Standard* and denied exhibition by many theaters across Britain because of its sadism, brutality, and sexual suggestiveness.

Instead, *The Krays* devotes much of its length speculating on the root causes of the twin's murderous psychology. But Philip Ridley's script doesn't provide much insight here, either, except to say that the twins' overprotective and coddling mum may have been most responsible for her boys' growing up believing they could do and get away with anything—and that listening to their uncle spin gruesome tales of Jack the Ripper's long-ago exploits in the neighborhood may have fired the impressionable lads' imaginations and appetite for bloodletting.

The Kemp brothers, former members of the British pop group Spandau Ballet, are adequate as the Krays, but, not being actors, they fail to bring much depth to

---

*Based on a novel by James Hadley Chase, the film was set in the United States but shot in Britain. Robert Aldrich returned the story to its American locale when he remade it in 1971 as *The Grissom Gang,* arguably the worst film of that talented director's career.

their roles. Also, they merely resemble one another and are not actual twins, whereas the real Krays were complete look-alikes who were often mistaken for one another and used this to their advantage. For example, when the mentally ill Ron was once institutionalized, brother Reg would visit and change places with him for short periods so that Ron could enjoy some vacation time on the outside.

As a chronicle of venality abroad, *The Krays* is more than passable. But it denies us a firm understanding of the twisted psyches of the Krays themselves—and of the society that may have bred them.

Warren Beatty gave a big, bold movie star performance as the gangster who founded Las Vegas in Bugsy *(1991). (Copyright © 1991 Tri-Star Pictures)*

CHAPTER 8

THE HOODS OF THE NEW HOLLYWOOD

It's become a truism in the bottom-line world of today's Hollywood that when studio chiefs tell writers and directors they want material that's new, what they really mean is that they want familiar material that can be *repackaged* as new.

The blockbuster mentality (pour all your money into a few big films in hopes of making a box-office killing on one of them) coupled with the astronomical costs of film production are chiefly responsible for the reluctance of today's major studios to break new cinematic ground. It simply makes greater economic sense to toil old fields, where new seeds may yield yet another rich harvest.

Except for the Western, there is probably no cinematic field with richer soil than the gangster genre. But the Western has yet to make a really big comeback; as for gangster films, they're still booming after all these years.

"WE ONLY KILL EACH OTHER"

In 1991, Benjamin "Bugsy" Siegel, one of the more popular real-life hoods of the old Hollywood, became *the* most popular screen hood of the new Hollywood. No less than three films were made about the legendary Bugsy Siegel that year: *The Marrying Man*, *Mobsters*, and Warren Beatty's *Bugsy*. A fourth Bugsy Siegel film slated to star Andy Garcia was also in the works by producer Steve Roth (the producer of *Mobsters*), but Roth abandoned the project when he learned of the Beatty film.

209

Why Hollywood's fascination with Bugsy? One reason, perhaps, is that Bugsy's extravagant life (and death) is more than just a good gangster tale. It's a glitzy show-biz story as well, for Bugsy Siegel's flamboyant career intersected the streets of Hollywood Gangland in a way that no other mobster's has before or since.

Along with boyhood pals Meyer Lansky, Frank Costello, and Charles "Lucky" Luciano, Siegel spearheaded the national crime "commission" that eventually became known as the syndicate. Siegel's unpredictable rages and appetite for violence gave rise to his legendary nickname—used by fellow mobsters and later picked up by the press, but never to Bugsy's face.

In the mid-1930s, Luciano, the syndicate's chieftain, sent Siegel to Hollywood to consolidate gambling operations on the West Coast. Linking up with his childhood pal George Raft, the suave, good-looking Siegel soon became a fixture in Hollywood's nightlife, a fast friend of Hollywood luminaries including Gary Cooper, Cary Grant, Howard Hughes, Jean Harlow, Clark Gable, and others. Siegel reportedly got so caught up in Hollywood's life that he entertained the idea of becoming an actor himself and even took a screen test—which only proved his onscreen talents woefully inadequate, so he dropped the idea and had eight-by-ten photos made of himself instead, which he passed out to people requesting autographs.

On the set of one of Raft's films, Siegel encountered bit player Virginia Hill, an aspiring actress and sometime paramour of many of Siegel's mobster friends (whom Hill frequently assisted as a bagwoman, delivering money overseas to the mobsters' Swiss bank accounts). Despite the fact that Siegel was married (his wife and children remained on the East Coast), the pair launched a stormy romance that endured until Siegel's death.

Committed to Hill, a woman whose temper was as fiery and unpredictable as his own, Siegel eventually divorced his wife and settled permanently on the West Coast, where his escapades became increasingly more visible in the press— much to the annoyance of his mob partners. He also began sinking more and more of the mob's cash into a plush resort hotel, called the Flamingo (Hill's nickname) that he was building in Las Vegas, a dirt-water desert town that Siegel dreamed of turning into a mecca for legalized gambling.

Deported for his criminal activities and relegated to a distanced high life in Cuba financed by money allegedly transferred overseas by Hill herself, Luciano learned that Siegel and Hill were embezzling mob funds and stashing them in a secret Swiss bank account. At a syndicate meeting in Havana, he, Meyer Lansky, and others voted to teach their flamboyant longtime partner a permanent lesson. And on the night of June 20, 1947, the forty-one-year-old Siegel was mowed down in the house he'd bought for Hill, killed by mob bullets fired through the living-room window. Grisly photos of Siegel's blood-spattered corpse filled the newspapers the next day. (The photos, showing Siegel with a bullet hole through the eye, may have provided Francis Ford Coppola and Mario Puzo with the inspiration for the grisly death of Moe Green, a character loosely based on Siegel, in their film *The Godfather*.)

Siegel henchman Mickey Cohen eventually took over the dead mobster's West Coast operations. Hill was later called to testify on mob activities before the Kefauver committee hearings into organized crime, but she proved to be a reluctant and irascible witness. Following the hearings, she emigrated to Europe, where she committed suicide in 1966.

To the end of his days, Bugsy Siegel could never understand the law's objections to his and his fellow gangsters' brutal behavior. After all, he told the press, "We only kill each other."

Scripted by Neil Simon, *The Marrying Man*, 1991's first Bugsy Siegel film, took up the legendary gangster's life and times after his nightclub had become a success and Las Vegas had become established as a gambling oasis—neither of which Siegel, in fact, lived to see. These inaccuracies can be excused, however, since *The Marrying Man* is less a movie about the real Bugsy Siegel than it is a nineties attempt at recreating the romance and humor of a typical 1930s- or 1940s-style gangland comedy, using the character of Bugsy (Armand Assante) as a menacing third banana to the film's main leads (Alec Baldwin and Kim Basinger).

In some ways, *The Marrying Man* is a reworking of Simon's earlier screen comedy *The Heartbreak Kid* (1972). The engaged-to-be-married title character (Baldwin) spends his last night of freedom partying with some pals in Las Vegas, where he meets the tempestuous Basinger, Bugsy's mistress and a singer in his club, and the pair attempt to carry on a romance under the gangster's nose.

Occasionally amusing but never as belly-laugh funny as some of its gangster-comedy forebears, *The Marrying Man* died a quick death at the box-office despite the highly publicized offscreen romance (and alleged on-set misbehavior) of stars Baldwin and Basinger—a situation that repeated itself when *Bugsy* stars Warren Beatty and Annette Bening got romantically involved offscreen, too. (Must be something in the material!) Assante makes a good Bugsy, though—and in fact looks more like the real Bugsy Siegel than either Beatty or Richard Grieco, the costar of 1991's next Bugsy film, *Mobsters*.

The story of *Mobsters* takes place well before Siegel's fateful sojourn to Hollywood and Las Vegas. It chronicles the rise of gangster pals Siegel, Meyer Lansky, Charles "Lucky" Luciano, and Frank Costello to the top of New York City's gambling, prostitution, and protection rackets during the lawless decade when the men (except the older Costello) were barely out of their teens. The Jewish Lansky (Patrick Dempsey) is the brains of the operation, headed by the wily Sicilian Luciano (Christian Slater); Siegel (Richard Grieco) and Costello (Costas Mandylor) are their enforcers. Under the tutelage of rackets czar Arnold Rothstein (F. Murray

*Richard Grieco as Bugsy
Siegel in* Mobsters
*(1991). With Lynette
Waldman. (Copyright ©
1991 Universal Pictures)*

Abraham), the quartet ruthlessly consolidates its power in the New York underworld. After their mentor, Rothstein, is murdered by mob bigwigs, the ambitious, vengeful young Turks mastermind a takeover of all East Coast operations by pitting mob bosses Giuseppe Masseria (Anthony Quinn) and Salvatore Maranzano (Michael Gambon)* against one another. After Masseria and Maranzano are out of the way, the boys assume leadership of the powerful New York City Mafia families, leading to the creation of a national crime syndicate—the point at which the film ends.

Mobsters was clearly intended as a vehicle for its rising young stars in the vein of *Young Guns* (1988) and *Young Guns II* (1990), two youth-oriented Westerns that featured another batch of young male stars in an MTV–styled rehash of the familiar saga of Billy the Kid. This led to *Mobsters* (whose original title was *Gangsters*) being cynically dubbed "Young Tommy Guns" by the press prior to its release. ("Our Gang" might have been equally appropriate.)

Luis Mandoki, the Mexican director of the acclaimed foreign film *Gaby—A True Story* (1987), starring Liv Ullmann, was producer Steve Roth's odd choice to transform the material into something more than just a youth-oriented rehash of well-worn gangster film clichés. But he was dismissed before shooting and replaced by Michael Karbelnikoff, a director of TV commercials and rock-music videos, whose style was more in keeping with what the producers were really after, even though Karbelnikoff had never directed a feature film before. Nicholas Kazan, the son of Oscar-winning director Elia Kazan, was given the task of turning the script into less of a history lesson and more of an entertainment. In doing so, Kazan freely admitted to being "not overly concerned with history," and indeed he wasn't: In one of the film's more obvious gaffes, Siegel's partners in crime affectionately call him Bugsy. (Siegel's partners and friends always called him Benny or Ben.)

Though handsomely produced, the film never quite gels, either as history or as entertainment, and it was an unexpected box-office flop. Wrote *Entertainment Weekly:* "[Nothing] could have saved *Mobsters*, a movie so synthetic it appears to have been based less on old gangster movies than on MTV videos based on old

---

*In the film, the name was changed to Feranzano—reportedly to avoid audience confusion, since the name of both gangsters started with the letter *M.* Who says this film wasn't made for the MTV generation?

gangster movies." Slater's Luciano and Dempsey's Lansky emerge less paper-thin than the film's other main characters, if only because they get more screen time than anyone else. Mandylor's Costello and Grieco's Bugsy Siegel fairly disappear into production designer Richard Sylbert's sumptuously recreated Prohibition decor, except when their services are needed to rub somebody out. Anthony Quinn's "Zorba the Godfather" routine as the obese, wheezy, pasta-gulping Don Masseria is alternately a hoot and an embarrassment. In all, the story of Luciano and company's bloody rise to underworld power and "glory" was chronicled more compellingly and truthfully (albeit as a roman à clef) in Coppola's *Godfather* films — and more entertainingly in Francesco Rosi's ultra-violent *Lucky Luciano* (1974), starring Gian-Maria Volonte.

Barry Levinson's Oscar-winning *Bugsy* combines the romantic comedy of *The Marrying Man* with the on-again, off-again adherence to history of *Mobsters*. Except for its frank language and graphic violence, the film even looks and feels like a glitzy, big-budget studio film of the 1930s or 1940s. It also suggests the type of movie role the starstruck Bugsy would likely have chosen for himself had his screen test panned out.

James Toback's witty script, written expressly for Warren Beatty, focuses exclusively on Siegel's ill-fated infatuation with Virginia Hill (Annette Bening) and his fatal Las Vegas dream. It picks up the gangster's saga as Luciano (terrifically played by the late rock promoter Bill Graham) and Lansky (Ben Kingsley) send him to Hollywood to coordinate the mob's West Coast activities. Upon his arrival, he renews acquaintances with childhood friend George Raft (Joe Mantegna), now an up-and-coming movie star. Raft introduces him to Hollywood's elite, including the Countess diFrasso, a woman with close ties to Benito Mussolini. Consumed by patriotic and romantic fervor, Bugsy carries on a brief affair with her in the hope that she'll arrange a meeting between him and Mussolini so that he can assassinate the Italian dictator. He gives up on the idea, though, when Mussolini's angry countrymen do the job instead. This is a funny bit, but Toback could have made it even funnier had he actually shown Bugsy's overseas trip to carry out his quixotic scheme; according to some accounts, Siegel actually went to Italy intending to sell Mussolini a new kind of explosive device. While there, it is said that he met visiting Nazi dignitaries Hermann Göring and Joseph Goebbels, whom he disliked instantly and decided to assassinate with his explosive device. But the device failed to work during a tryout. Mussolini passed on it and the disappointed Siegel scurried back to Hollywood.

Siegel's relationships with West Coast mobster Mickey Cohen (Harvey Keitel) and the ambitious Hill, whom he meets on the set of one of Raft's films, are the core of the film. His increasingly flamboyant business schemes with Cohen and all-consuming infatuation with Hill separate him more and more from his East Coast partners. The huge cost overruns of the syndicate-financed Flamingo Hotel

Beatty as Bugsy (1991).
(Copyright © 1991 Tri-
Star Pictures)

finally put him on the outs with the mob, which suspects that Hill is stashing some of the construction money in a Swiss bank account (without Siegel's knowledge, the film maintains). When bad weather dampens the expensive gambling casino's opening night and Siegel is forced to close the place down, the mob decides it's had enough of the loose cannon. Even Lansky, Siegel's chief protector, can no longer defend his friend's impetuous actions, and the syndicate unanimously votes to have Siegel killed and to take over the potentially lucrative hotel itself. In a scene reminiscent of the conclusion of *Casablanca* (not to mention *Bonnie and Clyde*), Siegel and Hill say their good-byes at the airport, their parting looks filled with longing and fatalism, and Siegel flies to Los Angeles to meet his doom. As the film ends, a title card informs us that Siegel's Las Vegas dream, which netted the visionary gangster nothing but a gruesome death, went on to make its syndicate heirs billions of dollars.

Beatty gives a big, bold movie-star performance as Bugsy Siegel that is perfectly in tune with the film's glitzy style and with Toback's theme—the tragedy (if indeed it can be called that) of a Jay Gatsby–like gangster who pays the ultimate price because he forgets that he *is* a gangster. The film lacks emotional resonance, however, because we don't really feel anything for Bugsy. He's by turns comic, frightening, endearing, and, in Hill's words, a "psychotic asshole." But he is never wholly empathetic. When he's gunned down, our reaction isn't one of shock, horror, or sympathy; it's simply that he's dead, and that's all. There is no powerfully communicated sense of loss—as there is, for example, at the conclusion of *The Godfather, Part III* when the aging and alone Michael Corleone slumps over dead in his chair. The love affair between Siegel and Hill lacks emotional resonance, too—because we're never sure if that's what it is. Their affair is tempestuous, sexy, funny, and torn by frequent outbursts of jealousy whenever one or the other makes eyes at someone else. But it seems more like a case of powerful physical attraction than a love affair. If there's more to it, the film doesn't fill us in. And since the film fails to show us Hill's reaction to Bugsy's death, we remain left without a clue. The not-bad 1974 TV movie *The Virginia Hill Story*, starring Dyan Cannon as Hill and Harvey Keitel as Siegel, offered considerably more insight into the depth of their relationship (particularly Hill's feelings for Siegel) than all two hours plus of *Bugsy*.

Still, the gangster genre has been good to Warren Beatty. It's given him his best film (*Bonnie and Clyde*), his most financially successful film (*Dick Tracy*, 1990), and his flashiest, most career-resuscitating role to date. He might not be unwise to stick with it.

The TV series "The Gangster Chronicles: An American Story" also dealt with the criminal rise of Luciano (who is mysteriously given the first name of Salvatore in the telefilm) and Siegel (Joe Penny). Inspired by the success of Coppola's *The Godfather*, the multiepisode series ran on NBC from February to May of 1981.

YAKUZAS

Though nowhere near as prevalent on the screen as Italian, Jewish, and Irish mobsters, Asian gangsters have not been overlooked by Hollywood, either. Martial-arts movies, especially those made in Hong Kong and Japan, have featured villainous Oriental gangster characters in film after film for decades. But in American movies, the Asian gangster is a relatively new hood on the block. Japan bashing notwith-standing, it remains to be seen how common a character the Asian gangster will become in the years ahead, however, since two of Hollywood's few remaining studios, Columbia and Universal, are now being run by Japanese parent companies. Very likely, an Oriental-themed *Little Caesar* or *Godfather* will not be coming our way anytime soon. Even simplistic American-made martial arts/gangland potboilers like *Showdown in Little Tokyo* (1991) may eventually become things of the past.

Maverick writer-producer-director Samuel Fuller, the auteur behind the B mob movie classic *Underworld U.S.A.* (1961), took picturesque advantage of the sights and sounds of teeming postwar Japan to create his colorful, wide-screen 1955 gangster film *House of Bamboo*. Although there are several shady underworld characters of Oriental extraction in the film, *House of Bamboo* is about the corruptive influence of American gangsters on postwar Japan. The villain is an American black marketeer (Robert Ryan) who stayed on after the war and now heads up a powerful numbers racket based in Tokyo. His partners in the organization are all former

GIs. Ryan's rules are unbending. Anyone who gets out of line is a dead man. Robert Stack plays an American detective sent to Tokyo to work with the Japanese police and security forces in toppling Ryan's criminal organization.

The script by Harry Kleiner is essentially a reworking of *White Heat* in an Eastern setting. Stack infiltrates the group to get close to Ryan, a paranoid psychopath in the mold of James Cagney's Cody Jarrett. Ryan comes to like Stack, bends the organization's ironclad rules to accommodate him, and begins relying on Stack more and more as both confidant and friend. Stack builds on the relationship to manipulate the gangster and eventually destroy him. When Ryan discovers Stack's duplicity, he, like Cody Jarrett, goes berserk. The conclusion of the film replaces *White Heat*'s apocalyptic petroleum-tank showdown with a lengthy shoot-out between the undercover cop and the doomed gangster in a Tokyo amusement park.

Gangster-movie veteran Robert Mitchum took on the Japanese mob in *The Yakuza* (1975), the Japanese word for *gangster* (literally, "good-for-nothing," or, if you will, "badfella"). Warner Brothers envisioned the film as a Japanese *Godfather* and snapped up the exotic script by Paul Schrader and his brother Leonard for a whopping $300,000, a record price for an original screenplay at the time. At the behest of director Sydney Pollack, however, the script's ethnicity was toned down and its violence toned up by Robert Towne (who shares screen credit with the Schraders); the Schraders, who went on to become directors themselves, have since disowned the film.

Although made in Japan, the film takes minimal advantage of its picturesque Japanese locale. Much of the action is confined indoors and could easily have been shot in Hollywood. Except for some graphically bloody scenes of arms and heads being lopped off by samurai swords and bodies being ripped open by shotgun blasts, Pollack's somber, moody style is more in keeping with 1940s noir. Mitchum's presence as the deceived and put-upon hero reinforces this link.

The excessively convoluted yet predictable plot hinges pretentiously on the "burden of obligation," an apparently venerated concept in Japanese and Yakuza culture. Retired cop Mitchum is obligated to army buddy Brian Keith for having set up his impoverished Japanese mistress (Eiko) in business after the war. Now a wealthy arms dealer, Keith has stiffed a Yakuza chieftain named Tono (Eiji Okada) on a valuable weapons shipment. Tono kidnaps Keith's daughter and threatens to kill her if Keith fails to fulfill his obligation and fork over the weapons. Keith calls in Mitchum's marker and sends him to Japan to bail him out of trouble. Mitchum looks up Eiko's estranged brother (Ken Takakura), an embittered veteran with ties to the Yakuza. Takakura is obligated to Mitchum for aiding his sister during the American occupation, and to fulfill his debt, Takakura helps Mitchum rescue Keith's daughter.

As the Yakuza code forbids one gangster from interfering in the affairs of

Ken Takakura takes on the Japanese mob, a.k.a. The Yakuza *(1975). (Copyright © 1975 Warner Bros.)*

another, Takakura finds himself on the outs with the mob and becomes a hunted man. Now feeling obligated to Takakura, Mitchum joins with him in taking on the Yakuza. Bodies and body parts pile up as the duo slaughter their way through the Yakuza underworld with gun and sword. Mitchum kills Keith after Keith puts a contract out on him, and Takakura is forced to kill his brother's (James Shigeta) gangster son. In keeping with Yakuza custom, Takakura amputates one of his fingers and offers it to Shigeta as a gesture of apology for the grief he has caused the man's family. When Mitchum learns that Eiko is, in fact, Takakura's wife and not his sister (a plot twist, like most in the film, we see coming a mile off), he realizes the grief he caused Takakura by taking the woman as his mistress. He, too, amputates a finger and offers it to Takakura as a gesture of apology. With all obligations and debts now settled, the former foes turned fingerless friends bow to one another at the airport and go their separate ways.

Except for the staging of the action sequences, which seem more Peckinpah than Pollack, *The Yakuza* squanders its exotic setting with a talky and routine mob melodrama.

Director Ridley Scott brought his own distinctive brand of noirish exotica to *Black Rain* (1989), an unacknowledged reworking of Don Siegel's cop thriller *Coogan's Bluff* (1968) in a Japanese setting.

In the Siegel film, Arizona cop Clint Eastwood is sent to New York City to transport an extradited killer (Don Stroud) home for trial. Stroud escapes from him, however, and disappears into the teeming crowds and mean streets of the

Big Apple, a world as alien to Eastwood as the dark side of the moon. Gruff
police lieutenant Lee J. Cobb orders Eastwood to stay out of the manhunt to
recapture the killer. But the big-city police department's bureaucratic methods of
getting the job done strike the maverick Eastwood as so crippled by rules and
procedure and alien to his own methods of police work that he gets fed up and
lights out to nail Stroud on his own.

The Eastwood character in *Black Rain* is played by Michael Douglas, a maverick
New York City cop under investigation from Internal Affairs for possibly accepting
a bribe. Douglas is charged with extraditing a Yakuza drug lord (Yusaku Matsuda)
back to Japan. Another cop, played by Andy Garcia, goes along to help out and
keep an eye on Douglas. At first, Douglas is resentful of Garcia, but eventually
they become pals.

Douglas delivers Matsuda into the hands of Japanese detectives aboard the
plane at the Osaka airport. But the detectives are bogus. They're really some of
Matsuda's Yakuza cohorts in disguise. When the bona fide authorities arrive, the
hapless Douglas realizes he's been duped and that his man has gotten away. Like
Eastwood in *Coogan's Bluff*, Douglas finds hmself a stranger in a strange land.
Frustrated by the Japanese police's alien ways of doing things, he quickly runs
afoul of the chief detective on the case (*The Yakuza*'s Ken Takakura again), who
attempts to rein in the hotheaded Yankee cop but with little success. When Garcia
is beheaded (a gaspingly realistic effect and the film's most shocking scene) by a
gang of motorcyclists, the death-dealing sword wielded by Matsuda himself, the

vengeful Douglas decides he's had enough, and, like Eastwood, resorts to his own methods to recapture or kill the brutal drug lord. He's assisted in his efforts by the expatriate American hostess (Kate Capshaw in a truly thankless role) of a Japanese nightclub where the Yakuza often hang out. Eventually, Takakura bends the rules and assists Douglas also. Together, the two lawmen take on the Yakuza mob and kill most of the gangsters, including Matsuda, in a final bloodbath. They also become mutually respectful colleagues and fast friends in the bargain.

As filtered through the directorial eye of Ridley Scott, whose nightmarish *Alien* (1979) and *Blade Runner* (1982) this film recalls in look and style, *Black Rain* is certainly no Japanese picture postcard. It's a travelogue for xenophobes in which Osaka, Japan's second-largest city and (according to Scott himself) one of the country's prettiest and least threatening to alien sensibilities, is portrayed as a noisy, smoky, steam-filled, rain-drenched, overcrowded, corruption-filled urban hell. Why anyone would choose to live in such an infernal landscape is the most interesting cultural mystery the film's simplistic and implausible (but admittedly exciting) script poses.

Akira Kurosawa's spellbinding 1963 crime drama *High and Low* deals with the Japanese underworld only in its second half. But the film's harrowing portrait of that world puts the synthetic terrors of Ridley Scott's *Black Rain* to shame.

High and Low is based on an American novel, *King's Ransom*, by Ed McBain, the author of the *87th Precinct* books. The first half of the film deals with a kidnapping. The main character is Kingo Gondo (Toshiro Mifune), an ambitious executive caught in a power struggle for control of the shoe company into which he has poured his life's blood. His greedy colleagues in the firm want to cut production costs and turn out an inferior product as a way to boost corporate profits. To thwart them, Gondo mortgages everything he owns to buy the extra shares of stock he requires to put him in control of the company. On the eve of closing the deal, Gondo's son is kidnapped and a king's ransom is demanded in exchange for the boy's life. Gondo agrees to pay up, then discovers that the kidnapper has snatched the chauffeur's child, his son's playmate, by mistake. The kidnapper demands that the ransom be paid anyway, however, and Gondo finds himself caught between a rock and a hard place. Even though paying the ransom money would have ruined him, he'd been willing to do so when his own son's life was at stake. Is the chauffeur's son's life worth the same sacrifice? At first, Gondo selfishly says no. But then his conscience gets the better of him. He agrees to pay the money and help the police nail the kidnapper. The boy is safely returned, but Gondo loses control of the company, his position in the firm, and his house to boot as his greedy colleagues and creditors move in swiftly for the kill.

In the film's second half, the police, who have developed a deep respect for Gondo, turn the manhunt for the kidnapper and the return of Gondo's money into a crusade. Echoing the film's title, their search takes them from the barren coastline overlooking scenic Mount Fuji to the teeming bars, brothels, and brutal drug alleys of Yokohama's hellish underworld. The kidnapper murders his gangland accomplices with an overdose of heroin to get them out of the way and grab all the money for himself. But the police plant a fake story in the newspapers that the accomplices are still alive. The kidnapper is drawn out into the open and caught, but most of the money is gone. There's enough left of it, however, for Gondo to open a small company of his own and start rebuilding his life.

Kurosawa's humanistic message is that despite the gulf that separates them, the victimized Gondo and the victimizing gangster kidnapper (Tsutomu Yamazaki) are inextricably bound together. This idea is reinforced in the film's powerful last scene, where Gondo and the kidnapper face one another for the first and last time and their faces merge in the prison-cell window that separates them. Gondo is at war with the greed of the corporate sharks who seek to undermine his pride in his life's work by taking control of the shoe company and turning out an inferior product. The kidnapper is at war with an affluent society that has undermined his pride by looking down on him—as Gondo's luxurious house does on the Yokohama slums where the kidnapper lives and operates—and refusing to take notice of him unless he takes violent action against that society and threatens its very fabric. The two men feed off one another. The gangster feeds his pride by lashing out at Gondo and is ultimately destroyed by his own hate. Gondo is destroyed at first but is ultimately reborn by the kidnapper's bold and brutal action and finds that he can no longer hate his lowly "twin."

Michael Cimino bounced back after *Heaven's Gate* with another pictorially striking but pretentious flop called *The Year of the Dragon* (1985), a modest tale of gang warfare on the streets of New York's Chinatown based on a novel by ex-cop Robert Daley, which Cimino tried to mushroom into a Chinese-American *Godfather*.

Mickey Rourke plays an embittered Vietnam vet turned tough cop charged with cleaning the mobsters and drug traffickers out of Chinatown after the brutal gangland slaying of the district's Chinese mayor. But Rourke's lack of compassion for—and racist attitudes toward—the ethnic population he's assigned to protect only exacerbate the problem. As rival gang lords John Lone and Victor Wong juggle for power, the streets of Chinatown erupt in gang warfare, leading to much bloodshed on both sides of the law, if not much excitement, before the final fade-out. Lone rubs out Wong and takes over but is toppled in a ferocious shoot-out with Rourke, who, by the end of the film, has finally recognized the error of his racist ways—sort of.

What *The Year of the Dragon* lacks in excitement (and involvement), it more than makes up for in atmosphere. Production designer Wolf Kroeger and art director Vicki Paul's vivid recreation of New York's Chinatown and other colorful sections of the Big Apple on the soundstages of producer Dino De Laurentiis's

North Carolina studios is a triumph. Oliver Stone's script is intriguing, as well; it hints at Stone's future films as a director with its theme of a man radicalized by exposure to a situation that shatters his beliefs. But the theme is insufficiently realized by Rourke's one-note performance.

For sheer visceral excitement, and over-the-top graphic violence, however, few gangster films made today either here or abroad come close to the work of Hong Kong writer-director John Woo, a twenty-year veteran of Oriental action cinema who began his career making martial arts movies with kung fu superstar Jackie Chan.

Woo shifted to bloody melodramas about his country's pervasive crime problems with *A Better Tomorrow* (1986), the tale of an ace counterfeiter gone straight who runs into brutal conflict with his ex-cronies in the mob and his younger brother, an ambitious cop on the Hong Kong police force whose career rise is threatened because of his brother's past reputation and criminal associations. One of the biggest box office successes in Hong Kong movie history, the film made a major star out of a charismatic Chinese actor in the Cagney mold named Chow Yuen Fat, who plays a crippled hit man and confidante of the film's protagonist. Fat and Woo teamed for an equally successful sequel, *A Better Tomorrow, Part 2*, in 1987, and the pair has been on an action-filled roll ever since, turning out one Hong Kong gangster film after another, with such titles as *Bullet in the Head* (1990), *Once a Thief* (1991), and *Hard-Boiled* (1992).

Their most widely released collaboration Stateside was 1990's *The Killer*, the story of a world-weary mob hitman (Fat) who suffers a crisis of conscience when he accidentally blinds a nightclub singer during a ferocious gangland shoot-out, and, in the manner of Bogart's Roy Earle in *High Sierra*, undertakes one last job to pay for an operation to restore her eyesight.

Woo's Hollywood gangster film-inspired plots are a mixture of ripe sentimentality and macho romance with a moral grounding in such virtues as friendship, loyalty, and duty to God and country. Like Sergio Leone, he treats the clichés of the genre as grand myths. But his most talked-about trademark is his skill at choreographing violent action set-pieces (often in slow motion) of a kind not seen on the screen since the passing of Sam Peckinpah, the director Woo seems to have been most influenced by. The climax of Peckinpah's *The Wild Bunch* erupted with what is still one of the most gut-wrenching, pyrotechnical displays of firepower and bloodletting ever put on the screen. Imagine if you will a director who stages all the action scenes—and they're virtually nonstop—in his films in the same balls-to-the-wall manner and you have a good idea of what the gangster films of John Woo are like. And why Hollywood finally imported him to breathe some new "life" into America's tired genre with *Hard Target*, a Woo-style updating of Richard Connell's classic tale of bloodsport, *The Most Dangerous Game*, which marked the Hong Kong action wiz's 1993 American film debut.

THE GANG'S ALL HERE

The more things change, the more they remain the same — an old adage that applies
as much to reel life as to real life. The same social ills that gave rise to gangs and
gangsterism and spawned public interest in movies about them during the early
decades of this century have not been eradicated. Poverty, drugs, bigotry, class and
ethnic warfare, homelessness, greed, and so on are all still with us. Inevitably, so
are the gangs and gangsters born of such ills. Their violent exploits continue to
fascinate us in real life and on the big screen, as well.

Today's gangster films are rougher, sexier, and more foulmouthed, but their
themes have changed remarkably little since the early days of Raoul Walsh's *The
Regeneration* and the golden days of Robinson, Cagney, and Bogart. Phil Joanou's
State of Grace (1990), for example — a tale of contemporary Irish mobsters battling
for a piece of the Mafia pie in New York's Hell's Kitchen (the setting of many
of Cagney's gangster movies) — recalls the ground-breaking Walsh film not only
in substance but even in the religious connotations of its title.

Like the hero of Walsh's film, Sean Penn's Tommy Noonan turns his back
on his past and tries to regenerate himself with the help of a good woman (Robin
Wright), his childhood sweetheart and the estranged sister of two gangster pals
(Ed Harris and Gary Oldman). Penn decides to become a cop. Knowing he will
inevitably be pitted against his old friends if he stays in Hell's Kitchen, he flees
the city and joins the Boston police. But a New York cop (the ubiquitous John
Turturro, who has appeared in more recent gangster movies than perhaps any other

actor) draws Penn back to his Hell's Kitchen roots years later for some undercover police work. Posing as an enforcer for hire, Penn rejoins the Harris/Oldman gang (based on the real-life Irish gang of the 1970s called the Westies) to inform on its activities and takes up his relationship with Wright where it left off. When she threatens to end the affair because he's gone back to his gangster ways, Penn reveals that he's an undercover man. But this only places a greater strain on their relationship, since the men he's after are her brothers; however much she detests their lifestyle and has removed herself from their influence, she still feels a sense of loyalty toward them. Penn (giving his customary sullen, droopy-eyed performance) suffers a crisis of conscience as well, since he feels a similar sense of loyalty toward Oldman, the hotheaded younger sibling and Penn's closest friend since childhood. Penn's crisis is resolved, though, when Harris kills Oldman to cement relations with his Mafia benefactors. In reprisal, Penn confronts Harris and his goons in an empty bar during New York's St. Patrick's Day parade and has it out with them in a bloody shoot-out. He kills them all; he is severely wounded himself, but he's done his duty (as he sees it), even though it's cost him his girl.

State of Grace came out the same year as *GoodFellas*, but equalled neither the commercial nor critical success of the Scorsese film—despite the movies' resemblances of technique, acting, graphic violence, and "never rat on your friends" subject matter. The dialogue of its inarticulate low-life characters is also quite similar. There are probably as many *fucks*, *fuck yous*, *fuckings*, *fuck offs*, and *fuck its* in *State of Grace* as there are in *GoodFellas*. It also resembles Scorsese's *Mean Streets* (Oldman's violent, none-too-bright Jack Flannery is practically a stand-in for De Niro's Johnny Boy in *Mean Streets*) and even Cagney's *The Public Enemy* and a host of other classic thirties gangster movies. The graphically bloody gunfight at the end, filmed in slow motion, is one-quarter Peckinpah and three-quarters Brian De Palma. Film-school grad Phil Joanou knows his medium: If nothing else, *State of Grace* is the complete film buff's gangster movie. (It could have been much more had Joanou taken a pair of scissors to Dennis McIntyre's script, which gets sidetracked much too often and spends far too much time obfuscating the slim but compelling story it has to tell.)

Nicholas St. John's script for *King of New York* (1990) is just plain vague. At one point in the film, the title character, Frank White (Christopher Walken), a former kingpin who's lost control of the city's drug rackets while in prison and determines to get it back, attends a performance of Eugene O'Neill's *The Emperor Jones* and sees his own situation mirrored on the stage. But the connection is tenuous at best.

Walken's gang is predominantly black and has remained loyal to him during his years in prison. We can see why when he's confronted (in one of the film's less diffuse scenes) on the subway by several black youths out to rob him. Instead of shooting them, he tosses them a wad of cash and tells them to report to his

Left: *Christopher Walken as the* King of New York *(1990).* (*Copyright © 1990 New Line Cinema*)

Right: *Cuba Gooding, Jr., clings to girlfriend Nia Long in despair over the seemingly endless violence in South Central Los Angeles in John Singleton's* Boys N the Hood *(1991).* (*Copyright © 1991 Columbia Pictures*)

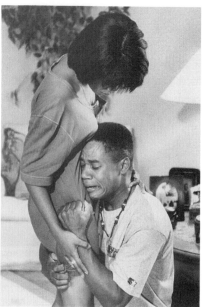

Plaza Hotel headquarters if they want more. Dispensing cash for loyalty is what made him king of New York—and it will make him that again.

Led by the silver-toothed, two gun–toting Jimmy (Larry Fishburne), Walken's longtime enforcer, the gang goes back into action and helps Walken rebuild his empire by decimating all the Mafia, Chinese, and Colombian competition in a series of bloody shoot-outs. The cops on the beat, a mixture of Irish and blacks, are unable to nail Walken or Fishburne for the murders, which Walken justifies in Bugsy Siegel fashion with the apologia, "I spent half my life in prison and I never killed anybody that didn't deserve it." He adds that the drug situation only got worse while he was in stir, not better. "I'm not your problem," he tells the cops. "I'm just the businessman."

When Walken becomes a media star by using some of the millions he's made from dealing drugs to finance the rebuilding of a community hospital in Harlem, the frustrated younger cops decide there's no way to bring this bad guy down except to play by his own rules and go out and kill him. Older cop Victor Argo counsels against this, but they proceed, anyway. And several of Walken's gang, including Fishburne, plus a number of cops are killed during the wild car chase and shoot-out, spectacularly staged in a torrential downpour, that follow. Walken escapes, however, and tells Argo he's put a contract of $1 million on the head of any cop who tries to get him or interferes with him in any way. All his criminal life he's been a target, he tells Argo. "Now you know what it's like." Argo engages him in a shoot-out and is killed. Walken is wounded, however, and goes out with a whimper when he slumps over dead in a cab in Times Square as dozens of men in blue close in on him. Elaborately staged by director Abel Ferrara, the scene is nevertheless not as kinetic or violent as most of the film's other major set pieces.

Larry Fishburne played a very different type of role in writer-director John Singleton's bitter *American Graffiti* for South Central Los Angeles, *Boyz n the Hood* (1991). (Award-winning cinematographer Ernest Dickerson offered an East Coast view of the same turbulent situation in *Juice,* 1992.) Fishburne plays Furious Styles, a divorced father trying to instill in his son (Cuba Gooding, Jr.) a sense of responsibility and hope in an environment beset by drugs, gangs, drive-by shootings, and the constant roar of surveilling police helicopters overhead. Furious is aptly named, but his is a quiet fury ruled by strength, the will to set a positive example, and the determination to keep his boy headed in the right direction — not the gun (although he has one and is not reluctant to use it when the criminal element invades his home).

Furious is a person, not a stereotype, and that's the most refreshing thing about the film. Singleton's directorial debut and a dual Oscar nominee, *Boyz N the Hood* is refreshingly devoid of the stereotypical black characters and stock black villains that have come to pervade modern films — especially gangster films — about urban violence and the drug menace. Singleton's theme is personal responsibility, at the grass roots but from the top down, as well. This message is compellingly stated in the film's powerful opening scene, where the young boys 'n the hood explore an abandoned playground cordoned off by crime-scene ribbons, the pavement covered with dried bloodstains, the walls covered with tattered Reagan/Bush 1984 campaign posters full of empty slogans and bullet holes. Steve Anderson's *South Central* (1992), filmed in the wake of the Los Angeles riots, and the Hughes brothers' *Menace II Society* (1993) have echoed the same theme.

It's back to stereotypes again, however, in *New Jack City* (1991), the directorial debut of actor Mario Van Peebles. Peebles plays no favorites, though. Blacks and every other ethnic group in this gangster-cum-horror film come across as lewd, crude, violence-loving, doped-out sleazeballs.

The film is set in The City (ostensibly New York but, by implication, every other urban sprawl in the United States, as well) during the years 1986 to 1989, when crack cocaine, the "new jack" of the title, first appeared on the nation's streets and crime lords everywhere began scrambling for exclusive rights to the profitable substance. One of them is flashy gang leader Nino Brown (Wesley Snipes), whose character seems modeled after Curtis Mayfield's definitive stud drug dealer in *Superfly* (1972). Snipes seizes the opportunity to violently edge out his Asian, Hispanic, and Mafia competition and build a powerful all-black criminal organization by cornering the market on crack production and distribution. He sets up shop in a huge apartment building where the drug is manufactured and dispensed to the city's crackheads and dealers if they have the necessary cash and

Sleazeball New Jack cops Judd Nelson and Ice-T make an arrest in New Jack City *(1991). (Copyright © 1991 Warner Bros.)*

credentials to get into the heavily fortified complex. Eventually, as the stoned-out crackheads mill about like zombies, the building's courtyard takes on the look of a George Romero movie. The entrepreneurial Snipes takes a leaf from the book of Capone and sets up food lines for the destitute and the hopeless (potential customers all) to win them over from the police. As the city erupts in a vicious drug war and the use of crack reaches epidemic proportions, cop Van Peebles takes a leaf from the book of *Pay or Die*'s Joseph Petrosino and persuades his superiors to let him put together a special team to win back the community's hearts and minds, bring down Snipes's empire, and return the crack- and violence-infested streets to safety. Except for Van Peebles himself, the multiethnic team of foulmouthed, gunslinging "new jack cops" is virtually unrecognizable from the scumballs it's up against. One of them is even a former crackhead, whose job is to infiltrate Snipes's armed fortress posing as a customer.

Like *Boyz n the Hood* and *South Central*, *New Jack City* is antidrug, proeducation, and propersonal responsibility. But its important message is lost in a sea of mayhem, melodrama, and cliché. The film seems to have been edited by a computer keyed to the average MTV viewer's attention span rather than narrative strength; virtually every other scene is a rock-music number. Action and exposition scenes alternate with numbing precision. The scourges it deals with may be new, but the film itself is just a throwback to such violence-with-a-beat "blaxploitation" epics of the 1970s as *Black Caesar* (1973), *Bucktown* (1975), and *Sweet Sweetback's Baadasssss Song* (1971, directed by and starring Van Peebles's father, Melvin). Wesley Snipes's swaggering gangster gets off a few good lines, though. "You gotta rob," he says, "to get rich in the Reagan era."

Director Bill Duke combined action and graphic gore with raucous humor in the grisly but funny gangland comedy *A Rage in Harlem* (1991), the story of a dim undertaker's assistant (Forest Whitaker) who falls for a femme fatale (Robin Givens) with a shady past and a trunkful of stolen loot. The film's macabre humor and oddball cast of swindler, con artist, killer, and mob kingpin characters recall the gangland farces of Edward G. Robinson and the popular action comedies *Cotton Comes to Harlem* (1970) and *Come Back, Charleston Blue* (1972), which chronicled the exploits of savvy but unorthodox Harlem police detectives Coffin Ed Johnson (Raymond St. Jacques) and Gravedigger Jones (Godfrey Cambridge). *A Rage in Harlem* brings back Coffin Ed and Gravedigger (played by different actors) for a walk-on and is set in the same 1950s time period; all three films were based on novels by expatriate African-American writer Chester Himes.

Black and Hispanic gangs clashed over territory, drugs, and assorted other things once more in *Colors* (1988), actor-director Dennis Hopper's gritty but cliché-ridden account of racial violence, law, and disorder in the ghettos and barrios of contemporary Los Angeles. Michael Schiffer's script focuses less on the causes of urban gang violence than on the stress of coping with it on two white police officers belonging to a special squad called CRASH (Community Resources Against Street Hoodlums). One officer, Bob Hodges (Robert Duvall), is an easygoing veteran approaching retirement. The other, Danny McGavin (Sean Penn), is an inexperienced eager beaver whose nickname, "Pacman," reflects his trigger-finger attitude and zealous approach to his work. It's fairly obvious from the beginning which of the duo will get killed and who will survive, having learned an important lesson in duty and compassion. In movies like this, it's always the experienced guy verging on retirement who wears a target on his back.

Penn is also mellowed when he falls for a Hispanic woman (Maria Conchita

Below, left: CRASH *officers Sean Penn and Robert Duvall make a key drug bust in* Colors *(1988). (Copyright © 1988 Orion Pictures Corp.)*

Right: Actor-director Edward James Olmos recreated the infamous "zoot suit riots" of 1943 Los Angeles in his ambitious American Me *(1992). (Copyright © 1992 Universal Pictures)*

Alonso) who gives him some much-needed insight into the conditions that have led to so much civil strife among her community's young people, as well as neighboring black youths. The film strives to be realistic and au courant, but the machinations of its melodramatic plot are soporific. The script's repetitive use of urban gang slang only adds to the boredom.

Actor-director Edward James Olmos offered a more insightful look at barrio culture and a more hard-hitting glimpse into the world of Mexican-American gangsters in *American Me* (1992), Olmos's and writers Floyd Mutrux's and Desmond Nakano's ambitious attempt at a Hispanic *Once Upon a Time in America*.

The film traces the rise and fall of three Hispanic hoodlums from the prewar years through the notorious zoot suit riots* of 1943 Los Angeles to the present day. The leader of the gang is Santana, played as a youth by Panchito Gomez and as an adult by Olmos. The other two hoods are Mundo (Richard Coca, Pepe Serna) and J. D. (Steve Wilcox, William Forsythe). *Entertainment Weekly*'s critic noted that the film's "...depictions of violence and degradation are sometimes powerful, especially in the scenes set in Folsom prison where Santana establishes his empire by selling drugs to prisoners," but that Olmos failed to reveal the sense of a lost human being beneath Santana's mask of ruthlessness. It strikes me, though, that the point Olmos is making is that Santana's ruthlessness *isn't* a mask. The conditions which gave rise to him haven't eroded his humanity over the years. They killed it early on.

THE MOB'S LOVE AFFAIR WITH THE MOVIES

Made right after his somewhat disappointing *The Krays*, Peter Medak's *Let Him Have It* (1991)† emerged as one of the most powerful gangster movies of recent vintage, and one of the richest—as well as one of the most neglected. Unlike *The Krays*, it received virtually no theatrical distribution in this country and went straight to video.

Let Him Have It is really two films. It's a wrenching docudrama about an actual murder case that led to the abolition of capital punishment in England in the mid-1950s. And it is also an insightful study of the adolescent nature of the gangster personality and how the veneer of that personality has been shaped over the years by the movies—a subject touched upon briefly in *The Krays*, as well. The film doesn't suggest that gangster movies are responsible for the problem of gangsterism

---

*Director Luis Valdez's gangland musical *Zoot Suit* (1981), also featuring Olmos, dealt powerfully with the same incident, which was sparked by the arrest and conviction of several Hispanic gang members (zoot suiters) for a murder they didn't commit.

†Not to be confused with the 1935 gangster film *Let 'em Have It*, directed by Sam Wood and starring Richard Arlen, which was another of Hollywood's paeans to the FBI made in the wake of Warner Brothers' popular *G-Men*.

in society. But it does suggest that gangsters have been influenced by the images of gangsterism they've seen flickering back at them from the big screen for the past sixty-plus years, which is why so many of them—from the big-time dons of New York to the street hoodlums we see on the nightly news broadcasts—seem like caricatures of their movie counterparts.

That Robinson, Cagney, Raft, and many other movie gangsters based their characters' style of dress, their mannerisms, and other behavioral tics on the famous gangster personalities of their age, we know. *Let Him Have It* explores the reverse angle, showing how gangsters, like children, have adopted many of the flamboyant characteristics of their screen idols over the years, as well, that they, too, are acting out roles in their own real-life gangster melodramas—albeit roles with very serious and often deadly consequences.

The film tells the story of Derek Bentley (heartbreakingly played by Christopher Eccleston), a withdrawn, epileptic nineteen-year-old lad with a low IQ and a yen for the good life. He was hanged in 1952 for the shooting of a policeman during a warehouse break-in. A hue and cry arose across England over the execution, because Bentley had not shot the policeman. He had no gun on him during the break-in and was, in fact, in the custody of police when the shooting occurred. The death-penalty sentence stemmed from an 1868 British law law proscribing execution for anyone involved in the murder of a policeman. Bentley was indeed involved, but only peripherally. The fatal bullet was fired by Bentley's partner in the break-in, Christopher Craig (Paul Reynolds), but since Craig was only sixteen at the time and fell into the juvenile-offender category to which the law did not apply, he was given a prison sentence, and Bentley got the noose.

Determined to set an example to other postwar youth bent on breaking the law (Britain was experiencing a wave of gangland violence at the time), the court justified its verdict of death by stating that while Bentley had not committed the actual murder, he was equally responsible and therefore equally guilty in the eyes of the law because he had incited his pal Craig to start shooting in the first place when he'd shouted "Let him have it, Chris!" after the first officer on the scene ordered Craig to turn over his gun. Bentley's counsel maintained (as does the film) that the court twisted the inference of Bentley's words to mean "Shoot him, Chris," whereas Bentley actually meant for Craig to comply with the officer's instructions. That the words were spoken by the docile and already-captured Bentley twenty minutes before the fatal shooting occurred prompted the jury to accept counsel's explanation and recommend leniency. But British justice at the time allowed no such option, and it let the benighted Bentley have it in the neck, anyway. Largely as a result of the storm of controversy created by the Bentley case (even the murdered policeman's widow argued for clemency), the law was repealed and the death penalty in Britain was soon abolished. According to one of the film's end titles, Bentley's sister Iris, who served as a special consultant on the production, is still working to have her brother's name cleared, but to no effect. Christopher Craig, on the other hand, was released from prison in 1962, and, according to another end title, has been a law-abiding citizen ever since.

Let Him Have It is a tragic tale, and Medak and his impeccable cast wring every ounce of emotion from it, without a drop of sentimentality. The scene of Bentley's execution is especially powerful because the manner in which the government's hangman (Clive Revill) goes about his ugly business isn't cruel or even inhumane. It's a dispassionate exercise in which the taking of a human life is reduced to a series of clinically efficient moves. Unlike similar scenes in so many other gangster and crime films, there is no harrowingly protracted last-mile walk to the gallows. "Just follow me, boy, and it'll be all right," the hangman says as he slips a hood over Bentley's head, the noose and straps hurriedly put in place, and springs the trap. Boom, boom, boom: The execution is over in seconds. But its awful legacy lingers as Medak cuts to the boy's home and shows his parents and sister huddled together by the fireplace as the clock on the mantel ticks 9:01, and they break down knowing the boy is gone. For Bentley, the pain is over. But for his grieving parents, it's only just begun.

Although *Let Him Have It* clearly presents the Bentley execution as a case of judicial murder — a wrongheaded effort on the part of the government to make sure that among the delinquent youth of Britain there would be no more "Chicago-style gun battles" (as the magistrate and the press luridly and inaccurately describe the warehouse break-in and aftermath) — the film is not primarily about the volatile issue of capital punishment. It's a character study of Bentley, of Craig, and, implicitly, of the gangster himself — a character the film sees as a gun-toting Peter Pan, a perpetual adolescent living in a world of fantasy whose style has been shaped, in part, by decades of gangster movies. In one of the film's subtlest expressions of this theme, Craig is shown shoving an old toy truck on the nightstand next to his bed out of the way with his brand new toy, a war-surplus revolver, and crying in childish bewilderment and anger over the "unfairness" of his brother's arrest and imprisonment.

Bentley and Craig *are* children. But the portrait applies to the film's adult gangsters, as well. A good example is Craig's older brother Niven (Mark McGann), a flashily dressed dude with the flaxen hair of a screen star. He seems stuck in time, forever locked inside his street kid's fantasy of what it means to be a big shot — a gun, plenty of cash and clothes, a big car, and a good-looking babe on your arm every night. Like most gangsters, he's stayed too long at the matinee — and he even speaks in gangster movie clichés. When he's arrested for dealing in contraband and hauled away by the coppers, he growls at his girlfriend: "You're gonna get it, bitch; you fingered me" — one of the hoariest of gangland threats, on and off the screen.

Aping their gangland elders, Bentley and Craig walk about in overcoats and fedoras like old-time movie gangsters and speak in similar clichés. Trapped by police on the roof of the warehouse, the pugnacious Craig twirls his gun and challenges, "Get back coppers" in the manner of his screen idols, Robinson and, especially, Cagney, whom Craig consistently imitates. At one point in the film, he and his pals even take in a reissue of the Cagney classic *White Heat*, which they've heard is a top-notch American gangster film, the type they like best because in Hollywood, they believe, makers of gangster movies "use real bullets."

The focus of the story, though, is Bentley and the ironic wheel of fortune (the title of his favorite pop tune and, the film suggests, the symbolic anthem of the gangster, as well) that leads him to his fate. Unlike Craig, Bentley is neither a violent youth nor even hostile to authority. Indeed, his reaction to being caught at the warehouse is an anguished "My dad's gonna kill me." And in his embarrassing courtroom appearance, he is so demonstrably slow-witted and intimidated that he can barely fathom the prosecutor's questions and effectively defend himself.

Bentley's motivation is a universal one: The yearning to make something of himself. But therein lies the trap—for him *and* for the gangsters he pathetically seeks to emulate. Because, like children, they both tend to perceive that goal in the most superficial terms and seek to achieve it by the shortest route possible, no matter what the risk.

As Craig says to him at one point: "Style don't come cheap, Derek." And another gang member knowingly chimes in, "In your case, it could become exorbitant."

SELECTED FILMOGRAPHY

CIN: cinematographer
DIR: director
MUS: music
PR: producer
SCR: screenplay

A BOUT DE SOUFFLE (aka Breathless, 1959)
Films Around the World
PR: Georges de Beauregard; DIR: Jean-Luc Godard; SCR: Jean-Luc Godard, from an idea by François Truffaut; MUS: Martial Sotlal; CIN: Raoul Coutard
CAST: Jean-Paul Belmondo, Jean Seberg, Daniel Boulanger, Jean-Pierre Melville, Liliane Robin, Henri-Jacques Huet, Jean-Luc Godard

AL CAPONE (1959)
Allied Artists
PR: John H. Burrows and Leonard J. Ackerman; DIR: Richard Wilson; SCR: Malvin Wald and Henry Greenberg; MUS: David Raksin; CIN: Lucien Ballard
CAST: Rod Steiger, Fay Spain, Murvyn Vye, James Gregory, Nehemiah Persoff, Lewis Charles, Joe De Santis, Louis Quinn, Martin Balsam

AMERICAN ME (1992)
Universal Pictures
PR: Sean Daniel, Robert M. Young, and Edward James Olmos; DIR: Edward James Olmos; SCR: Floyd Mutrux and Desmond Nakano; MUS: Dennis Lambert; CIN: Reynaldo Villalobos
CAST: Edward James Olmos, Pepe Serna, William Forsythe, Panchito Gomez, Richard Coca, Steve Wilcox, Evelina Fernandez, Vira Montes, Sal Lopez

ANGELS WITH DIRTY FACES (1938)
Warner Brothers

PR: Sam Bischoff; DIR: Michael Curtiz; SCR: John Wexley and Warren Duff, from a story by Rowland Brown; MUS: Max Steiner; CIN: Sol Polito
CAST: James Cagney, Pat O'Brien, Humphrey Bogart, Ann Sheridan, George Bancroft, Billy Halop, Bobby Jordan, Leo Gorcey, Bernard Punsley, Gabriel Dell, Huntz Hall, Edward Pawley

ASPHALT JUNGLE, THE (1950)
MGM
PR: Arthur Hornblow, Jr.; DIR: John Huston; SCR: Ben Maddow and John Huston, based on the novel by W. R. Burnett; MUS: Mikos Rozsa; CIN: Harold Rosson
CAST: Sterling Hayden, Louis Calhern, Jean Hagen, James Whitmore, Sam Jaffe, Marc Lawrence, Barry Kelley, Anthony Caruso, John McIntire, Marilyn Monroe

BABY FACE NELSON (1957)
United Artists
PR: Al Zimbalist; DIR: Don Siegel; SCR: Daniel Mainwaring; MUS: Van Alexander; CIN: Hal Mohr
CAST: Mickey Rooney, Carolyn Jones, Sir Cedric Hardwicke, Christopher Dark, Ted De Corsia, Leo Gordon, Emile Meyer, Anthony Caruso, Jack Elam, John Hoyt

BAD SLEEP WELL, THE (1960)
Toho
PR: Tomoyuki Tanaka and Akira Kurosawa; DIR: Akira Kurosawa; SCR: Shinobu Hashimoto, Hideo Oguni, Ryuzo Kikushima, Eijiro Hisaita, and Akira Kurosawa; MUS: Masaru Sato; CIN: Yuzuru Aizawa
CAST: Toshiro Mifune, Takeshi Kato, Masayuki Mori, Takashi Shimura

BIG BROTHER (1923)
Paramount–Famous Players–Lasky
DIR: Allan Dwan; SCR: Paul Sloane, based on the story "Big Brother" in the collection *Big Brother and Other Stories* by Rex Beach; CIN: Hal Rosson
CAST: Tom Moore, Edith Roberts, Raymond Hatton, Joe King, Mickey Bennett, Charles Henderson, Paul Panzer, Neill Kelley, William Black, Martin Faust, Milton Herman, Florence Ashbrook, Yvonne Hughes, Charles Hammond

BIG CITY, THE (1928)
MGM
DIR: Tod Browning; SCR: Tod Browning and Waldemar Young; CIN: Henry Sharp
CAST: Lon Chaney, Marceline Day, James Murray, Betty Compson, Matthew Betz, John George, Virginia Pearson, Walter Percival, Lew Short, Eddie Sturgis

BIG HEAT, THE (1953)
Columbia Pictures

PR: Robert Arthur; DIR: Fritz Lang; SCR: Sydney Boehm, based on the novel by William P. McGivern; MUS: Daniele Amfitheatrof; CIN: Charles Lang
CAST: Glenn Ford, Gloria Grahame, Jocelyn Brando, Alexander Scourby, Lee Marvin, Jeanette Nolan, Peter Whitney, Willis Bouchy

BLACK BIRD, THE (1926)
MGM
DIR: Tod Browning; SCR: Tod Browning and Waldemar Young; CIN: Percy Hilburn
CAST: Lon Chaney, Renée Adorée, Doris Lloyd, Andy MacLennon, William Weston, Eric Mayne, Sidney Bracy, Ernie S. Adams, Owen Moore, Lionel Belmore, Billy Mack, Peggy Best

BLACK CAESAR (1973)
American International Pictures
PR: Larry Cohen; DIR: Larry Cohen; SCR: Larry Cohen; MUS: James Brown; CIN: Fenton Hamilton and James Signorelli
CAST: Fred Williamson, D'Urville Martin, Gloria Hendry, Art Lund, Val Avery, Minny Gentry, Julius W. Harris, Phillip Roye

BLACK HAND, THE (1950)
MGM
PR: William H. Wright; DIR: Richard Thorpe; SCR: Luther Davis; MUS: Alberto Colombo; CIN: Paul C. Vogel
CAST: Gene Kelly, J. Carroll Naish, Teresa Celli, Marc Lawrence, Frank Puglia, Barry Kelley, Mario Siletti, Carl Milletaire, Peter Brocco, Gracia Narciso

BLOOD FEUD (1983)
Twentieth Century–Fox Television
PR: Daniel Selznick and Joel Glickman; DIR: Mike Newell; SCR: Robert Boris; MUS: Fred Steiner
CAST: Robert Blake, Cotter Smith, Danny Aiello, Edward Albert, Brian Dennehy, Douglas Dirkson, Sam Groom, Lance Henrickson, Michael Lerner, Forrest Tucker, Michael V. Gazzo, Jose Ferrer, Michael C. Gwynne

BONNIE AND CLYDE (1967)
Warner Brothers/Seven Arts
PR: Warren Beatty; DIR: Arthur Penn; SCR: David Newman and Robert Benton; MUS: Charles Strouse; CIN: Burnett Guffey
CAST: Warren Beatty, Faye Dunaway, Gene Hackman, Michael J. Pollard, Estelle Parsons, Denver Pyle, Gene Wilder, Evans Evans, Dub Taylor

BONNIE PARKER STORY, THE (1958)
American International Pictures

PR: Stanley Shpetner; DIR: William Witney; SCR: Stanley Shpetner; MUS: Ronald Stein; CIN: Jack Marta
CAST: Dorothy Provine, Jack Hogan, Richard Bakalyan, Joseph Turkel, William Stevens, Ken Lynch, Douglas Kennedy, Patti Huston

BORSALINO (1970)
Paramount Pictures
PR: Alain Delon; DIR: Jacques Deray; SCR: Jean-Claude Carrière, Claude Sautet, Jacques Deray, and Jean Cau, based on the book *Bandits à Marseilles* by Eugene Soccomare; MUS: Claude Bolling; CIN: Jean-Jacques Tarbès
CAST: Jean-Paul Belmondo, Alain Delon, Michael Bouquet, Catherine Rouvel, Françoise Christophe, Corinne Marchand

BRINK'S JOB, THE (1978)
Universal Pictures
PR: Ralph Serpe; DIR: William Friedkin; SCR: Walon Green, based on the book *Big Stick-Up at Brink's* by Noel Behn; MUS: Richard Rodney Bennett; CIN: A. Norman Leigh
CAST: Peter Falk, Gene Rowlands, Peter Boyle, Warren Oates, Allen Goorwitz, Paul Sorvino, Sheldon Leonard, Gerald Murphy, Kevin O'Connor

BROADWAY (1929)
Universal Pictures
PR: Carl Laemmle, Jr.; DIR: Paul Fejos; SCR: Edward T. Lowe and Charles Furthman, based on the play by Jed Harris, Philip Dunning, and George Abbott; MUS: Howard Jackson; CIN: Hal Mohr
CAST: Glenn Tryon, Evelyn Brent, Merna Kennedy, Thomas Jackson, Robert Ellis, Otis Harlan, Paul Porcast, Leslie Fenton

BROTHERHOOD (1968)
Paramount Pictures
PR: Kirk Douglas; DIR: Martin Ritt; SCR: Lewis John Carlino; MUS: Lalo Schifrin; CIN: Boris Kaufman
CAST: Kirk Douglas, Alex Cord, Irene Papas, Luther Adler, Susan Strasberg, Murray Hamilton, Eduardo Cianelli, Joe De Santis

BUGSY (1991)
Tri-Star Pictures
PR: Mark Johnson, Barry Levinson, and Warren Beatty; DIR: Barry Levinson; SCR: James Toback; MUS: Ennio Morricone; CIN: Allen Daviau
CAST: Warren Beatty, Annette Bening, Harvey Keitel, Ben Kingsley, Joe Mantegna, Bill Graham, Elliott Gould

BULLETS OR BALLOTS (1936)
Warner Brothers–First National

DIR: William Keighley; SCR: Seton I. Miller, based on a story by Seton I. Miller and Martin Mooney; MUS: Heinz Roemheld; CIN: Hal Mohr
CAST: Edward G. Robinson, Joan Blondell, Barton McLane, Humphrey Bogart, Frank McHugh, Joseph King, Richard Purcell, George E. Stone

CITY GONE WILD, THE (1927)
Paramount–Famous Players–Lasky
PR: Adolph Zukor and Jesse L. Lasky; DIR: James Cruze; SCR: Jules Furthman; CIN: Bert Glennon
CAST: Thomas Meighan, Marietta Millner, Louise Brooks, Fred Kohler, Duke Martin, Charles Mailes, Nancy Phillips, Wyndham Standing

CITY STREETS (1931)
Paramount Pictures
PR: E. Lloyd Sheldon; DIR: Rouben Mamoulian; SCR: Oliver H. P. Garrett, from an original screen story by Dashiell Hammett; CIN: Lee Garmes
CAST: Gary Cooper, Sylvia Sidney, Paul Lukas, William "Stage" Boyd, Guy Kibbee, Stanley Fields, Wynne Gibson

DEAD END (1937)
Samuel Goldwyn
PR: Samuel Goldwyn; DIR: William Wyler; SCR: Lillian Hellman, based on the play by Sidney Kingsley; MUS: Alfred Newman; CIN: Gregg Toland
CAST: Joel McCrea, Sylvia Sidney, Humphrey Bogart, Wendy Barrie, Claire Trevor, Allen Jenkins, Marjorie Main, Billy Halop, Huntz Hall, Bobby Jordan, Leo Gorcey, Gabriel Dell, Bernard Punsley

DESPERATE (1947)
RKO
PR: Michel Kraike; DIR: Anthony Mann; SCR: Harry Essex; MUS: Paul Sawtell; CIN: George E. Diskant
CAST: Steve Brodie, Audrey Long, Raymond Burr, Douglas Fowley, William Challee, Jason Robards

DESPERATE HOURS, THE (1955)
Paramount
PR: William Wyler; DIR: William Wyler; SCR: Joseph Hayes, based on his novel and play; MUS: Gail Kubik; CIN: Lee Garmes
CAST: Humphrey Bogart, Fredric March, Arthur Kennedy, Martha Scott, Dewey Martin, Gig Young, Mary Murphy, Richard Eyer, Robert Middleton

DILLINGER (1945)
Monogram Pictures

PR: Frank and Maurice King; DIR: Max Nosseck; SCR: Philip Yordan; MUS: Dimitri Tiomkin; CIN: Jackson Rose
CAST: Lawrence Tierney, Edmund Lowe, Anne Jeffreys, Eduardo Cianelli, Marc Lawrence, Elisha Cook, Jr., Ralph Lewis, Ludwig Stossel

DOORWAY TO HELL (1930)
Warner Brothers
DIR: Archie Mayo; SCR: George Rosener, based on the story "A Handful of Clouds" by Rowland Brown; MUS: Leo F. Forbstein; CIN: Barney "Chick" McGill
CAST: Lew Ayres, Charles Judels, Dorothy Matthews, Leon Janney, Robert Elliott, James Cagney

DRAG NET, THE (1928)
Paramount–Famous Players–Lasky
PR: B. P. Schulberg; DIR: Josef von Sternberg; SCR: Jules and Charles Furthman; CIN: Harold Rosson
CAST: George Bancroft, Evelyn Brent, William Powell, Fred Kohler, Francis McDonald, Leslie Fenton

DRESSED TO KILL (1928)
Fox Film Corporation
PR: William Fox; DIR: Irving Cummings; SCR: Howard Estabrook; CIN: Conrad Wells
CAST: Edmund Lowe, Mary Astor, Ben Bard, Robert Perry, Joe Brown, Tom Dugan, John Kelly, Robert E. O'Connor, R. O. Pennell, Ed Brady, Charles Morton

ENFORCER, THE (1951)
Warner Brothers
PR: Milton Sperling; DIR: Bretaigne Windust and [uncredited] Raoul Walsh; SCR: Martin Rackin; MUS: David Buttolph; CIN: Robert Burks
CAST: Humphrey Bogart, Zero Mostel, Ted de Corsia, Everett Sloane, Roy Roberts, Lawrence Tolan, King Donovan, Bob Steele

EXCLUSIVE RIGHTS (1926)
Preferred Pictures
PR: J. C. Bachmann; DIR: Frank O'Connor; SCR: Eve Unsell, based on the book *Invisible Government* by Jerome N. Wilson; CIN: André Barlatier
CAST: Gayne Whitman, Lillian Rich, Gloria Gordon, Raymond McKee, Gaston Glass, Grace Cunard, Sheldon Lewis, Charles Mailes

FINGER POINTS, THE (1931)
Warner Brothers–First National
DIR: John Francis Dillon; SCR: Robert Lord, W. R. Burnett, and John Monk Saunders; CIN: Ernest Haller

CAST: Richard Barthelmess, Fay Wray, Regis Toomey, Clark Gable, Robert Elliott, J. Carrol Naish

FOOLS' HIGHWAY (1924)
Universal Pictures
PR: Carl Laemmle; DIR: Irving Cummings; SCR: Lenore J. Coffee and Harvey Gates, based on the book *My Mamie Rose: The Story of My Regeneration* by Owen Kildare and the play *The Regeneration* by Owen Kildare; CIN: William Fildew
CAST: Mary Philbin, Pat O'Malley, William Collier, Jr., Lincoln Plummer, Edwin J. Brady, Max Davidson, Kate Price, Charles Murray, Sherry Tansey, Steve Murphy, Tom O'Brien

GANGSTER, THE (1947)
Allied Artists
PR: Maurice King and Frank King; DIR: Gordon Wiles; SCR: Daniel Fuchs, based on his novel *Low Company*; MUS: Louis Gruenberg; CIN: Paul Ivano
CAST: Barry Sullivan, Belita, Joan Lorring, Akim Tamiroff, Henry Morgan, John Ireland, Fifi D'Orsay, Virginia Christine, Sheldon Leonard, Charles McGraw, Elisha Cook, Jr.

GET CARTER (1971)
MGM
PR: Michael Klinger; DIR: Mike Hodges; SCR: Mike Hodges, based on the novel *Jack's Return Home* by Ted Lewis; MUS: Roy Budd; CIN: Wolfgang Suschitzky
CAST: Michael Caine, Ian Hendry, Britt Eklund, John Osborne, Tony Beckley, George Sewell, Geraldine Moffatt, Dorothy White

G-MEN (1935)
Warner Brothers–First National
PR: Lou Edelman; DIR: William Keighley; SCR: Seton I. Miller, based on *Public Enemy No. 1* by Gregory Rogers; MUS: Leo F. Forbstein; CIN: Sol Polito
CAST: James Cagney, Ann Dvorak, Margaret Lindsay, Robert Armstrong, Barton MacLane, Lloyd Nolan, William Harrigan, Russell Hopton

GODFATHER, THE (1972)
Paramount Pictures
PR: Albert S. Ruddy; DIR: Francis Ford Coppola; SCR: Mario Puzo and Francis Ford Coppola, based on Puzo's novel; MUS: Nino Rota; CIN: Gordon Willis
CAST: Marlon Brando, Al Pacino, James Caan, Richard Castellano, Robert Duvall, Sterling Hayden, Diane Keaton, Richard Conte, Talia Shire, John Cazale, John Marley, Al Martino

GODFATHER, THE, PART II (1974)
Paramount Pictures
PR: Francis Ford Coppola; DIR: Francis Ford Coppola; SCR: Mario Puzo and Francis Ford Coppola, based on Puzo's novel; MUS: Nino Rota; CIN: Gordon Willis

CAST: Al Pacino, Robert Duvall, Diane Keaton, Robert De Niro, John Cazale, Talia Shire, Lee Strasberg, Michael V. Gazzo, G. D. Spradlin

Godfather, THE, PART III (1990)
Paramount Pictures
PR: Francis Ford Coppola; DIR: Francis Ford Coppola; SCR: Mario Puzo and Francis Ford Coppola; MUS: Carmine Coppola; CIN: Gordon Willis
CAST: Al Pacino, Diane Keaton, Talia Shire, Andy Garcia, Eli Wallach, Joe Mantegna, Bridget Fonda, George Hamilton, Sofia Coppola

GOODFELLAS (1990)
Warner Brothers
PR: Irwin Winkler; DIR: Martin Scorsese; SCR: Nicholas Pileggi and Martin Scorsese, based on the book *Wiseguy* by Nicholas Pileggi; CIN: Michael Ballhaus
CAST: Robert De Niro, Ray Liotta, Joe Pesci, Lorraine Bracco, Paul Sorvino, Frank Sivero, Tony Darrow, Mike Starr, Frank Vincent, Henny Youngman

GUN CRAZY (1949)
United Artists
PR: Frank and Maurice King; DIR: Joseph H. Lewis; SCR: MacKinlay Kantor and Millard Kaufman, based on Kanter's story; MUS: Victor Young; CIN: Russell Harlan
CAST: Peggy Cummins, John Dall, Barry Kroeger, Morris Carnovsky, Anabel Shaw, Harry Lewis, Nedrick Young, Rusty Tamblyn

HARDER THEY FALL, THE (1956)
Columbia Pictures
PR: Philip Yordan; DIR: Mark Robson; SCR: Philip Yordan, based on the novel by Budd Schulberg; MUS: Hugh Friedhofer; CIN: Burnett Guffey
CAST: Humphrey Bogart, Rod Steiger, Jan Sterling, Mike Lane, Max Baer, Jersey Joe Walcott, Edward Andrews, Harold J. Stone, Nehemiah Persoff

HIGH AND LOW (1963)
Toho
PR: Tomoyuki Tanaka and Ryuzo Kikushima; DIR: Akira Kurosawa; SCR: Ryuzo Kikushima, Hideo Oguni, Choichi Naki, and Akira Kurosawa, based on the novel *King's Ransom* by Ed McBain; MUS: Masaru Sato; CIN: Asakazu Nakai
CAST: Toshiro Mifune, Kyoko Kagawa, Tatsuya Nakadai, Takashi Shimura, Yutaka Sada, Tsutomu Yamazaki

HIGH SIERRA (1941)
Warner Brothers–First National
PR: Hal B. Wallis and Mark Hellenger; DIR: Raoul Walsh; SCR: John Huston and W. R. Burnett, based on the novel by Burnett; MUS: Adolph Deutsch; CIN: Tony Gaudio

CAST: Humphrey Bogart, Ida Lupino, Alan Curtis, Arthur Kennedy, Joan Leslie, Henry Hull, Henry Tavers, Jerome Cowan, Baron MacLane, Cornel Wilde

KEY LARGO (1948)
Warner Brothers–First National
PR: Jerry Wald; DIR: John Huston; SCR: Richard Brooks and John Huston, based on the play by Maxwell Anderson; MUS: Max Steiner; CIN: Karl Freund
CAST: Humphrey Bogart, Lauren Bacall, Edward G. Robinson, Lionel Barrymore, Claire Trevor, Thomas Gomez, Marc Lawrence, Dan Seymour

KILLER, THE (1990)
Circle Releasing Corp. (U.S. release 1991)
PR: Tsui Hark; DIR: John Woo; SCR: John Woo; MUS: Lowell Lo; CIN: Wong Wing Hang and Peter Pao.
CAST: Chow Yuen Fat, Danny Lee, Sally Yeh, Chu Kong, Tsang Kong, Shing Fui On.

KILLERS, THE (1946)
Universal Pictures
PR: Mark Hellinger; DIR: Robert Siodmak; SCR: Anthony Veiller and [uncredited] John Huston, based on the story by Ernest Hemingway; MUS: Mikos Rozsa; CIN: Woody Bredell
CAST: Burt Lancaster, Edmond O'Brien, Ava Gardner, Albert Dekker, Sam Levene, William Conrad, Charles McGraw, John Miljan

KILLING, THE (1956)
United Artists
PR: James B. Harris; DIR: Stanley Kubrick; SCR: Stanley Kubrick and Jim Thompson, based on the novel *Clean Break* by Lionel White; MUS: Gerald Fried; CIN: Lucien Ballard
CAST: Sterling Hayden, Coleen Gray, Marie Windsor, Elisha Cook, Jr., J. C. Flippen, Vince Edwards, Ted de Corsia, Joe Sawyer, Joseph Turkel, Timothy Carey

KING OF THE ROARING TWENTIES: THE STORY OF ARNOLD ROTHSTEIN (1961)
Allied Artists
PR: Samuel Bischoff and David Diamond; DIR: Joseph M. Newman; SCR: Jo Swerling, based on *The Big Bankroll* by Leo Katcher; MUS: Franz Waxman; CIN: Carl Guthrie
CAST: David Janssen, Diane Foster, Mickey Rooney, Jack Carson, Diana Dors, Dan O'Herlihy, Mickey Shaughnessy, Keenan Wynn, Joseph Schildkraut, William Demarest, Murryn Vye

KISS OF DEATH (1947)
Twentieth Century–Fox
PR: Fred Kohlmar; DIR: Henry Hathaway; SCR: Ben Hecht and Charles Lederer; MUS: David Buttolph; CIN: Norbert Brodine

CAST: Victor Mature, Richard Widmark, Brian Donlevy, Coleen Gray, Taylor Holmes, Karl Malden, Mildred Dunnock, Millard Mitchell

LAST GANGSTER, THE (1937)
MGM
PR: J. J. Cohn; DIR: Edward Ludwig; SCR: John Lee Mahin, based on a story by William A. Wellman and Robert Carson; MUS: Edward Ward; CIN: William Daniels
CAST: Edward G. Robinson, James Stewart, Rose Stradner, Lionel Stander, Douglas Scott, John Carradine, Sidney Blackmer, Edward Brophy

LE SAMOURAI (aka *The Godson*, 1967–1972)
Artists International
PR: Eugene Lepicier; DIR: Jean-Pierre Melville; SCR: Jean-Pierre Melville, based on the novel *The Ronin* by Joan McLeod; MUS: Françoise de Roubaix; CIN: Henri Decaë
CAST: Alain Delon, Nathalie Delon, François Périer, Cathy Rosier, Jacques Leroy, Jean-Pierre Posier

LET HIM HAVE IT (1991)
Fine Line Features
PR: Luc Roeg and Robert Warr; DIR: Peter Medak; SCR: Neal Purvis and Robert Wade; MUS: Michael Kamen; CIN: Oliver Stapleton
CAST: Christopher Eccleston, Paul Reynolds, Eileen Atkins, Tom Bell, Clare Holman, Tom Courtenay, Michael Gough, Mark McGann, Clive Revill, James Villiers

LIGHTS OF NEW YORK (1928)
Warner Brothers
DIR: Bryan Foy; SCR: Hugh Herbert and Murray Roth, from a story by Charles L. Gaskill; CIN: Ed Du Par
CAST: Helene Costello, Cullen Landis, Gladys Brockwell, Mary Carr, Eugene Pallette, Wheeler Oakman, Robert Elliott, Tom Dugan, Tom McGuire

LINEUP, THE (1958)
Columbia Pictures
PR: Jaime Del Valle; DIR: Don Siegel; SCR: Stirling Silliphant; CIN: Hal Mohr
CAST: Eli Wallach, Robert Keith, Warner Anderson, Richard Jaeckel, Mary La Roche, William Leslie, Emile Meyer, Marshall Reed

LITTLE CAESAR (1930)
Warner Brothers–First National
DIR: Mervyn LeRoy; SCR: Francis Faragoh, based on the novel *Little Caesar* by W. R. Burnett; MUS: Erno Rapee; CIN: Tony Gaudio
CAST: Edward G. Robinson, Douglas Fairbanks, Jr., Glenda Farrell, Ralph Ince, William Collier, Jr., George E. Stone, Thomas Jackson, Stanley Fields

LITTLE GIANT, THE (1933)
Warner Brothers
PR: Raymond Griffith; DIR: Roy Del Ruth; SCR: Robert Lord and Wilson Mizner, based on a story by Lord; MUS: Leo Forbstein; CIN: Sid Hickox
CAST: Edward G. Robinson, Helen Vinson, Mary Astor, Russell Hopton, Kenneth Thomson, Shirley Grey, Donald Dillaway, Louise Mackintosh

LITTLE MISS MARKER (1934)
Paramount Pictures
PR: B. P. Schulberg; DIR: Alexander Hall; SCR: William R. Lipman, Sam Hellman, and Gladys Lehman, based on a story by Damon Runyon; CIN: Alfred Gilks
CAST: Adolphe Menjou, Charles Bickford, Shirley Temple, Dorothy Dell, Lynne Overman, Willie Best

LONG GOOD FRIDAY, THE (1980)
Embassy Pictures/Handmade Films
PR: Barry Hanson; DIR: John Mackenzie; SCR: Barrie Keefe; MUS: Francis Monkman; CIN: Phil Meheux
CAST: Bob Hoskins, Helen Mirren, Eddie Constantine, Dave King, Bryan Marshall, Stephen Davies, Derek Thompson, Paul Freeman, Pierce Brosnan, George Coulouris

LOST CAPONE, THE (1990)
Turner Pictures
PR: Eva Fyer; DIR: John Gray; SCR: John Gray; MUS: Mark Snow; CIN: Paul Elliott
CAST: Adrian Pasdar, Ally Sheedy, Titus Welliver, Eric Roberts, Martia Pitillo, Anthony Crivello, Dominic Chianese, Jimmy F. Skaggs, Barton Heyman, William Andrews

LOVE ME OR LEAVE ME (1955)
MGM
PR: Joe Pasternak; DIR: Charles Vidor; SCR: Daniel Fuchs and Isobel Lennart; MUS: various; CIN: Arthur E. Arling
CAST: James Cagney, Doris Day, Cameron Mitchell, Robert Keith, Tom Tully, Harry Bellaver, Peter Leeds, Richard Gaines, Claude Stroud

MALTESE FALCON, THE (1941)
Warner Brothers–First National
PR: Hal B. Wallis; DIR: John Huston; SCR: John Huston, based on the novel by Dashiell Hammett; MUS: Adolph Deutsch; CIN: Arthur Edeson
CAST: Humphrey Bogart, Mary Astor, Sidney Greenstreet, Peter Lorre, Barton MacLane, Lee Patrick, Ward Bond, Elisha Cook, Jr.

MARKED WOMAN (1937)
Warner Brothers–First National

PR: Louis F. Edelman; DIR: Lloyd Bacon; SCR: Robert Rossen and Abem Finkel; MUS: Bernhard Kuhn and Heinz Roemheld; CIN: George Barnes
CAST: Bette Davis, Humphrey Bogart, Lola Lane, Isabel Jewell, Eduardo Cianelli, Rosalind Marquid, Mayo Methot, Jane Bryan, Allen Jenkins

MEAN STREETS (1973)
Warner Brothers
PR: Jonathan T. Taplin; DIR: Martin Scorsese; SCR: Martin Scorsese and Mardik Martin; CIN: Kent Wakeford
CAST: Harvey Keitel, Robert De Niro, David Proval, Amy Robinson, Richard Romanus, Cesare Danova, Victor Argo, David Carradine, Robert Carradine, Catherine Scorsese, Martin Scorsese

ME, GANGSTER (1928)
Fox Film Corporation
PR: William Fox; DIR: Raoul Walsh; SCR: Charles Francis Coe and Raoul Walsh, based on the book *Me — Gangster* by Charles Francis Coe; CIN: Arthur Edeson
CAST: June Collyer, Don Terry, Anders Randolf, Stella Adams, Burr McIntosh, Walter James, Gustav von Seyffertitz, Al Hill, Carole Lombard, Nigel De Brulier, Arthur Stone, Herbert Ashton, Bob Perry, Harry Castle, Joe Brown

MOUTHPIECE, THE (1932)
Warner Brothers
DIR: James Flood and Elliott Nugent; SCR: Earl Baldwin, based on a story by Frank Collins; CIN: Barney McGill
CAST: Warren Williams, Sidney Fox, Aline MacMahon, William Janney, John Wray, J. Carrol Naish, Polly Walters, Ralph Ince

MURDER, INC. (1960)
Twentieth Century–Fox
PR: Burt Balaban; DIR: Burt Balaban and Stuart Rosenberg; SCR: Irv Tunick and Mell Barr, based on *Murder, Inc.: The Story of the Syndicate* by Burton Turkus and Sid Feder; MUS: Frank De Vol; CIN: Gayne Rescher
CAST: Stuart Whitman, May Britt, Henry Morgan, Peter Falk, David J. Stewart, Simon Oakland, Morey Amsterdam, Vincent Gardenia

MUSKETEERS OF PIG ALLEY, THE (1912)
Biograph Company
PR/DIR: D. W. Griffith; SCR: D. W. Griffith; CIN: G. W. "Billy" Bitzer
CAST: Lillian Gish, Elmer Booth, Walter Miller, Spike Robinson, Harry Carey, Robert Harron

NARROW MARGIN, THE (1952)
RKO

PR: Stanley Rubin; DIR: Richard Fleischer; SCR: Earl Felton; CIN: George E. Diskant
CAST: Charles McGraw, Marie Windsor, Jacqueline White, Gordon Gebert, Queenie
Leonard, Peter Virgo

ONCE UPON A TIME IN AMERICA (1984)
Warner Brothers
PR: Arnon Milchan; DIR: Sergio Leone; SCR: Leonardo Benvenuti, Piero De Bernardo,
Enrico Medioli, Franco Arcalli, Franco Ferrini, and Sergio Leone, based on the book *The
Hoods* by Harry Grey; MUS: Ennio Morricone; CIN: Tonino Delli Colli
CAST: Robert De Niro, James Woods, Elizabeth McGovern, Treat Williams, Tuesday
Weld, Burt Young, Joe Pesci, William Forsythe, James Hayden, Darlanne Fleugel, Richard
Bright

ON THE WATERFRONT (1954)
Columbia Pictures
PR: Sam Spiegel; DIR: Elia Kazan; SCR: Budd Schulberg, based on a series of magazine
articles by Malcolm Johnson; MUS: Leonard Bernstein; CIN: Boris Kaufman
CAST: Marlon Brando, Eva Marie Saint, Lee J. Cobb, Karl Malden, Rod Steiger, James
Westerfield, Pat Henning, Tony Galento, Martin Balsam

OUT OF THE PAST (1947)
RKO
PR: Warren Duff; DIR: Jacques Tourneur; SCR: Geoffrey Homes, based on his novel
Build My Gallows High; MUS: Roy Webb; CIN: Nicholas Musuraca
CAST: Robert Mitchum, Jane Greer, Kirk Douglas, Rhonda Fleming, Steve Brodie, Richard
Webb, Paul Valentine, Virginia Huston, Dickie Moore

OUTSIDE THE LAW (1921)
Universal Pictures
PR: Carl Laemmle; DIR: Tod Browning; SCR: Lucien Hubbard and Tod Browning; CIN:
William Fildew
CAST: Priscilla Dean, Ralph Lewis, Lon Chaney, Wheeler Oakman, E. A. Warren, Stanley
Goethels, Melbourne MacDowell, Wilton Taylor

OUTSIDE THE LAW (1930)
Universal Pictures
PR: Carl Laemmle; DIR: Tod Browning; MUS: David Broekman; SCR: Tod Browning
and Garrett Fort; CIN: Roy Overbaugh
CAST: Edward G. Robinson, Mary Nolan, Owen Moore, Edwin Sturgis, John George,
Delmar Watson, DeWitt Jennings, Rockliffe Fellowes, Frank Burke, Sidney Bracy

PARTY GIRL (1958)
MGM

PR: Joe Pasternak; DIR: Nicholas Ray; SCR: George Wells; MUS: Jeff Alexander; CIN: Robert Bronner
CAST: Robert Taylor, Cyd Charisse, Lee J. Cobb, John Ireland, Kent Smith, Corey Allen, David Opatoshu, Claire Kelly, Lewis Charles

PAY OR DIE (1960)
Allied Artists
PR: Richard Wilson; DIR: Richard Wilson; SCR: Richard Collins and Bertram Millhausser; MUS: David Raksin CIN: Lucien Ballard
CAST: Ernest Borgnine, Zohra Lampert, Alan Austin, Renata Vanni, Bruno Della Santina, Franco Corsaro, Robert F. Simon, Howard Caine, John Duke, John Marley, Mario Siletti, Mimi Doyle, Paul Birch

PENALTY, THE (1920)
Goldwyn Distributing Corp.
PR: Samuel Goldwyn; DIR: Wallace Worsley SCR: Charles Kenyon and Philip Lonergan, based on the novel *The Penalty* by Gouverneur Morris; CIN: Don Short
CAST: Lon Chaney, Ethel Grey Terry, Claire Adams, Kenneth Harlan, James Mason, Edouward Trebaol, Milton Ross, Wilson Hummel, Montgomery Carlyle

PERSONS IN HIDING (1939)
Paramount Pictures
PR: Edward T. Lowe; DIR: Louis King; SCR: Horace McCoy and William Lipman, based on the book by J. Edgar Hoover (ghosted by Courtney Riley Cooper); MUS: Bons Morros; CIN: Harry Fischbeck
CAST: Lynne Overman, Patricia Morison, J. Carrol Naish, Helen Twelvetrees, Richard Denning, William Frawley, William Collier, Sr.

PETE KELLY'S BLUES (1955)
Warner Brothers
PR: Jack Webb; DIR: Jack Webb; SCR: Richard L. Breen; MUS: various; CIN: Hal Rosson
CAST: Jack Webb, Janet Leigh, Edmond O'Brien, Peggy Lee, Andy Devine, Lee Marvin, Ella Fitzgerald, Martin Milner, Than Wyenn, Jayne Mansfield

PETRIFIED FOREST, THE (1936)
Warner Brothers–First National
PR: Henry Blanke; DIR: Archie Mayo; SCR: Charles Kenyon and Delmer Daves, based on the play by Robert E. Sherwood; MUS: Bernhard Kaun; CIN: Son Polito
CAST: Leslie Howard, Bette Davis, Humphrey Bogart, Genevieve Tobin, Dick Foran, Joseph Sawyer, Porter Hall, Charles Grapewin

PRIZZI'S HONOR (1985)
Twentieth Century–Fox

PR: John Foreman; DIR: John Huston; SCR: Richard Condon and Janet Roach, based on the novel by Richard Condon; MUS: Alex North; CIN: Andrzej Bartkowiak
CAST: Jack Nicholson, Kathleen Turner, Anjelica Huston, Robert Loggia, John Randolph, William Hickey, Lee Richardson, Michael Lombard

PUBLIC ENEMY, THE (1931)
Warner Brothers
DIR: William A. Wellman; SCR: Kubec Glasmon, John Bright, and Harvey Thew, from the novel *Beer and Blood* by Bright; MUS: David Mendoza; CIN: Dey Jennings
CAST: James Cagney, Edward Woods, Jean Harlow, Joan Blondell, Beryl Mercer, Donald Cook, Mae Clarke, Leslie Fenton, Robert Emmett O'Connor

QUEEN OF THE MOB (1940)
Paramount Pictures
DIR: James Hogan; SCR: Horace McCoy and William Lipman, based on the book *Persons in Hiding* by J. Edgar Hoover (ghosted by Courtney Riley Cooper); CIN: Theodor Sparkuhl
CAST: Ralph Bellamy, Blanche Yurka, Jack Carson, James Seay, Paul Kelly, Richard Denning, J. Carol Naish, Jeanne Cagney, Hedda Hopper, Billy Gilbert

RACKET, THE (1928)
Paramount–Famous Players–Lasky
PR: Howard Hughes; DIR: Lewis Milestone; SCR: Harry Behn and Del Andrews, based on the play *The Racket* by Bartlett Cormack; CIN: Tony Gaudio
CAST: Thomas Meighan, Marie Prevost, Louis Wolheim, George Stone, John Darrow, Skeets Gallagher, Lee Moran, Lucien Prival, Tony Marlo, Henry Sedley, Sam De Grasse, Burr McIntosh, G. Pat Collins

RACKET, THE (1951)
RKO
PR: Edmund Grainger; DIR: John Cromwell; SCR: William Wister Haines and W. R. Burnett, based on the play *The Racket* by Bartlett Cormack; MUS: Constantin Bakaleinikoff; CIN: George E. Diskant
CAST: Robert Mitchum, Robert Ryan, Lizabeth Scott, William Tallman, Ray Collins, Joyce MacKenzie, Robert Hutton, William Conrad, Les Tremayne, Don Porter

RAW DEAL (1948)
Reliance Pictures/Eagle Lion
PR: Edward Small; DIR: Anthony Mann; SCR: Leopold Atlas and John C. Higgins, based on the story *Corkscrew Alley* by Arnold B. Armstrong and Audrey Ashley; MUS: Paul Sawtell; CIN: John Alton
CAST: Dennis O'Keefe, Claire Trevor, Marsha Hunt, John Ireland, Raymond Burr

REGENERATION, THE (1915)
Fox Film Corporation

PR: William Fox; DIR: R. A. (Raoul) Walsh; SCR: R. A. Walsh and Carl Harbaugh, based on the book *My Mamie Rose: The Story of My Regeneration* by Owen Kildare and the play *The Regeneration* by Owen Kildare and Walter Hackett; CIN: Georges Benoit
CAST: Rockliffe Fellowes, Anna Q. Nilsson, William Sheer, Carl Harbaugh, James Marcus, Maggie Weston, John McCann, H. McCoy, Peggy Barn

RESERVOIR DOGS (1992)
Miramax Films
PR: Lawrence Bender and Harvey Keitel; DIR: Quentin Tarantino; SCR: Quentin Tarantino; CIN: Andrzej Sekula
CAST: Harvey Keitel, Tim Roth, Chris Penn, Steve Buscemi, Lawrence Tierney, Michael Madsen, Quentin Tarantino

RIFIFI (1955)
United Motion Picture Organization
PR: René G. Vuattoux; DIR: Jules Dassin; SCR: Jules Dassin, René Wheeler, Auguste le Breton, based on the novel *Du Rififi chez les Hommes* by Auguste le Breton; MUS: Georges Auric; CIN: Philippe Agostini
CAST: Carl Mohner, Jean Servais, Robert Manuel, Perlo Vita (Jules Dassin), Marie Sabouret, Marcel Lupovici, Robert Hossein

RISE AND FALL OF LEGS DIAMOND, THE (1960)
Warner Brothers
PR: Milton Sperling; DIR: Budd Boetticher; SCR: Joseph Landon; MUS: Leonard Rosenman; CIN: Lucien Ballard
CAST: Ray Danton, Karen Steele, Elaine Stewart, Jesse White, Simon Oakland, Robert Lowery, Judson Pratt, Warren Oates, Frank De Kova

ROGER TOUHY, GANGSTER (1944)
Twentieth Century–Fox
PR: Lee Marcus; DIR: Robert Florey; SCR: Crane Wilbur and Jerry Cady; MUS: Hugo W. Friedhofer; CIN: Glen MacWilliams
CAST: Preston Foster, Victor McLaglen, Lois Andrews, Kent Taylor, Anthony Quinn, William Post, Jr., Henry Morgan, Reed Hadley, John Archer, George E. Stone, Byron Foulger

ROMANCE OF THE UNDERWORLD (1928)
Fox Film Corporation
PR: William Fox; DIR: Irving Cummings; SCR: Douglas Doty, based on the play *A Romance of the Underworld* by Paul Armstrong; CIN: Conrad Welles
CAST: Mary Astor, Ben Bard, Robert Elliott, John Boles, Oscar Apfel, Helen Lynch, William H. Tooker

ROAD TO MANDALAY, THE (1926)
MGM
DIR: Tod Browning; SCR: Elliott Clawson; CIN: Merritt Gerstad
CAST: Lon Chaney, Lois Moran, Owen Moore, Henry B. Walthall, Sojin, John George

ROARING TWENTIES, THE (1939)
Warner Brothers
PR: Hal B. Wallis; DIR: Raoul Walsh; SCR: Jerry Wald, Richard Macaulay, Robert Rossen, from a story by Mark Hellinger; MUS: Heinz Roemheld; CIN: Ernest Haller
CAST: James Cagney, Humphrey Bogart, Jeffrey Lynn, Priscilla Lane, Gladys George, Frank McHugh, Paul Kelly, Joseph Sawyer, Abner Biberman

RUBY (1992)
Triumph Releasing
PR: Sigurjon Sighvatsson and Steve Golin; DIR: John Mackenzie; SCR: Stephen Davis, based on his play *Love Field*; MUS: John Scott; CIN: Phil Meheux
CAST: Danny Aiello, Sherilyn Fenn, Arliss Howard, Tobin Bell, Marc Lawrence

SCARFACE MOB, THE (1959)
Desilu Productions, Inc.
PR: Quinn Martin; DIR: Phil Karlson; SCR: Paul Monash, based on the novel [*sic*] *The Untouchables* by Eliot Ness and Oscar Fraley; MUS: Wilbur Hatch; CIN: Charles Straumer
CAST: Robert Stack, Keenan Wynn, Barbara Nichols, Pat Crowley, Neville Brand, Bruce Gordon, Bill Williams, Joe Mantell, Peter Leeds, Eddie Firestone, Robert Osterloh, Abel Fernandez, Paul Picerni, John Beradino

SCARFACE: THE SHAME OF A NATION (1932)
United Artists
PR: Howard Hughes; DIR: Howard Hawks and Richard Rosson; SCR: Ben Hecht, Seton I. Miller, John Lee Mahin, and W. R. Burnett, based on the novel *Scarface* by Armitage Trail; MUS: Adolph Tandler and Gus Arnheim; CIN: Lee Garmes and L. William O'Connell
CAST: Paul Muni, Ann Dvorak, Karen Morley, Osgood Perkins, Boris Karloff, C. Henry Gordon, George Raft, Vince Barnett, Purnell Pratt, Tully Marshall

SECRET SIX, THE (1931)
MGM
DIR: George Hill; SCR: Frances Marion; CIN: Harold Wenstrom
CAST: Wallace Beery, John Mack Brown, Lewis Stone, Jean Harlow, Marjorie Rambeau, Clark Gable, Ralph Bellamy

SHOCK, THE (1923)
Universal Pictures
PR: Carl Laemmle; DIR: Lambert Hillyer; SCR: Arthur Statter and Charles Kenyon; CIN: Dwight Warren

CAST: Lon Chaney, Virginia Valli, Jack Mower, William Welsh, Henry Barrows, Christine Mayo, Harry Devere, John Beck, Walter Long

SLIGHT CASE OF MURDER, A (1938)
Warner Brothers–First National
PR: Hal B. Wallis; DIR: Lloyd Bacon; SCR: Earl Baldwin and Joseph Schrank, based on the play by Damon Runyon and Howard Lindsay; MUS: M. K. Jerome and Jack Scholl; CIN: Sid Hickox
CAST: Edward G. Robinson, Jane Bryan, Allen Jenkins, Ruth Donnelly, Willard Parker, John Litel, Edward Brophy, Harold Huber, Paul Harvey

SMART MONEY (1931)
Warner Brothers
DIR: Alfred E. Green; SCR: Kubec Glasmon and John Bright, based on a story by Lucien Hubbard and Joseph Jackson; MUS: Leo Forbstein; CIN: Robert Kurrie
CAST: Edward G. Robinson, James Cagney, Evalyn Knapp, Ralf Harolde, Noel Francis, Margaret Livingston

SOME LIKE IT HOT (1959)
Universal Pictures
PR: Billy Wilder; DIR: Billy Wilder; SCR: Billy Wilder and I. A. L. Diamond, from a screen story by R. Thoeren and M. Logan; MUS: Adolph Deutsch; CIN: Charles Lang, Jr.
CAST: Tony Curtis, Jack Lemmon, Marilyn Monroe, George Raft, Pat O'Brien, Joe E. Brown, Nehemiah Persoff, George E. Stone, Mike Mazurski

STATE'S ATTORNEY (1932)
RKO
PR: David O. Selznick; DIR: George Archainbaud; SCR: Gene Fowler and Rowland Brown, from a story by Louis Stevens; CIN: Leo Tover
CAST: John Barrymore, Helen Twelvetrees, William "Stage" Boyd, Jill Esmond, Mary Duncan, C. Henry Gordon, Oscar Apfel, Ralph Ince

ST. VALENTINE'S DAY MASSACRE, THE (1967)
Twentieth Century–Fox
PR: Roger Corman; DIR: Roger Corman; SCR: Howard Browne; MUS: Fred Steiner; CIN: Milton Krasner
CAST: Jason Robards, Jr., George Segal, Ralph Meeker, Jean Hale, Clint Ritchie, Frank Silvera, Bruce Dern, Joseph Campanella, Richard Bakalyan, David Canary, Harold J. Stone, Kurt Krueger, Paul Richards, Joseph Turkel, Jack Nicholson

THEY LIVE BY NIGHT (1949)
RKO Pictures

PR: John Houseman; DIR: Nicholas Ray; SCR: Charles Schnee, based on the novel *Thieves Like Us* by Edward Anderson; MUS: Leigh Harline; CIN: George E. Diskant
CAST: Cathy O'Donnell, Farley Granger, Howard da Silva, Jay C. Flippen, Helen Craig, Will Wright, Marie Bryant, Ian Wolfe

THIEVES LIKE US (1974)
United Artists
PR: Jerry Bick; DIR: Robert Altman; SCR: Calder Willingham, Joan Tewkesbury, and Robert Altman, based on the novel by Edward Anderson; CIN: Jean Boffety
CAST: Keith Carradine, Shelley Duvall, John Schuck, Bert Remsen, Louise Fletcher, Ann Latham, Tom Skerritt, Al Scott, John Roper

THIS GUN FOR HIRE (1942)
Paramount Pictures
PR: Richard M. Blumenthal; DIR: Frank Tuttle; SCR: Albert Maltz and W. R. Burnett, based on a novel by Graham Greene; MUS: David Buttolph; CIN: John Seitz
CAST: Veronica Lake, Robert Preston, Alan Ladd, Laird Cregar, Tully Marshall, Marc Lawrence

THUNDERBOLT (1929)
Paramount–Famous Players–Lasky
DIR: Josef von Sternberg; SCR: Jules Furthman and Herman J. Mankiewicz; CIN: Henry Gerrald
CAST: George Bancroft, Fay Wray, Richard Arlen, Tully Marshall, Eugénie Besserer, James Spottiswoode, Fred Kohler, Robert Elliott, E. H. Calvert, George Irving, Mike Donlin

T-MEN (1947)
Eagle Lion
PR: Aubrey Schenck; DIR: Anthony Mann; SCR: John C. Higgins and [uncredited] Anthony Mann, based on a story by Virginia Kellogg; MUS: Paul Sawtell; CIN: John Alton
CAST: Dennis O'Keefe, Mary Meade, Alfred Ryder, Wallace Ford, June Lockhart

UNDERWORLD (1927)
Paramount–Famous Players–Lasky
PR: Hector Turnbull; DIR: Josef von Sternberg; SCR: Robert N. Lee; CIN: Bert Glennon
CAST: George Bancroft, Clive Brook, Evelyn Brent, Larry Semon, Fred Kohler, Helen Lynch, Jerry Mandy, Karl Morse

UNHOLY THREE, THE (1925)
MGM
PR: Louis B. Mayer; DIR: Tod Browning; SCR: Waldemar Young, based on the play *The Unholy Three* by Clarence Aaron Robbins; CIN: David Kesson

CAST: Lon Chaney, Mae Busch, Matt Moore, Victor McLaglen, Harry Earles, Harry Betz, Edward Connelly, William Humphreys, A. E. Warren, John Merkyl, Charles Wellesley

UNHOLY THREE, THE (1930)
MGM
DIR: Jack Conway; SCR: J. C. and Elliott Nugent, based on the play *The Unholy Three* by Clarence Aaron Robbins; CIN: Percy Hilburn
CAST: Lon Chaney, Lila Lee, Elliott Nugent, Harry Earles, John Miljan, Ivan Linow, Clarence Burton, Crawford Kent

UNTOUCHABLES, THE (1987)
Paramount Pictures
PR: Art Linson; DIR: Brian De Palma; SCR: Davie Mamet; MUS: Ennio Morricone; CIN: Steven H. Burum
CAST: Kevin Costner, Sean Connery, Andy Garcia, Robert De Niro, Charles Martin Smith

VALACHI PAPERS, THE (1972)
Columbia Pictures
PR: Dino De Laurentiis; DIR: Terence Young; SCR: Stephen Geller, based on the book by Peter Maas; MUS: Riz Ortolani; CIN: Aldo Tonti
CAST: Charles Bronson, Lino Ventura, Gerald S. O'Loughlin, Mario Pilar, Fred Valleca, Guido Leontini, Walter Chiari, Angelo Infanti, Alessandro Sperli

WHILE THE CITY SLEEPS (1928)
MGM
DIR: Jack Conway; SCR: A. P. Younger; CIN: Henry Sharp
CAST: Lon Chaney, Anita Page, Carroll Nye, Wheeler Oakman, Mae Busch, Polly Moran, Lydia Yeamans Titus, William Orlamond, Richard Carle

WHITE HEAT (1949)
Warner Brothers–First National
PR: Louis F. Edelman; DIR: Raoul Walsh; SCR: Ivan Goff and Ben Roberts, based on a story by Virginia Kellogg; MUS: Max Steiner; CIN: Sid Hickox
CAST: James Cagney, Virginia Mayo, Edward O'Brien, Margaret Wycherly, Steve Cochran, John Archer, Fred Clark, Wally Cassell

WHOLE TOWN'S TALKING, THE (1935)
Columbia Pictures
PR: Lester Cowan; DIR: John Ford; SCR: Jo Swerling and Robert Riskin, based on the novel by W. R. Burnett; CIN: Joseph August
CAST: Edward G. Robinson, Jean Arthur, Wallace Ford, Arthur Byron, Donald Meek, Arthur Hohl, Paul Harvey, Edward Brophy, Etienne Giradot

You Only Live Once (1937)
United Artists
PR: Walter Wanger; DIR: Fritz Lang; SCR: Gene Towne and Graham Baker; MUS: Alfred Newman; CIN: Leon Shamroy
CAST: Henry Fonda, Sylvia Sidney, Barton MacLane, Jean Dixon, William Gargan, Jerome Cowan, Margaret Hamilton, John Wray, Jonathan Hale

SELECTED
BIBLIOGRAPHY

PERIODICALS

Anonymous. "Cimino's Bandit." *Premiere,* November 1987, 58–59.

Biskind, Peter. "Breathless for Dick Tracy." *Premiere,* June 1990, 85–88.

———. "Warren and Me." *Premiere,* July 1990, 50–60, 103–105.

Braudy, Leo. "In the Criminal Style." *American Film,* July–August 1980, 53–55.

Collins, Max Allan. "The Grifters." *Mystery Scene,* April 1991, no. 29: 58, 60.

Drew Bernard. "The Man Who Paid His Dues." *American Film,* December–January 1979, 22–27.

Dunne Philip. "An Offer He Couldn't Refuse." *American Film,* March 1987, 63–64.

Gleiberman, Owen. "A Night at the Opera." *Entertainment Weekly,* January 1991, 38–40.

Hoberman, J. "The Movie Within Me." *Premiere,* September 1990, 46, 117.

———. "Something Wilder." *Premiere,* September 1988, 80–84.

Kornbluth, Jesse. "The Untouchables: Shot-By-Shot." *Premiere,* July–August 1987, 35–40.

Levy, Steven. "Miller's Crossing." *Premiere,* March 1990, 63–68.

McCormick, Bret. "Fred Williamson." *Psychotronic,* Summer 1991, vol. 2, no. 10: 22–34.

Pond, Steve. "Babies in Gangland." *Premiere,* August 1991, 68–74.

———. "Black Rain: Shot-By-Shot." *Premiere,* October 1989, 104–108.

———. "The Hero's a Hired Gun." *Premiere,* July–August 1987, 42–43.

Queenan, Joe. "The Lonely Raging Bull." *Movieline,* April 1990, 39–43, 87–88.

Richardson, John H. "The Joel & Ethan Coen Story." *Premiere,* October 1990, 94–101.

Ryan, Elizabeth E. "Acting Teacher: William Hickey." *Premiere,* August 1991, 38, 40.

Sporkin, Elizabeth. "Three Faces of Bugsy." *People,* May 1991, 133.

Stivers, Cyndi. "Family Reunion." *Premiere,* January 1991, 76–84, 106.

Thomson, David. "Leonesque." *American Film,* September 1989, 26–31.

BOOKS

American Institute Catalog of Motion Pictures Produced in the United States, Feature Films, 1921–1930. New York: Bowker, 1971.

Anderson, Robert G. *Faces, Forms, Films: The Artistry of Lon Chaney.* New York: A. S. Barnes & Co., Inc., 1971.

Baxter, John. *The Gangster Film.* New York: A. S. Barnes & Co., Inc., 1970.

Beck, Calvin Thomas. *Heroes of the Horrors.* New York: Macmillan Publishing Co., Inc., 1975.

Bergan, Ronald. *The United Artists Story.* New York: Crown, 1986.

Bogdanovich, Peter. *Allan Dwan: The Last Pioneer.* New York: Praeger Publishers, Inc., 1971.

Brownlow, Kevin. *Behind the Mask of Innocence.* New York: Alfred A. Knopf, 1990.

—— and John Kobal. *Hollywood: The Pioneers.* New York: Alfred A. Knopf, 1979.

Dickens, Homer C. *The Complete Films of James Cagney.* Secaucus, N.J.: Citadel Press, 1972, 1989.

Eames, John Douglas. *The MGM Story.* New York: Crown, 1979.

——. *The Paramount Story.* New York: Crown, 1985.

Hanke, Ken. *Early Talkies from Hollywood.* Jefferson, N.C.: McFarland & Company, Inc., 1993.

Henderson, Robert M. *D. W. Griffith: His Life and Work.* New York: Oxford University Press, 1972.

——. *D. W. Griffith: The Years at Biograph.* New York: Farrar, Straus and Giroux, 1970.

Hirschhorn, Clive. *The Columbia Story.* New York: Crown, 1989.

——. *The Universal Story.* New York: Crown, 1983.

— — —. *The Warner Bros. Story.* New York: Crown, 1979.

Jewell, Richard B. and Vernon Harbin. *The RKO Story.* New York: Arlington House, 1982.

Kaminsky, Stuart M. *Don Siegel: Director.* New York: Curtis Books, 1973.

LeRoy, Mervyn. *Mervyn LeRoy: Take One.* New York: Hawthorn Books, 1974.

McArthur, Colin. *Underworld U.S.A.* New York: The Viking Press, 1972.

McCarty, Clifford. *Bogey: The Films of Humphrey Bogart.* Secaucus, N.J.: Citadel Press, 1975.

McCarty, John. *The Complete Films of John Huston.* Secaucus, N.J.: Citadel Press, 1991.

——. *Thrillers: Seven Decades of Classic Screen Suspense.* Secaucus, N.J.: Citadel Press, 1992.

McGill, Frank N. *McGill's Survey of Cinema, Silent Films.* New Jersey: Salem Press, 1982 (3 vols).

McGilligan, Patrick. *Robert Altman: Jumping off a Cliff.* New York: St. Martin's Press, 1989.

Marill, Alvin H. *The Complete Films of Edward G. Robinson*. Secaucus, N.J.: Citadel Press, 1990.

Miller, Don. *"B" Movies*. New York: Curtis Books, 1973.

New York Times Film Reviews, 1913–1990. New York: New York Times/Arno Press, 1970–1990.

Parrish, James Robert and Michael R. Pitts. *The Great Gangster Pictures*. Metuchen, N.J.: Scarecrow Press, 1976, 1987 (2 vols).

Pye, Michael and Lynda Myles. *The Movie Brats*. New York: Holt, Rinehart and Winston, 1979.

Riley, Philip J. *A Blind Bargain*. Atlantic City, N.J.: MagicImage Filmbooks, 1988.

———. *London After Midnight*. New York: Cornwall Books, 1985.

Rosenthal, Stuart and Judith M. Kass. *Tod Browning and Don Siegel*. New York: A. S. Barnes & Co., Inc., 1975.

Sann, Paul. *The Lawless Decade*. New York: Crown, 1957.

Sarris, Andrew. *The American Cinema*. New York: E. P. Dutton & Co., Inc., 1968.

Schickel, Richard. *D. W. Griffith: An American Life*. New York: Simon and Schuster, 1984.

Schumach, Murray. *The Face on the Cutting Room Floor*. New York: William Morrow and Company, 1964.

Shipman, David. *The Story of Cinema*. New York: St. Martin's Press, 1982.

Sifakis, Carl. *The Encyclopedia of American Crime*. New York: Facts on File, 1982.

Stack, Robert (with Mark Evans). *Straight Shooting*. New York: Macmillan Publishing Co., Inc., 1980.

Thomas Tony and Aubrey Solomon. *The Films of 20th Century–Fox*. Secaucus, N.J.: Citadel Press, 1985, 1979.

Sternberg, Josef von. *Fun in a Chinese Laundry*. New York: Macmillan Publishing Co., Inc., 1965.

Walsh, Raoul. *Each Man in His Time*. New York: Farrar, Straus and Giroux, 1974.

Warren, Doug (with James Cagney). *Cagney*. New York: St. Martin's Press, 1983.

Weinberg, Herman G. *Josef von Sternberg*. New York: E. P. Dutton & Co., Inc., 1967.

Wood, Robin. *Arthur Penn*. London: Studio Vista, Ltd., 1967.

About the Author

JOHN MCCARTY is the author of numerous books on film, including the cult classic *Splatter Movies: Breaking the Last Taboo of the Screen* (St. Martin's Press, 1984) — which *Fangoria* magazine has called "The definitive history of the gore film"; its companion volumes, *John McCarty's Official Splatter Movie Guide*, vols. 1 and 2 (St. Martin's Press, 1989, 1992); *Thrillers: Seven Decades of Classic Film Suspense* (Carol Publishing, 1992); and *The Modern Horror Film: Fifty Contemporary Classics* (Carol Publishing, 1990). His supernatural thriller *Deadly Resurrection* (St. Martin's Press, 1990) earned a recommendation for a Bram Stoker Award as Best First Novel by the Horror Writers of America. Mr. McCarty is married and lives in upstate New York.

INDEX